FASHION BEFORE I

Dress cultures

Series Editors: Reina Lewis & Elizabeth Wilson

Advisory Board: Christopher Breward, Hazel Clark, Joanne Entwistle, Caroline Evans, Susan Kaiser, Angela McRobbie, Hiroshi Narumi, Peter McNeil, Özlem Sandikci, Simona Segre Reinach, Arti Sandhu

Dress Cultures aims to foster innovative theoretical and methodological frameworks to understand how and why we dress, exploring the connections between clothing, commerce and creativity in global contexts.

Published:

Delft Blue to Denim Blue: Contemporary Dutch Fashion
edited by Anneke Smelik

Dressing for Austerity: Aspiration, Leisure and Fashion in Post War Britain
by Geraldine Biddle-Perry

Experimental Fashion: Performance Art, Carnival and the Grotesque Body
by Francesca Granata

Fashion in European Art: Dress and Identity, Politics and the Body, 1775–1925
edited by Justine De Young

Fashion in Multiple Chinas: Chinese Styles in the Transglobal Landscape
edited by Wessie Ling and Simona Segre Reinach

Modest Fashion: Styling Bodies, Mediating Faith
edited by Reina Lewis

Niche Fashion Magazines: Changing the Shape of Fashion
by Ane Lynge-Jorlen

Styling South Asian Youth Cultures: Fashion, Media and Society
edited by Lipi Begum, Rohit K. Dasgupta and Reina Lewis

Thinking Through Fashion: A Guide to Key Theorists
edited by Agnès Rocamora and Anneke Smelik

Veiling in Fashion: Space and the Hijab in Minority Communities
by Anna-Mari Almila

Wearing the Cheongsam: Dress and Culture in a Chinese Diaspora
by Cheryl Sim

Fashioning Indie: Popular Fashion, Music and Gender in the Twenty-First Century
by Rachel Lifter

Revisiting the Gaze: The Fashioned Body and the Politics of Looking
edited by Morna Laing and Jacki Willson

Reading Marie al-Khazen's Photographs: Gender, Photography, Mandate Lebanon
by Yasmine Nachabe Taan

Wearing the Niqab: Muslim Women in the UK and the US
by Anna Piela

Fashioning the Modern Middle East: Gender, Body, and Nation
edited by Reina Lewis and Yasmine Nachabe Taan

Fashion, Performance, & Performativity: The Complex Spaces of Fashion
edited by Andrea Kollnitz and Marco Pecorari

Silhouettes of the Soul: Meditations on Fashion, Religion, and Subjectivity
edited by Otto von Busch and Jeanine Viau

The Women of 'Little Paris': Women's Fashion in Interwar Bucharest
by Sonia-Doris Andras

Fashion in Altermodern China
by Feng Jie

Fashioning the Afropolis: Histories, Materialities and Aesthetic Practices
edited by Kerstin Pinther, Kristin Kastner and Basile Ndjio

Jews in Suits: Men's Dress in Vienna, 1890–1938
by Jonathan C. Kaplan-Wajselbaum

Fashion Before Plus-Size: Bodies, Bias, and the Birth of an Industry
by Lauren Downing Peters

Reina Lewis: reina.lewis@fashion.arts.ac.uk
Elizabeth Wilson: elizabethwilson.auth@gmail.com

FASHION BEFORE PLUS-SIZE

BODIES, BIAS, AND THE BIRTH OF AN INDUSTRY

Lauren Downing Peters

BLOOMSBURY VISUAL ARTS

LONDON • NEW YORK • OXFORD • NEW DELHI • SYDNEY

BLOOMSBURY VISUAL ARTS
Bloomsbury Publishing Plc
50 Bedford Square, London, WC1B 3DP, UK
1385 Broadway, New York, NY 10018, USA
29 Earlsfort Terrace, Dublin 2, Ireland

BLOOMSBURY, BLOOMSBURY VISUAL ARTS and the Diana logo
are trademarks of Bloomsbury Publishing Plc

First published in Great Britain 2023
Reprinted 2024
Paperback edition published in 2025

Series design by BRILL
Cover image: Ad for Associated Stylish Stout Wear Makers, Inc.
in *Women's Wear New York* magazine, 1918

A catalogue record for this book is available from the British Library.

A catalog record for this book is available from the Library of Congress.

ISBN: HB: 978-1-3501-7254-8
          PB: 978-1-3503-9937-2
          ePDF: 978-1-3501-7255-5
          eBook: 978-1-3501-7256-2

Typeset by Integra Software Services Pvt. Ltd.
Printed and bound in Great Britain

To find out more about our authors and books visit www.bloomsbury.com
and sign up for our newsletters.

For Jon, with love

CONTENTS

Contents

ILLUSTRATIONS

ACKNOWLEDGMENTS

It's a solitary and oftentimes lonely thing, researching and writing a book; however, I could not have completed this project without the support of my extended network of colleagues, collaborators, friends, and, most importantly, family. I'd like to begin by thanking some of the wonderful people who helped me along the way.

Fashion Before Plus-Size began as a doctoral dissertation, which I completed at the Centre for Fashion Studies at Stockholm University under the supervision of Hazel Clark, Caroline Evans, Andrea Kollnitz, and Klas Nyberg and, at an earlier stage, Paul von Wachenfeldt and Louise Wallenberg. Their generous guidance, delivered with patience, compassion, and enthusiasm from the shaky first drafts through to my public defense, gave shape and weight to this research and I will be forever grateful for their support. While at Stockholm University, I had the distinct privilege of being immersed in an international community of emerging scholars. I feel lucky to have had the opportunity to workshop ideas and drafts with them, but more so for their friendship, especially when the writing got tough and the self-doubt began to creep in. I owe special thanks to Hanne Eide, Lisa Ehlin, Chiara Faggella, Ulrika Kyaga, Emma Lindblad, Marco Pecorari, Sara Skillen, Natalie Snoyman, Patrick Steorn, Annamari Vänskä, and Philip Warkander for the thoughtful feedback they offered on chapter drafts. I owe a special debt of gratitude to my "opponents" (the unnecessarily aggressive Swedish term for external reviewers), Christopher Breward and Reina Lewis, who provided invaluable comments on the full draft manuscript and who helped me to imagine the form this research might take as a book.

I began the process of transforming the dissertation into a book shortly after joining the faculty at Columbia College Chicago. Although I began with an optimistic goal of completing the project in just twelve short months, I quickly learned that it is no small task to juggle research and writing with the demands of being a newly minted tenure track professor! This fact was not lost on my exceptional and exceptionally kind department chair, Colbey Reid, who has been an unwavering champion of my research and a tireless guardian of my time and energy. I'm thankful for the mentorship of Ames Hawkins and Debra Parr, both of whom taught me the invaluable lesson that it is OK to say no sometimes. I'm also grateful for the camaraderie of my writing group friends, Melanie Chambliss, Khalid Long, Grace Overbeke, and Molly Schneider. Thanks to the four of you for holding me accountable and for always holding space to celebrate the small wins. I also owe a huge thank you to the Office of the Provost for providing me with generous financial support for archival visits, image licensing fees, and indexing fees, without which this book would be far less rich.

Acknowledgments

I want to recognize and thank the Dress Cultures series editors, Reina Lewis and Elizabeth Wilson, for encouraging me to submit a proposal and for their most excellent suggestions for the title of this book. Thanks as well to my Bloomsbury editor, Frances Arnold, and her editorial assistant, Rebecca Hamilton, for their incredible kindness and patience throughout the production process. It's truly an understatement to say that this book couldn't have come to fruition without their help and guidance. I also want to thank my blind peer reviewers, whoever they may be, for providing such constructive and helpful feedback, both on the proposal and on the full draft manuscript.

This is a subject in which I have been immersed for a very long time. Thus, although this is an original work, some of the ideas presented here were initially explored in other journals and edited volumes, but are more fully fleshed out and contextualized in the pages that follow. Several concepts and case studies discussed in Chapter 2 can be found in my 2019 article "Flattering the Figure: Fitting in: The Design Discourses of Stoutwear, 1915–1930," published in the journal *Fashion Theory*, and in my 2020 article "Body as Architecture: Designing the Stout Body in the Age of Standardization," published in the journal *Fashion Studies*. Portions of the conclusion, and specifically my reflections on an epistemology of "fat clothes," were first explored in a 2022 article published in *Design Issues* titled "On Fat Clothes: Unraveling Plus-Size Design Discourse."

I'm grateful to have had the opportunity to share different versions and stages of this work at the University of Georgia, Toronto Metropolitan University, Donghua University, the University of Helsinki, the University of Southern Denmark, the American University in Paris, the Fashion Research Network, the Fashion Institute of Technology, the University of Illinois at Urbana-Champaign, and the Stanford University Humanities Center. Each of these invitations to present my research was a growth opportunity that helped me to clarify and strengthen my writing.

The writing and editing of this book occurred, by and large, during the scariest, most uncertain, and most isolated days of the Covid-19 pandemic. I am so, so grateful to Chloe Chapin, Emma McClendon, Debra Parr, and Colbey Reid for somehow finding the time and energy to read and provide such helpful feedback on my chapter drafts over the last couple of years. I'm also so incredibly grateful for the support and friendship of my *Fashion Studies Journal* family, including Sara Idacavage, Natalie Nudell, Anthony Palliparambil, Lara Snelgrove, and Olivia Warschaw, who provided a sense of stability and normalcy during those first terrible months of the pandemic.

It is my wonderful friends and family, however, to whom I owe the largest debt of gratitude. To the Pink Ladies, the Beaches, the Peters family, The Colonels, and my parents, thank you for your words of encouragement and unwavering support, even when it was probably unclear to you why, exactly, I was so down on myself. Last but not least, thank you to my husband, Jon, for being my champion, my friend, and my sometimes editor. I love you very much, and this book is for you (and Lemmy and Dolly).

INTRODUCTION

In a 1923 interview with the *South Bend Tribune*, the French couturier Paul Poiret shared his concerns about American women who, the designer believed, had grown alarmingly fat (Figure I.1). Whereas French women were "desirous of being beautiful and ... slim," Poiret had observed that a significant proportion of American women had abandoned their claims to beauty for the comforts of avoirdupois. In his opinion, American manufacturers were at least partly to blame for this, for they had misled the nation's fat women into thinking that "a line here and a color there" could effect a slender and stylish appearance. The idea that one could simply dress their way to slenderness was, in Poiret's estimation, merely a snare and a delusion. "If you weigh 180 pounds you will look 180, and not 179. To be sure, the fat woman can look neat and pleasing," he acquiesced, "but stylish and beautiful? Never!" Speaking on behalf of all French designers, Poiret went on to state the following:

> We do not pay much attention to fat women. They are the infirm among the fashionable. We cannot do anything special for them. They have merely to trail along the path of La Mode. Their case is not for the dress designer—it is for the physician.[1]

With these remarks, Poiret was inserting himself into a national conversation about weight that had been growing more alarmist since the last quarter of the nineteenth century, and which by the 1920s had come to focus almost exclusively on women.[2] As the "high priest of feminine fashion," the *Tribune* believed that his statements would not go unnoticed among the scores of American women for whom "weight is always a topic of discussion." Alongside fad diets and exercise regimens, the precept of "dressing to look slender," which Poiret so gruffly dismissed in this interview, was promoted as a salve to the problem of overweight; however, if it was so apparent to Poiret that fat women were "hopeless," how had they come to believe that beauty was within their grasp in the first place?

Eight years earlier, *Women's Wear* reported that so-called "stoutwear" was to become one of the fastest-growing sectors of the burgeoning ready-made garment industry in the United States.[3] Catering to an estimated 35 percent of the adult female population, stoutwear manufacturers sought to address endemic consumer discontent by providing fat women with affordable, well-made, and well-fitting clothing in an expanded range of sizes.[4] Even as manufacturers, advertisers, and journalists referred to her in the trade press as a "freak" and a "monster," they also cynically realized the fat woman's business to be "tremendously worthwhile."[5] Although the industry's contempt for her

Figure I.1 "'Fat Women Hopeless,' Says Poiret—Is He Right?," *South Bend Tribune* (January 14, 1923), 36. Published with permission from Newspapers.com.

was thinly veiled, over the span of just a few short years, the fat woman was brought in from what one manufacturer described as "fashion's muddy edges."[6] Suddenly more visible within the spaces and places of fashion, by the second decade of the twentieth century fat women could walk into most department stores around the country and buy everything from underwear to dresses off-the-rack.[7]

As Poiret aptly observed, however, stoutwear manufacturers were selling far more than ready-made clothing in an expanded range of sizes. They were also selling the promise that fat women could mitigate the appearance of excess body fat, and therefore evade the social stigma of overweight, with little more than some self-restraint, a bit of good taste, and, perhaps most importantly, a wardrobe of specially designed stoutwear. Superseding stoutwear manufacturers' claims to greater freedom of choice and the ease of a perfect fit was the more elusive promise of sartorial salvation. So great was the pressure to reduce in early twentieth-century America that *Vogue* even went so far as to tell its readers in a 1918 beauty column that it is "far better … to commit any number of petty crimes than to be guilty of the sin of growing fat."[8] For fat women who shouldered the heavy burden of overweight in an increasingly fatphobic society, the promise that the "sin" of fat could be mitigated, if not eradicated, through dress alone would have seemed too good to be true, and in many ways it was.

As with most products that promised fast and effective solutions to the problem of fat, the claims made by stoutwear manufacturers would prove to be overstated. In the trade press, stoutwear was heralded as an important harbinger of change in the American fashion industry toward greater segmentation and specialization.[9] Yet, despite their claims to the contrary, stoutwear manufacturers proved to be less interested in challenging the status quo—that is, to make the fashion industry more inclusive of diverse bodies—than in bringing the fat female body more in line with prevailing standards of beauty and fashionability, and namely with the ascendant slender ideal. The general principles of stoutwear design were perhaps best summarized by Albert Malsin—a figure described in the fashion media as "the master of lines for stout figures"—who stated that clothing for fat people should be designed in such a way as to "conceal the defects of their figures."[10] Yet, even as figures like Malsin touted the high-minded notion that design could be employed to diminish the appearance of overweight, thereby allowing fat women to evade weight stigma, underlying stoutwear design was the core assumption that the fat body was inherently flawed. Although the absolute certainty with which stoutwear manufacturers upheld slenderness as the central pillar around which all design decisions were made is in itself striking, the stigmatization of fat within stoutwear design discourse was hardly unique or exceptional.

In a nation that, to borrow Amy Erdman Farrell's phrasing, is as historically and "extraordinarily 'fat aware'" as the United States, weight bias is something of a cherished, if taken-for-granted, national tradition.[11] Although there persists a romantic perception that there was a moment in the not-too-distant past when fatness was venerated as a symbol of power, prosperity, and even beauty, the truth is that there are exceedingly few moments in American history in which fatness has been regarded as anything less than a profound moral or aesthetic failing.[12] Weight bias became such a cornerstone of American life and culture during the early twentieth century that it shaped not just the national ethic, informing how and to what extent fat people could participate in civic life as full citizens, but also its institutions and industries. While there is a growing body of literature that explores the history of fat and its cultural, political, and economic effects, there has yet to be a book-length historical investigation into how weight bias affects fashion systems and practices, nor into the key roles that fashion and dress have played in shaping public opinion about fat during the twentieth century. By exploring the wider contexts from which the large-size dress sector first emerged, this book frames fashion as an important if overlooked site for investigating the nature and nuances of fat in American life—one in which the medium of dress has been used less to mitigate the stigma of overweight than to design fat out of existence altogether.

Fashion Before Plus-Size

Straddling the disciplines of cultural history, dress history, and fashion studies, this book explores the ways that fashion—as object, industry, and embodied practice—has materialized and perpetuated weight bias in the United States. Spanning the first decades of the twentieth century, this study is chronologically bookended on one end by *Women's Wear's* 1915 predictions about stoutwear's rosy future and on the other by its resignation in 1930 that, due to new fads in dieting, exercise, and fashion, "there are no more stout women."[13] It also overlaps with the period during which most historians agree that modern ideas about deviant fatness had become well entrenched in the minds of Americans. By necessity, however, this brief fifteen-year time frame is truncated and artificial. Before *Women's Wear* discussed the growth potential of stoutwear in 1915 and even after it declared its demise in 1930, there were garments being produced for women of larger sizes on a mass scale.[14] Yet, this period is particularly notable for the extent to which it laid the foundations for the plus-size fashion industry in the late twentieth century, as well as for the remarkable tenor of optimism that suffused industry discourse. While this book examines the time "before" plus-size fashion, it also seeks out the resonances between then and now, or the ways that the echoes of the past reverberate in the present.

This book is, in many ways, a Foucauldian "genealogy" of plus-size fashion, or history written through the lens of present-day concerns in order to reveal the historical mechanisms and power struggles through which certain practices, institutions, conflicts, and ideologies emerged.[15] As David Garland summarizes, genealogy enables the historian to "suggest ... by presenting a series of troublesome associations and lineages ... that institutions and practices we value and take for granted today are actually more problematic or more 'dangerous' than they otherwise appear."[16] To be certain, *Fashion Before Plus-Size* is a book about what existed before the plus-size fashion industry as we know it today. The impetus for writing this book, however, came from the present controversies surrounding size inclusivity in fashion and my desire to locate what Michel Foucault describes as their processes of "descent" and "emergence," or the "erratic and discontinuous process whereby the past became the present."[17] For many readers, the ideas and debates discussed in the following chapters will undoubtedly feel remarkably, if not uncannily, familiar and generally little changed. That is because, as Elizabeth Wilson, Caroline Evans, and Ulrich Lemann have each observed, contemporary fashion sits on the bedrocks of late nineteenth- and early twentieth-century technological innovations, commercial relations, and, as is especially pertinent to this study, social anxieties.[18] Not only is the contemporary fashion system (and specifically plus-size fashion) an outgrowth of ideas and practices that can be traced back more than a century, the echoes of the past, as Evans has so poetically written, have a tendency to "surface in the present like the return of the repressed."[19]

It is during the early twentieth century, for instance, that plus-size standard bearer Lane Bryant shifted its attention away from maternity wear to design some of the earliest specially designed stoutwear garments.[20] This period also witnessed manufacturers devise innovative sizing and grading systems that took into account the different ways that women carry fat on their bodies—the basic principles of which persist in plus-size fashion design and patternmaking to this day. Indeed, many of the key institutions and apparatuses of contemporary plus-size fashion can be traced back to the early twentieth century. So too, however, can some of the more harmful assumptions and ideologies that have stunted the growth of this sector and buttressed the perception of the fat female body as excessive and unruly and therefore in need of design intervention. Merchandising norms such as segregated departments and fat taxes have their origins in the early twentieth century, as do the moralizing design precepts of "slenderizing" and "figure flattery." As an outgrowth of the nation's nascent ready-made garment industry, however, stoutwear provided fat women the opportunity to, for the first time, participate in an essential experience of modernity: buying clothing in standardized sizes off-the-rack.

Before stoutwear, fat women either relied upon their faculties as home sewers or enlisted the help of tailors and seamstresses in the creation of bespoke and made-to-measure garments.[21] While the issue of good fit was less of a concern—for women had their clothes fit to their bodies, rather than fitting their bodies to their clothes—custom clothing was both expensive and slow to produce. Fat women in particular had to suffer multiple indignities when commissioning garments, from tedious fittings to embarrassing interactions with seamstresses that only grew worse as weight bias further calcified in American society and as the preference for ready-made dress supplanted that for the tailor-made.[22] More generally, bespoke and tailor-made dress reinforced class hierarchies wherein those on the lower rungs of the socioeconomic ladder were resigned to wear clothing of lesser quality, cast-offs, and hand-me-downs. The ready-made revolution, as it were, heralded what historians Claudia Kidwell and Margaret Christman have deemed the "democratization of clothing in America" wherein the quality and affordability of American clothing "served to obliterate ethnic origins and blur social distinctions" so that Americans became the "best-dressed average people in the world."[23] Stoutwear was an industry born from the democratic idealism of American mass manufacturing, which held that all citizens should have access to an abundance of affordable, well-made goods.[24] Yet, even as fat women were presented with more options in the way of ready-made dress, this greater freedom of choice was not without its trade-offs. Where ready-made dress obfuscated class status and ethnic origins, it also reified beauty norms and perpetuated weight-based stereotypes.

In addition to being a product of America's shift away from the custom-made to the ready-made, stoutwear was born from the unique ideological climate of the early twentieth century, and specifically of Americans' evolving attitudes toward fat. Although it stands to reason that stoutwear was the product of increased demand, the average

American woman had not suddenly grown fatter at the turn of the century.[25] Rather, it was more so that tolerances for even moderate amounts of overweight had begun to narrow so that people who in previous decades would not have been considered problematically fat suddenly were.[26] As will be discussed in greater depth in the following chapter, this narrowing of tolerances was partly facilitated by new technologies for measuring and quantifying body weight, such as the scale, height and weight charts, and standardized sizing. Cumulatively, these technologies gave shape to the "normal" or "standard" body, against which all other bodies were measured. In turn, there emerged new ways to speak about and quantify bodily deviance. Feminine fatness—once vaguely defined through the relative ampleness of a woman's curves—came into sharper relief both through comparison and, as is the thesis of this book, through the discourses and practices of fashion. The technology of standardized sizing in particular provided a seemingly objective basis for determining who classified as overweight. For women, this threshold was a forty-four-inch bust and a thirty-inch waist, or what would (at least at the waist) roughly correspond to a contemporary US size ten or a UK size fourteen.[27] No less important than sizing, however, was the fact that, as *Vogue* claimed in a 1923 column, increasingly streamlined fashions "demanded" streamlined bodies.[28]

During the last quarter of the nineteenth century, highly tailored, two-piece dresses rendered in heavy, luxurious textiles were at the height of fashion. Supported by an armature of rigid undergarments that variously amplified and diminished the body's natural curves, these fashions forcibly reshaped women's bodies into artificial silhouettes, such as the hourglass and the S-bend. By 1910, however, the sumptuous fashions of the Gilded Age gave way to simpler one-piece dresses and lighter, more flexible undergarments that allowed greater freedom of movement, but less room for the body to deviate from the ever-slenderer beauty ideal.[29] While the new fashions were less sophisticated in terms of construction and therefore easier to fit to a variety of body shapes than those of previous decades, they also revealed more of the body than ever. This, along with the growing popularity of standardized, mass-manufactured garments, only intensified the requirement for bodily conformity.

Stoutwear could not have emerged anywhere but in the United States—a prosperous, industrialized, and increasingly secular consumer society that, as historian Hillel Schwartz has written, was so "perplexed or intimidated by its abundance" that it had to devise strategies to offset or atone for this abundance.[30] Within a society still holding if only by a thread to the Protestant virtues of temperance and asceticism, weight loss became a compensatory strategy for overconsumption and overindulgence in other aspects of American life.[31] By the 1920s, the once marginal practices of secular fasting and dieting were commonplace, as was the use of more expedient quick fixes and cure-alls.[32] Over a few short decades, countless products materialized that promised faster, more pleasurable, and, perhaps most importantly, *more profitable* routes to weight loss. While most early twentieth-century fat-melting products—from rubber chin straps to vibrating abdominal belts—were harmless if inefficacious gimmicks, amphetamine-laced diet pills and experimental abdominal lipectomy surgeries were among the more dangerous ways to shed unwanted pounds during this period.[33] As many Americans would come to realize, however, the sensational claims made by advertisers about the effectiveness and permanence of these approaches were at best exaggerated, and at worst outright lies.

Although stoutwear was not a weight-loss product, many of the claims made by stoutwear manufacturers and advertisers were scarcely different from those made by companies hawking diet pills and rubber corsets. Yet, within the commercial weight-loss landscape, stoutwear was unique to the extent that it sold women the promise that they could achieve the appearance of slenderness without actually having to diet, exercise, ingest experimental drugs, or undergo surgery. Ostensibly, all one had to do to look slender was slip on a specially designed stoutwear dress. As with other slimming products, however, stoutwear would only more deeply entrench weight bias in American society to the extent that it framed body fat as something that could, and should, be eradicated.

Re-fashioning Fat History

The idea that the fashion system has played a crucial role in establishing and cementing modern standards of beauty, and, in particular, the slender ideal, is well-trodden territory in the scholarly literature.[34] The history of fat and the causes of weight bias, likewise, have been exhaustively explored from multiple disciplinary perspectives.[35] Less acknowledged, however, is the role that fashion *specifically* has played in producing and perpetuating weight bias in American life. Within the published histories of fat, many scholars frame fashion as but one piece of a larger puzzle in the construction of modern attitudes toward fat, and a somewhat frivolous one at that. Perhaps most explicitly, in his seminal history of fat, *Never Satisfied* (1986), Hillel Schwartz describes fashion as but a "small part" of the broader constellation of factors that have shaped public opinion about weight and weight loss during the twentieth century. Fashion, he argues,

> has to do with shape and texture, posture and quality of skin, not with weight. Our century's unique confusion of dimension, proportion, mass and weight has been compounded by fashion and fashion writing, but styles in clothing and cosmetics do not of themselves have causal priority.[36]

More important than fashion, according to Schwartz, are the complex relays between science, politics, technology, and the diet industrial complex. While I do not go so far as to claim that fashion should be given causal priority, I do believe that fashion should at least be given equal consideration in any investigation into America's complicated relationship with health and overweight. This is because it is the body that ultimately lies at the center of any investigation into the history of, or meanings attached to, fat. In his own scholarship, Schwartz even acknowledges this fact, stating that "the body ... what it is, what it seems to be, what it could turn out to be" must be employed to understand the "shared fictions" about fat.[37] Histories of fat are always, and necessarily, histories of the body.

As Roy Porter observes, histories of the body "rescue the body from neglect and disrepute" in the discipline of history, and in doing so reposition the body at "the crossroads between self and society." Histories of the body also acknowledge that the body, and the way humanity conceives of the body, is neither neutral nor static.[38] Foucauldian genealogies, discussed previously, fall within the remit of body history for they are also concerned with the body as it is embroiled within and shaped by power struggles. As Foucault writes in his essay "Nietzsche, Genealogy, History," "Genealogy, as analysis of descent, is thus situated within the articulation of the body and history. Its task is to expose a body totally imprinted by history and the process of history's destruction of the body."[39] Since the 1970s, there has been a particular interest in recovering histories of bodies traditionally subordinated to the margins of scholarly inquiry, such as the queer body and the disabled body. The goal of this scholarship, which is deeply indebted to the work of Foucault, is to conceptualize the body "as a flesh upon which the micro-physics of power leave their mark."[40] Histories of the fat body, for their part, meaningfully reframe fat as an organizing principle in society, rather than something experienced by a small subset of the population. To the extent that they reframe bodies as the effects of historical power struggles, however, body histories frequently succumb to what Porter describes as a tendency "float off into the stratosphere of discourse analysis," thereby losing sight of the physical experience of embodiment. This, he argues, is due in large part to a neglect of the more "tangible materials" at the disposal of the historian—that is, the stuff of life.[41] Alongside the many records of human embodiment that Porter offers up for analysis—from hospital registers to personal snapshots—I would also present fashion as a means of bringing body history back down to earth, so to speak; not rarefied high fashion or *haute couture*, but ordinary, everyday dress. As with other bodily ephemera, dress can help us to answer key questions Porter poses, such as, "How have people made sense of the mysterious link between 'self' and its extensions?" and, "How have they managed the body as an intermediary between the self and society?"[42] Yet, despite the intimate proximity of dress to the body and all that dress can reveal about bodies of the past, many historians fail to recognize the central role that dress plays in mediating human embodiment.

"Human bodies," as Joanne Entwistle observes, "are *dressed* bodies."[43] While this may seem like an obvious point, it is one that is consistently glossed over outside of the interdisciplinary field of fashion studies, and understandably so. What constitutes "fashion" may vary within different cultural contexts, but the practice of adorning the human body is universal. While some choose to engage in more exuberant or subversive performances of self-fashioning, the act of dressing in daily life is reflexive to the point of banality. Indeed, we take for granted the fact that it is unacceptable in nearly all contexts to forego clothing altogether. It therefore makes sense that dress would tend to go overlooked in studies about fat and weight bias, but this doesn't make its omission any less egregious.

Beyond merely covering the body, Entwistle argues that it is dress that makes the body "recognizable and meaningful to a culture." By turn, "bodies which do not conform, bodies which flout the conventions of their culture and go without the appropriate clothes are subversive of the most basic social codes and risk exclusion, scorn or ridicule."[44] Echoing this idea, Elizabeth Wilson has remarked upon the deeply ambivalent nature of twentieth-century fashion. According to Wilson, twentieth-century fashion is as much an aesthetic and expressive medium as it is a cover or container for the flesh. In addition to fulfilling our individual, and somewhat contradictory, desires for both belonging and self-differentiation, fashion and dress create clear boundaries between bodies and culture, self and other, inside and outside. Drawing upon the work of the anthropologist Mary Douglas, she notes how humans are deeply uncomfortable with the "dangerous" margins of the biological, fleshy body. Dress and dress codes therefore serve the important function of "strengthening" and "reinforcing" these bodily boundaries. By turn, the sense of unease we experience when someone is improperly dressed "reminds us that the naked body underneath the clothes … is somehow unfinished, vulnerable and leaky at the margins."[45]

The most flagrant example of a sartorially subversive body, as many have observed, is that of the nudist; however, transgressions of dress in daily life are typically much more subtle. This is because the "rules" of appropriate dress are themselves often quite mundane. At their most basic, they boil down to wearing the right thing at the right moment. During the intimate act of getting dressed, an individual must make a series of decisions based on where they are going, who they are seeing, and what the weather is like, among other things. As inconsequential as these each of these considerations may seem individually, together they evince the entanglements of the body, identity, the environment, and culture. Employing Foucault's theories about the interdependent nature of power and knowledge—and specifically his contention that bodies are invested with and shaped by regimes of knowledge via discourse—Entwistle observes that individuals always get dressed "within the bounds of a culture and its particular norms [and] expectations about the body, and about what constitutes a 'dressed' body."[46] Dress, in other words, materializes discursive regimes of power (i.e., beliefs, values, social norms, etc.), while the physical act of *getting dressed* is the process through which bodies are invested with that power. It is for these reasons, Entwistle argues, that "dress in everyday life cannot be separated from the living, breathing, moving body it adorns." Said differently, the dressed body should be regarded as an object of culture—one that bears the weight of the norms and expectations of its culture, and which is constrained by the finite resources of consumer culture.[47]

While consumer culture has since the early twentieth century sold the interrelated promises of infinite choice and a product to solve every problem, our options are not actually as boundless as advertisers would have us believe. This is particularly true within the fashion industry wherein the assortment of goods on offer, as Paolo Volonté argues, is determined less by the creative whims of individual designers than by the "tyranny" of beauty ideals and by the technological limitations of mass manufacturing.[48] Entwistle touches on this point as well, writing that "choices over dress are always defined within a particular context: the fashion system and what it provides as the 'raw material' of our choices."[49] Not unlike the written and unwritten "rules" of dress, garments (as designed objects) are themselves always invested with the values of the cultures in which they are created. Fashion is therefore always a limited and *limiting* medium of expression. Not only are we constrained by the norms of the cultures in which we live; we are also constrained by what, in any given moment, is available for purchase within the marketplace.

Over the long twentieth century and even into the twenty-first, the slender beauty ideal has played an outsize role in shaping the discourses and practices of fashion and, more specifically, the style and fabrication of fashionable garments.[50] One could even argue that it is *the* central pillar around which modern fashion revolves. Rebecca Arnold summarizes this well when she writes, "Fashion colludes in society's obsession with thinness," determining everything from which bodies are upheld as beautiful in the fashion media, to the shape of the fashionable silhouette, to the comforts individuals willingly forego in order to achieve the appearance of slenderness. Not only do fashion and dress reflect this cultural preoccupation with slenderness, they uphold and perpetuate it, for fashion, as Arnold writes, "is rather a form of seductive and beautiful coercion into believing the miracle of perfection that awaits those faithful to its decrees."[51] For all but the privileged few who possess a body that fits neatly within the bounds of that which is considered ideal (or are intrepid enough to flout cultural norms altogether), the act of getting dressed goes hand-in-hand with "self-care" and "bodywork" regimens that actively intervene in the body to change its physical shape and contours.[52] To the extent that it is undergirded by slenderizing design principles, stoutwear and plus-size fashion make fat bodies culturally intelligible by bringing them more in line with accepted beauty norms.

Although fashion has in many ways come to be regarded as a "solution" to the "problem" of fat, fashion and fat occupy a similar place in the cultural imaginary. Like "fashion," which Valerie Steele famously deemed the *other* "F-word," fat is generally perceived as excessive, unnecessary, and even frivolous.[53] Richard Klein takes this comparison even further, writing,

> Fat has always been conceived as a kind of cancerous growth, inessential to the body or its image, an excrescence, a corruption of the flesh whose removal [leaves] the body intact and in better shape. Fat is something we wear; it is on the outside of our inside.[54]

As Klein observes, fat—as much as it regarded as a superfluous substance that is effectively "worn" on the outside of the body—is not actually so different from fashion. Although fat, as anyone who has ever attempted a diet can attest, cannot literally be taken off like a garment, it is nevertheless conceived as something ancillary to the body proper. This idea, however, could not be farther from the truth. Just as fashion is an essential component of human embodiment, so too is fat. As will be discussed in greater depth in the following section, fat (not unlike a transgression of dress) "marks" the body as abject and Other and mediates fat people's experience of being in the world. Extending this idea, it stands to reason that because fat is an extension of the human body, and because human bodies are dressed bodies, fashion and dress are therefore inextricable from the experience of fat embodiment. It is for these reasons that fashion and dress should not be brushed aside as but a "small part" of the histories of fat and weight bias.

According to Heike Jenß, "fashion" can refer to objects (e.g., garments, accessories, etc.), to a collective belief system, or to an aesthetic economy. As a verb, however, "fashion" connotes an active practice unmoored from the creative field of fashion. To fashion is thus "to form, mold, shape (either a material or immaterial object)."[55] Sophie Woodward has provided a similar definition, writing that "the process of fashioning in part produces what is fashionable, yet is also produced by the system of fashion."[56] Both definitions acknowledge fashioning as a social dynamic, as a process, and as a dispersed system of power relations. The project of "re-fashioning" fat history therefore involves not merely repositioning the fat body as dressed, nor in foregrounding fashion within the history of fat—that is, by recovering the history of large-size dress, and specifically stoutwear. Rather, it also requires a repositioning of stoutwear less as an effect of weight bias than as one of the key sites in which weight bias was produced or *fashioned*.

The Slender Ideal, Fat Stigma, and Weight Bias

While an investigation into the ebbs and flows of the large-size dress sector throughout the twentieth and twenty-first centuries can reveal much about America's ever-evolving relationship with fat, stoutwear in particular lays bare the myriad ways that fashion has not just been a mirror for but has actively perpetuated weight bias, or "negative weight-related attitudes, beliefs, assumptions and judgements toward individuals who are 'overweight' or 'obese.'"[57] For instance, stoutwear provided a material basis for weight bias by effectively marking bodies as "stout" during a time when the threshold between fat and thin was growing ever finer and increasingly ambiguous. Likewise, dressmaking and tailoring tools such as sizing tables, proportional systems, and flexible tape measures were, alongside scales, some of the more widely adopted means of measuring and quantifying body weight and size. As the contours of deviant fatness came into sharper relief, so too, however, did those of the slender body. Beauty norms, as Volonté has observed, are both relational and asymmetrical. Although slenderness is upheld as ideal in American culture, it is by no means objectively more aesthetically appealing than fatness; it is a social construct.[58] By neglecting and marginalizing non-slender bodies, fashion naturalizes the slender beauty ideal while also producing and perpetuating negative ideas about fatness. Standards of what constitutes a "problematically fat" or an "ideally slender" body in any given era are shaped through comparison and, as is relevant to the current study, reified through fashion discourses and practices.

To be clear, however, the denigration of fat bodies is not unique to the field of fashion, nor is the slender ideal the product of fashion discourses and practices irrespective to external forces, beliefs, and ideologies. Rather, fashion was one site among many that fortified the societal aversion to fat bodies in the early twentieth century and which elevated slenderness as ideal. The origins of weight bias, on the other hand, have much deeper roots.

In the United States, the slender ideal is inextricably linked with ideas about gender, race, ethnicity, and citizenship, and in particular beliefs about what constitutes an appropriately "American" body. Sabrina Strings has traced these linkages and in doing so has demonstrated that Americans' aversion to fatness is deeply entwined with racism and, specifically, with anti-Blackness. In *Fearing the Black Body* (2019), she identifies the first stirrings of this ideology not within the contexts of medical discourse and modernity, as have been suggested elsewhere, but amid the growth of the transatlantic slave trade and the spread of Protestantism in the eighteenth and nineteenth centuries. Whereas "racial and scientific rhetoric about slavery linked fatness to 'greedy' Africans … religious discourse suggested that overeating was ungodly." She therefore argues that, in the United States, "the phobia about fatness and the preference for thinness have not, principally or historically, been about health," nor have various attempts to control, contain, and eradicate fat. Rather, they have been employed to create social distinctions, legitimate constructions of Americanness, and to sustain racist ideologies. With the fat Black body framed as both "coarse" and "immoral," the slender body became the singular model of feminine beauty for white American women.[59] Like the "unruly" bodies of enslaved African women, those of immigrants provided another point of contrast in the constitution of appropriate feminine embodiment. This idea has been furthered by Katharina Vester, who observes that within the context of mass migration in the nineteenth century, "the 'obese,' foreign and exoticized woman was used as a contrast to the self-restrained and self-controlled [American] woman signifying advancement and progress."[60] More than a fear of the negative health effects of overweight, both Strings and Vester conclude that it was deep-seated fears of the Black body and the immigrant Other that first propelled the adoption of the slender feminine ideal in the United States.

In some instances, the racist and xenophobic origins of weight bias could clearly be glimpsed within fashion discourses. In an August 1920 interview with the trade journal *Printers' Ink*, for instance, a stoutwear manufacturer was quoted as having said, "while no class of society is immune, women of foreign birth seem to be more inclined to stoutness than do the more pure-blooded Americans."[61] In her own work, Strings found multiple instances in which fashion and beauty columnists quite explicitly framed appetite suppression as a practice of cultivated white women and therefore a mark of racial superiority.[62] By the first decades of the twentieth century, however, explicit correlations between ethnic origins, skin color, and fat were supplanted by the qualities and behaviors associated with those groups. Laziness, greed, immorality, uncleanliness, and stupidity were all traits that were first associated with the "unruly" and "uncivilized" bodies of racial and ethnic Others but which inevitably came to be ascribed to those of fat white people, too.[63] As they became increasingly unmoored from their racialized origins, the negative stereotypes associated with overweight assumed different meanings. Where excess body fat was described in nineteenth-century ethnographic and anthropological literature as a hallmark of the "uncivilized" bodies of "savages," Farrell observes that the twentieth-century fat was more generally regarded as a symbol of "greedy and uncontrolled impulses—a sign that the excesses of modernism could not be handled."[64]

The stigmatization of body fat, or the negative social and psychological traits associated with the appearance of excessive body weight, is productive of weight bias. Although he does not focus on fatness in his work, body fat meets the definitions of what Erving Goffman has referred to as both a "visible stigma" and an "abomination of the body." Visible stigmas are physical attributes that mark bodies as different from those which are regarded as "normal" within societies, and which reduce individuals "from a whole and usual person to a tainted, discounted one."[65] As with other visible stigmas—from physical disabilities to one's race or ethnicity—the meanings assigned to fat are historically contingent. While moderate amounts of overweight were acceptable and even desirable throughout much of human history, for all the reasons outlined above, Americans have, since at least the early nineteenth century, ascribed meanings to bodily fatness that are separate from, or bear no relation to, the physical trait itself. Excess body fat, for instance, does not confer stupidity or laziness. It does, however, provide the preconditions for discrediting bodies that do not fit neatly within a prescribed social order.

Because of their size relative to those who are considered "normal," fat people face potential social ostracization and forms of discrimination that render them undeserving of the same rights and freedoms as more "normatively-sized" people. Indeed, this is how weight bias manifests in everyday life. So great is the stigma of overweight in American culture that individuals will go to great lengths to reduce their weight or to diminish the appearance of body fat. Such acts of "self-regulation" or "self-discipline" may include dieting and exercise, but also encompass individual dress practices that are variously undertaken in order to attain some semblance of beauty and therefore social acceptance. With the exception of the last chapter, which focuses on the dress practices of self-identifying fat women, however, this book is less concerned with stigma management than the fashion discourses and practices that produced and perpetuated weight bias.

A History of Fashion without Fashion

"What does it mean to study a history of fashion *without* fashion?" This was a question Professor Caroline Evans asked in a research seminar I attended at the Centre for Fashion Studies at Stockholm University in 2016.[66] Although Evans asked the question rhetorically (and somewhat off-handedly), it was nevertheless a question that weighed heavily on me throughout the course of researching and writing this book. As others who have studied fat fashion from a historical vantage point can attest, the material record is scanty at best and non-existent at worst.[67] This is because large-size dress objects are more likely to end their lives in donation or rag bins than in the archives. Through a protracted period during which I reached out to historical fashion and costume collections in the United States, I learned that the frequency with which large-size dress objects are collected pales in comparison to standard- and small-size garments. With few exceptions, my inquiries into an institution's large-size dress holdings were answered with polite apologies, even though I suspected that many of these institutions likely had examples of large-size dress hiding in plain sight, with some collection managers and curators suffering from a sort of "size astigmatism." Indeed, because what constitutes fat in any given era is so mutable, what to contemporary eyes might seem average or even small would have, in its time, been considered stout- or plus-size.[68] Even still, the fact remains that clothing worn by fat people has not been collected with any particular zeal by any major American fashion or costume archive.[69] This dearth of surviving objects can be attributed to a number of institutional, political, and practical reasons, from tight budgets that do not allow for the acquisition of specialized dress forms and mannequins in a diverse range of sizes, to the conscious and unconscious biases of donors and curators, to simply not knowing what to look for. Although they varied from institution to institution, the reasons given for these archival silences affirmed Carolyn Steedman's observation that archives are not neutral spaces of discovery but rather are powerful microcosms of social and cultural values that are subject to the priorities and values of their collecting bodies, curators, and conservators.[70]

The absence of large-size dress within these spaces has led to a deeply entrenched survival bias that has naturalized the notion that fat women have been excluded from fashion or, worse, that there were no large-sized women in the past.[71] When large-size garments are collected and conserved, they tend to be technically odd or exceptional, materially valuable, or attributed to a notable designer or wearer (e.g., Queen Victoria's mourning attire or "Mama" Cass Elliot's colorful bespoke kaftans).[72] While the dearth of stoutwear and plus-size fashion in archives and museums has obvious implications for inclusivity and representation in fashion curation, it has also contributed to the marginalization of fat bodies within the fashion literature given historians' tendency to "lead out" from the garment.[73] Due to the lack of surviving large-size dress in costume archives, I was forced to return to Evans' question, albeit slightly rephrased: How does one recover a history of fat fashion *without* fat fashion?

In brief, it requires an eclectic approach, an open mind, and a great deal of patience. This, as Annabella Pollen and Charlotte Nicklas have remarked, is not so uncommon within the interdisciplinary field of fashion studies in which researchers are frequently required to adopt "ad hoc" approaches as they turn ever more "to unusual or unresearched historical sources."[74] Evans has echoed this point with her metaphor, drawn from Walter Benjamin's *Arcades Project*, for fashion historians as "ragpickers" who must combine different methods, primary sources, and ways of thinking in order to capture the inherently dynamic, "semiotically unstable" nature of fashion.[75] In devising my own ad hoc method, I began by first reading the seminal histories of fat with a particular attention to the role that fashion played in these accounts. While it was rare that fashion was omitted altogether, it was most often lumped together with beauty products as an effect, rather than a cause, of weight bias. In an effort to understand why fashion amounted to little more than a footnote in these histories, I returned to the fashion and dress historical literature where, with few exceptions, the early history of large-size dress was similarly glossed over or incomplete.[76] Although the field of fashion studies encourages incisive, curious, and critical approaches to the study of fashion and its "multiple meanings and interpretations," as evidenced by its neglect of the fat body, dress history and fashion studies are not entirely unaffected by the fashion industry's hierarchies and value systems.[77] Just as fashion was neglected in the published histories of fat, fat was similarly marginalized in the histories of fashion.

With only hints to the role that fashion played in the perpetuation of weight bias and no formal fashion or dress archive to work in, I turned to a diverse and dispersed range of sources that spoke to fashion as industry, object, idea, and practice, and which lent clues to how stoutwear was conceived by designers and manufacturers and experienced by fat women in everyday life. Rarely, for the reasons previously discussed, were these sources canonical fashion objects but rather "traces," or the "refuse," of fashion history. As Evans writes, the concept of historical traces can be located in Benjamin's *Arcades Project*, where he uses the term to describe the marks that remain when the objects of bourgeois domesticity are moved or disturbed. For the fashion historian, however, Evans argues that such traces can be used for a new kind of cultural analysis—one that reveals overlooked histories as well as the messy and fragmented relays between the past and the present.[78] My own historical traces were found in digitized online archives, regional libraries, and, less frequently, museums and university costume collections. In these archives, I consulted literary sources such as biographies, autobiographies, fashion magazines, and fashion trade journals; visual sources such as street photography, portraits, satirical prints, and cartoons; commercial sources like catalogs, mailers, and advertisements; and, when available, surviving dress objects. No less important, however, were the primary sources, or "fashion ephemera," that evaded collection even within these less formal fashion archives—from style guides to personal snapshots—and which I took to purchasing myself from estate sales and online auction websites in the creation of my own ad hoc archive.[79]

Facing a similar paucity of surviving dress objects in his research into the history of masculine consumption in fin de siècle London, Christopher Breward proposed collapsing disciplinary boundaries that typically exist, for instance, around literary sources and those that might be considered social, legal, or political. The goal of this approach was to "[reconcile] oppositional methodological positions and sources" in order to recover evidence of fashion discourses and practices that were never recorded or that had been lost to time and to memory. Although Breward notes that while it is necessary to recognize the status, reliability, and intentions of a primary source, such a collapsing of disciplinary boundaries can help to reveal connections, patterns, and themes that might otherwise go unnoticed. It is the "tensions" and "spaces between" disparate sources, and especially between those that have been viewed as "the most shaky" or that have been "attacked for their lack of integrity," that Breward finds particularly evocative. By combining evidence from sources as diverse as novels, catalogs, trade publications, cartes de visite, and street photography, he was able to reveal the nuances of how fashion and dress are experienced in everyday life.[80] Echoing this point, Cheryl Buckley and Hazel Clark note that in their research into fashion in everyday life, the use of quotidian, ephemeral, and ordinary sources, placed in conversation with one another, helped not only to address the silences in formal costume collections but to reveal how fashion was practiced and experienced.[81]

Following Evans, Breward, and Buckley and Clark, this book weaves together a wide and eclectic array of primary sources or "traces" in order to reveal both the discursive and material mechanisms through which the fashion industry participated in the construction and perpetuation of weight bias. This book is therefore less an exhaustive history of stoutwear—although some aspects of this history are discussed—than it is about behaviors, beliefs, biases, beauty ideals, and bodies. Indeed, while the material qualities, design, representation, and promotion of stoutwear are discussed in the pages that follow, these discussions are had in the service of unravelling the webs of power in which the fat woman was entangled—that is, how fashion and dress defined and delimited the contours of the fat female body and, to a lesser extent, how fat women themselves navigated this fraught terrain.

A Note on Terminology

The language employed throughout this book has been chosen with great care and with attention to avoiding anachronistic slippages in, for instance, applying contemporary terms and phrasings to historical objects, bodies, ideas, and phenomena. This, however, was not without its difficulties. Although this book is embedded within the historical context of the early twentieth century, as previously discussed, the circumstances, debates, and discourses discussed throughout will feel to the reader if not highly contemporary then little changed. Throughout the process of writing this book, it was all too easy to see the contemporary plus-size woman mirrored in the historical stout woman given the way that each has existed in her own time as fashion's forgotten Other. Likewise, early discussions about how to refer to the stout woman within consumer advertising almost begged to be compared with similar conversations that are being had today about whether or not to abolish the term "plus-size" in favor of more inclusive language. At the same time, however, plus-size fashion and stoutwear are products of completely different sociohistorical circumstances and, as a result, studies of stoutwear and plus-size fashion should each be afforded their own space. It is ahistorical to conflate the two periods, even as we might acknowledge the correspondences between them.

Although this is a historical and theoretical investigation, throughout this book, I have chosen to follow the lead of contemporary fat activists who have called for the reclamation of the term "fat" as a neutral descriptor for referring to bodies and body weight. This is different from how fat is employed within the sources I reference where it is most commonly used to mark larger bodies as abject and unruly. Beginning in the late twentieth century, "fat" was replaced by "obese" as the preferred, and (some would argue) more politically correct, term with which to label larger bodies; however, activists have observed that it has only further stigmatized bodily fatness for the manner in which it medicalizes human diversity and fuels discrimination under the guise of scientific objectivity.[82] In order to resolve these debates, fat activists and fat studies scholars, pointing to the fact that the "O-word is neither neutral nor benign," have made a concerted effort to reclaim fat as a political identity and as the preferred term within scholarly work.[83] This convention has been widely adopted throughout the literature, and as such, throughout this book I avoid invoking the "O-word," or place it in scare quotes when using it at all.

Even as the term "fat" has been embraced within the academic literature, as Don Kulick and Anne Meneley point out, "The tone with which the word fat is still uttered [in public] is often concerned, ashamed, alarmist or condemnatory."[84] As a result, there has been no shortage of alternatives conceived throughout the twentieth century, many of them within fashion, to refer to fat bodies. The terms "plus-size," "curvy," "full-figured," "voluptuous," "chubby," and "stout," among others, have all been employed by fashion manufacturers, advertisers, and retailers in various moments to effectively repackage fat and sell an ideal back to consumers.[85] Much like the "O-word," however, terms like "voluptuous" and "curvy," while decidedly more euphemistic, are themselves neither neutral nor benign. Whereas fat studies scholars call for such euphemisms to similarly be placed within scare quotes due to the extent to which they "falsely put a positive spin on a negative view of fatness," I have chosen to forego this particular convention due to the frequency with which these terms are used in my primary source materials and appear in this text.[86]

Chapter Outline

In Chapter 1, "Creating Consumers," I build upon ideas sketched out in this Introduction. I do so by situating stoutwear at the center of growing concerns about the perceived fattening of American women in the early twentieth century, as well as a number of ascendant technologies for measuring and quantifying the body that established clearer boundaries around "normal" and "deviant" body weight. Through this investigation, I challenge the presumption that the stoutwear industry was the result of a suddenly fatter society by pursuing the contrary notion that the limitations of mass manufacturing incited a demand for larger sizes, and that stoutwear was, in part, the product of the search for new markets. I argue that it is a result of these interrelated forces that the stoutwear consumer, and by proxy, the fat woman, was effectively *created*.

In Chapters 2, 3, and 4, I explore a different aspect of fashionable production (i.e., design, advertising, and fashion journalism) in order to reveal the specific mechanisms through which the fashion industry perpetuated weight bias in early twentieth-century America. In Chapter 2, "Designing for Disorder," I consider the underlying ideology of stoutwear design, and namely the precept that the fat female body was disorderly and in need of design intervention. Through an investigation of stoutwear design discourse, I reveal stoutwear's unlikely intersections with modernist and architectural design thinking, and namely the notion, furthered by male industrialists, that fashion design could transcend its feminized origins to solve social problems. Beyond just meeting the fit needs of fat female consumers, I argue that stoutwear manufacturers endeavored to design fat out of existence altogether. In Chapter 3, "Fitting the Mind," I consider the limitations of "consumer citizenship" by positioning stoutwear advertising within the emerging discipline of consumer psychology. In their attempts to translate fat women's desires and anxieties into sales, advertisers strategically stoked concerns about the social repercussions of overweight while touting the miraculous slenderizing capacities of scientifically designed stoutwear. This, I argue, was essential to the economic viability of stoutwear but had the adverse effect of pathologizing feminine fatness. In Chapter 4, "Parables of Overweight," I focus on the ways that fat was discussed within the women's and fashion press in the early twentieth century. Drawing upon Agnès Rocamora's conceptualization of "fashion media discourse," I identify four "parables of overweight" that expose how other concerns, from ageing to surveillance culture, were mapped onto the fat female body. Taken together, these three chapters begin to unravel the webs of power in which fat women were entangled, and the ways that fashion not only reflected but also produced negative ideas about overweight.

In Chapter 5, "The Forgotten Woman," I foreground the dress practices of three self-identifying fat women. Taking an eclectic methodological approach, I place personal snapshots, biographies, and style guides, among other ephemeral materials, in conversation in order to reconstruct stories that have largely been lost to history. Yet, even as the dress practices of the women discussed in this chapter may have been forgotten, their names will likely be familiar to many readers. The sartorial biographies of the vaudeville performer Sophie Tucker and the blues singer Gertrude "Ma" Rainey, along with the lesser-known Jane Warren Wells, reveal that, although fat women were conceived within the industry as a monolith—that is, as insecure, emotionally stunted, and unintelligent—their experiences with fashion and dress were as diverse as their lived experiences, and intersected with, among other things, race, ethnicity, and class.[87]

In the Conclusion I consider how the legacies of stoutwear manifest in contemporary fashion systems and practices, namely through the imposition of what I describe as fashion's "slenderness imperative." In particular, I address the extent to which moralizing design precepts persist within plus-size and curve design in spite of the massive strides by fat activists and allies in resignifying fat embodiment in recent decades and within the context of the mainstream Body Positivity Movement. In a final reflection, I also explore what a more radically inclusive approach to large-size garment design might entail.

CHAPTER 1
CREATING CONSUMERS

On June 11, 1915, *Women's Wear* published an article titled "How Many Fat Women in Your Town?" With a subheading that read "You Don't Know, But Enough to Pay Well for Special Attention," it foreshadowed a shift in the way large-size women's garments would be designed, manufactured, and sold to fat women for decades to come. In exploring the lucrative future of a new sector of the American fashion industry known as "stoutwear," the article recounts the experiences of a manager from a Midwestern department store who had successfully expanded his product assortment. As he told the publication,

> Every once in a while ... a stout customer used to ask me while I was waiting on her, or used to ask the salesgirls: "Don't you ever buy anything for fat women?" Whatever the response we made was bound to be a lame one, because the simple truth in the matter was that I didn't think there were enough fat women to make it pay. After a while though, I began to ... keep my eyes peeled for the stout ones ....
>
> You haven't any idea how many fat women there are in the world until you begin to sell something they want. The proportion of fat women is greater than the proportion of fat men, probably because many of them lead lives more sedentary than their husbands. Whatever the reason, the fact is undisputable—at least in this town and in every other town where I have ever been.[1]

In a cartoon that accompanied the article (Figure 1.1), a mob of fat women is depicted spilling into an urban shopping corridor, suggesting their ostensibly sudden arrival onto the American fashion scene. The women are rendered in larger-than-life and less-than-flattering proportions—their features exaggerated to accentuate their physical departures from the ascendant slender beauty ideal. The effect is further heightened by the presence of a man, over whom they loom. Ushering them into a storefront emblazoned with the words "Your Store?" he stands before the women as a proxy for the retailers who would stand to benefit from their patronage. The growing stigma of overweight in the early twentieth century is personified by their enormous proportions and appearance, written on their bodies for all to see. So too, however, is their perceived hunger to consume.

In the long history of plus-size fashion, this article is a watershed as it is among the first to discuss the unrealized potential of a specialized category of clothing for fat women. As the department store manager recounted to *Women's Wear*, although he was not unaccustomed to encountering the occasional fat female customer, he simply had not realized that "there were enough fat women" to financially justify carrying larger sizes. After having become aware of the limitations of his inventory, however, he suddenly became more conscious of fat women's presence and more attuned to the fact

You have no idea now many fat women there are until you begin to sell something they want.

Figure 1.1 "How Many Fat Women in Your Town?," *Women's Wear* (June 11, 1915), 3. Published with permission of ProQuest LLC. Further reproduction is prohibited without permission.

that they looked "too big" in their clothes—a symptom, perhaps, of the constraints of conventional sizing systems. The article concluded with the following prediction:

> It is probable that the "stouts" will continue to rank as the most important of the special classes of "freaks" in the ready-to-wear trade. With all the consideration in

the world for them and appreciation of their self-conscious distress, which is very real, women like these offer possibilities in the way of business.[2]

Having been previously neglected by the makers of mass-manufactured garments, the "discovery" of the fat woman in 1915 marked a turning point in American fashion toward greater market segmentation and, one could argue, inclusivity. Yet, even as retailers and manufacturers saw an opportunity in the fat woman's patronage, their opinion of her was clearly ambivalent at best. This begs the question: Why at a time when anti-fat sentiment was on the rise was there paradoxically more room for the fat woman in fashion than ever before?

In exploring answers to this question, this chapter investigates the broader social and cultural contexts in which the stoutwear industry emerged during the first two decades of the twentieth century. In doing so, it draws principally upon articles from the trade press—or journals, magazines, and articles written by and for manufacturers, advertisers, and retailers rather than for the general public—that offer a revealing, and oftentimes unvarnished, backstage glimpse into the decisions, practices, and debates that gave rise to this new sector of the American fashion industry. Far from emerging from a vacuum as is suggested in the *Women's Wear* article, however, this chapter describes an industry intimately bound up with and responding to rapidly shifting attitudes toward health and fat in the United States, as well as developments in mass manufacturing and consumer culture. It also begins to cast light on the ways in which fashion discourses and practices helped to more clearly define the threshold between "normal" and "overweight." This chapter therefore challenges the presumption that the large-size dress sector emerged in response to a suddenly fatter society by pursuing the contrary notion that the conditions of garment manufacturing actually incited a demand for larger sizes. In working out the problem of how to produce larger sizes, however, manufacturers had to first map out the contours of the fat woman's body in order to delimit how and to what extent her curves deviated from those of the "normal" or "average" woman. It is through this process that manufacturers gave shape to or *created* the "stout consumer."

The notion of "creating consumers" is borrowed from the historian Stuart Ewen who describes the process through which a desiring buying public was identified in order to meet the productive capacity of mass manufacturing in the United States in the early twentieth century.[3] Before mass manufacturing, American industry catered to a small, affluent market. With a growing capacity to produce goods cheaply and quickly, however, there needed to be an equivalent increase in consumers to purchase those goods if mass manufacturing were to ever be profitable. "As the question of expanding old and creating new markets became a function of the massification of industry," Ewen writes, "foresighted businessmen began to see the necessity of organizing their businesses not merely around the production of goods, but around the creation of a buying public."[4] Just as industrialists like Henry Ford were identifying and targeting new markets for their assembly line-produced automobiles, so too were captains of flexible industries like fashion, which was undergoing its own convulsions during the early twentieth century. In particular, the notion of the "standard" body—or the foundation from which mass-manufactured clothing was sized and graded—proved to be ill equipped for meeting the fit needs of a diverse population.

This chapter argues that while stoutwear was first and foremost a response to the inefficiencies of mass garment manufacturing, it was also the product of a search for new markets amid the expansion of the American fashion industry. As was reported in a 1922 *Women's Wear* article, the success of stoutwear was notable less for the quality and style of goods on offer than for "the great consumer demand that has been built up" by manufacturers and advertisers. Continuing, the article explains how "the wave of new stoutwear houses in the field this season … is ample evidence that the existence of this new market and this new demand is an actual fact."[5] As will be discussed later in this chapter, however, fat women were not necessarily a "new market." Rather, fat women had always been there; the real and imagined shortcomings of standardized ready-made dress merely allowed them to be seen with greater clarity, while the needs of an expanding market transformed them into desirable consumers.

The New Normal

In the fashion literature, the early twentieth century is identified as the period during which cumbersome silhouettes gave way to their more streamlined counterparts that, in their simplicity, revealed more of the "natural" body. Too often, though, this fact is extended in order to support the notion that, prior to the twentieth century, fatness—or more precisely, voluptuousness—was generally upheld as ideal.[6] Yet, to conflate voluptuousness with fat ignores the fact that fat is essentially an affliction of the abdomen.[7] Certainly, more or less voluptuous silhouettes have gone in and out of vogue in the history of fashion, but the appearance of corpulence at the waist has itself never been an ideal at least from the end of the seventeenth century onward.[8] Even during the abundant Gilded Age, when the bustle achieved its most exaggerated form and corsets were engineered to greatly enhance the fullness of the breasts, the waist remained trim and rigidly confined.[9] Although the popularity of curvaceous stage beauties such as Lillian Russell and Fanny Davenport would seem to suggest otherwise, outright fatness was not a common hallmark of feminine beauty in the mid- to late nineteenth century.[10] At the same time, however, those who carried some extra weight on their bodies prior to about 1890 were unlikely to be the subjects of ridicule or censure. Instead, the cultural consensus about fat prior to this moment was one of ambivalence, with excess weight largely being regarded as an inevitable by-product of advancing age.[11]

It is during the last decade of the nineteenth century that there occurred a rapid and dramatic shift in the ways about which fat was thought. While a number of historians have speculated on what happened in this moment to make fat go from being an individual affliction to a societal threat, the increased availability of nutritious food, an influx of immigrants, the rising popularity of fad diets, and a more youthful beauty ideal are frequently cited as culprits.[12] While it was in all likelihood some combination of all of these factors that turned fatness into a turn-of-the-century target, what's indisputable is the fact that a growing number of Americans with the means to do so had, by this time, begun trying to shed extra pounds. Fad diets such as Bantingism and Fletcherism rose in popularity and "reducing" became a uniquely American obsession.[13] It was not the promise of improved health that motivated individuals to pursue weight loss during this period, however. Rather, it was the social stigma of fat that propelled weight-loss faddism, and which fortified the slender ideal. Indeed, so great was the desire to reduce that one doctor was compelled to remark in a 1907 *The New York Times* article that "all America has gone perfectly daft on the subject of having a figure like a walking stick."[14]

Amid rising concerns about the American physique, a new feminine beauty ideal emerged that fueled new anxieties. The enormous popularity of the lithe, youthful Gibson Girl created by the illustrator Charles Dana Gibson marked the formal transition from the more curvaceous Gilded Age ideal to the ascetic archetype of the twenties. In contrast to her forerunners, the Gibson Girl was often pictured in the pages of *Life* magazine and *Harper's Weekly* as a body in motion, frequently strolling along a New England beach, riding a bicycle, playing golf, or swimming (Figure 1.2). As Lois Banner has written, she was tall and willowy, had a slim waist, and possessed a youthful naturalism that set her apart from the trussed-up matrons of a the previous generation (Figure 1.3).[15] According Martha H. Patterson, however, the Gibson Girl was far more than a pretty face. As she appeared in Gibson's work, "she both promised and threatened to effect sociopolitical change as a consumer, as an instigator of evolutionary and economic development, as a harbinger of modern technologies [and] as an icon of successful assimilation into dominant Anglo-American culture."[16] To the extent that she was the fictional embodiment of the "New Woman," she was a threat both to the old symbolic order of things and to old beauty ideals. In Gibson's illustrations, the

Figure 1.2 "Different Styles in Bathing Suits," Charles Dana Gibson, 1907. Chronicle/Alamy.

Figure 1.3 "The Jury Disagrees," Charles Dana Gibson, 1904. Science History Images/Alamy.

fat woman was often presented as a literal and symbolic counterweight to the Gibson Girl—her hunched posture, outmoded dress, and overall rumpled appearance standing in stark contrast to the Gibson Girl's breezy elegance. Somewhat contradictorily, hers was both the "civilized" and the "natural" body in a society increasingly concerned with the stigma and burden of overweight and in which slenderness was increasingly becoming a manifestation of the belief in American exceptionalism. Fatness, by contrast, had become synonymous with immigrant and non-white women whose bodies were symbols of the dilution of a unifying American identity and an impediment to progress within a rapidly industrializing and modernizing society.[17]

Yet, even as the more slender beauty ideal embodied by the Gibson Girl revealed the textures and contours of early twentieth-century weight bias, it did not address why fat went from being understood as an individual affliction to a societal problem. To understand why attitudes toward fat changed so dramatically and in such a short span of time, the tools that enabled deviations from the new normal to be more easily measured and observed must be discussed.

In his seminal history of fat, *Never Satisfied* (1986), Hillel Schwartz argues that it was ultimately the invention of new technologies for both measuring and surveilling the body that lent scientific objectivity to the emotional, spiritual, and moral dimensions of American weight bias.[18] The early twentieth century saw the invention of myriad technologies for measuring the body, including the stethoscope, the ophthalmoscope, the X-rays, the polygraph, and, perhaps most importantly, the scale. Emerging first on city streets in the 1880s as an object of amusement, by the 1920s the scale was a ubiquitous presence in American domestic bathrooms.[19] The arrival of this new and novel technology into American homes meant that people were weighing themselves with greater frequency and measuring deviations from their "baseline" or "normal" weight with greater acuity. As they were advertised in the women's and fashion press, they were explicitly marketed as accurate and discrete tools for both monitoring the figure for "unbecoming pounds" and answering the "relentless call of fashion," as was noted in one advertisement (Figure 1.4).

Figure 1.4 Detecto Scale advertisement, *Vogue* (April 1, 1926), 163. Published with permission from *Vogue*, © Condé Nast.

For some women, however, even having scales in their own bathrooms didn't offer enough privacy for this increasingly anxiety-laden practice. A 1925 *The New York Times* article reported on an emergent phenomenon in which some women, fearing judgment from their husbands, were retreating to the feminized spaces of department store bathrooms to perform their weekly weigh-ins.[20] While body weight had previously been only a vague indicator of overall health used principally by doctors, the possibility for the individual to be able to routinely and cheaply monitor minute fluctuations in body weight precipitated what Mark Seltzer has described as a "conversion of individuals into numbers and cases" in the early twentieth century that signaled a confluence of "two of the crucial control technologies of machine culture: statistics and surveillance."[21] Through the increasingly commonplace practice of weighing the body in public, overweight came to be less of a matter of natural bodily variance than one of bodily deviance, thereby cementing the categories of "normal" and "overweight." The question of exactly how much they should weigh, however, remained unresolved in the minds of many American women.

The boundaries between normal and deviant weight were more clearly defined through another important somatic tool: height and weight charts, or the early twentieth-century precursors to the Body Mass Index (BMI). Around the turn of the century, the life insurance industry, with the support of the medical establishment, attempted to compose a clearer image of the "normal" American body, and in doing so, they created an ideal body type that was markedly thinner than that of the previous century.[22] Within a five-volume report entitled the *Medico-Actuarial Mortality Investigation*, the two entities collaborated to publish statistical data on the heights and weights of over 700,000 insured men and women compiled between 1885 and 1908.[23] The main aim of the study was to create a reliable basis for the comparison of health data to be used by actuaries to more accurately assess the mortality rates of, and therefore extract higher premiums from, their policyholders. Although the report was created as a reference tool, it also established a seemingly sound basis for comparing the relative health of not just policyholders but patients, too. The raw data included in the report, however, were highly unreliable. Among the report's many oversights—including the fact that its subject pool was heavily swayed toward the urban, white middle class—perhaps one of the most egregious was the fact that some measures, and particularly those of women's bodies, were based on mere visual estimations.[24]

In spite of the many biases embedded within the data, the report confidently concluded that "there is an apparent steady advance in relative mortality with increasing weight."[25] With excess weight signaling early mortality according to the new height and weight tables, policy underwriters as well as physicians were armed with data that permitted them to encourage below average weights to, as they argued, increase life span. As a result of the report's spurning of averages in favor of low body weights, Amanda Czerniawski argues that modern conceptions of bodily normalcy and deviancy came into sharper focus.[26] With the publication of this report, over half of the American population over the age of thirty-five could be newly qualified as "overweight" according to the actuarial tables, even if there was no concrete basis for such an assessment.[27] The soundness of the science behind the charts, however, ultimately proved immaterial. By the 1910s, height and weight charts had established a quantitative, measurable basis for the moral dimensions of weight bias.

Sizing up Stoutness

During the second decade of the twentieth century, the slender ideal further entrenched itself in American culture and, more precisely, within women's and fashion media—so much so that one would be forgiven for thinking that the voluptuous Gilded Age matron had all but been eclipsed by the ideal embodied by the New Woman. With new tools to measure and quantify fat, more people than ever were monitoring their body weight, trying to understand the causes of overweight, and seeking out quick fixes for even moderate amounts of fat. In the fashion trade press, this cultural preoccupation with quantifying weight manifested within discussions about how many American women were overweight. Between 1915 and 1920, various trade publications, seeking to establish a grounded, quantitative rationale for manufacturers and retailers to enter into this untested sector, estimated that somewhere between 20 and 50 percent of American women were overweight. Most, however, seemed to land somewhere in the range of 25 to 35 percent.[28] Punctuating commentaries on the statistical argument for a specialized stoutwear sector were speculative discussions about the circumstances that led the fattening of American women. Among them, the comforts of modern life—and particularly those increasingly enjoyed by middle-class women—were framed as common culprits that led to the putting on of fat.

In a 1919 *Women's Wear* article, for instance, an anonymous, New York-based manufacturer admonished the ready-to-wear industry for its longtime neglect of fat women in spite of evidence to suggest that they were an expanding population, conjecturing, "I am sure the percentage of numbers of stout women and girls in this city must be growing. Flat life, the automobile and candy eating is surely producing obvious results, but as a class our merchants seem to be overlooking this fact."[29] A health and beauty lecturer made similar observations in a 1922 *Women's Wear* article in which she described how it had come to her attention "that there is certainly an increase in the number of fat women. They ride too much in automobiles and never take any exercise, and this together with an unrestricted diet accounts for the added avoirdupois."[30] Nowhere were the circumstances that led to the fattening of American women more clearly articulated, however, than in a 1917 *The New York Times* feature in which a stoutwear wholesaler explained,

While there is today undoubtedly a larger proportion of stout figures than was the case a decade or so ago, the natural process of evolution has developed an entirely new type of stout figure. Success in acquiring the material things of life usually manifests itself in a gradual physical development that is more or less abnormal. Inactivity and leisure result in a gradual taking on of weight, and it is these conditions that have created the new type of figure referred to. Higher standards of living, less worry and less household drudgery have done their part in increasing feminine avoirdupois, as have the more general introduction of motor cars and the growth of club life with its gastronomic and other pleasures.[31]

As these quotations demonstrate, the fat woman was understood as both a victim and a product of her historical and social circumstances, and namely the comforts conferred by a rapidly modernizing society. While more leisure time, less worry, and "less household drudgery" might otherwise be considered net positives, these sentiments evince a certain ambivalence toward or even fear of social and technological progress and the perceived effects they had on the body. Within the mainstream fashion media, fatness was no longer regarded as an age-related inevitability. Instead, leisure time, motorized transportation, and labor-saving devices were framed as threats to the American woman's physique.

While historians and epidemiologists do not deny an upward trend in average body weight throughout the twentieth century, they have also acknowledged that it is not as if American women were suddenly growing fatter after 1900.[32] As discussed previously, it was more so that a number of new technologies allowed for even moderate amounts of overweight to be measured and tracked. Scales and height and weight charts played a significant role, certainly, but so too did the infrequently discussed technology of standardized sizing. With the emergence of standard sizing in the last quarter of the nineteenth century, a forty-four-inch bust became the concrete threshold that separated the "normal" body from the "stout" body. From 1915 onward, however, the market for large-size dress opened up as manufacturers recognized just how lucrative this sector could be. Yet, as would be discussed extensively in the trade press, fitting the fat woman correctly went far beyond merely carrying extended sizes. Although there were clear financial incentives to producing stoutwear, manufacturers would quickly come to realize that doing so was not as simple as grading up standard sizes.

The problem of sizing was the focus of a 1915 *Women's Wear* article titled "Ready for the Big Ones: A New Angle on the Fat Woman's Wants," which recounted the experiences of a department store manager who had recently started carrying large-sized garments. As he told the publication,

There are lots and lots of fat women. Where they come from or why they get fat I don't know. But there are lots of them; more and more all the time. I have lost business in the past because I wasn't able to supply the wants of these women. They resent their flesh to a greater or less degree and they never are more conscious of it when they are endeavoring to get into a ready-to-wear garment that is not roomy enough …. No waist cut from a 44 pattern that is a little over-size is going to please a fat woman with a 52 circumference whatever size label is put in it.[33]

Here, the buyer argues that, on the one hand, there's a great deal of money to be made from this forgotten consumer class. On the other, however, he also suggests that these gains are immaterial unless manufacturers shift their focus toward the matter of fit, arguing that simply sticking a large-size tag into a dress that is improperly graded will do little to satisfy fat consumers.

The "stoutwear revolution," as it were, was founded on the idea that mass-manufacturing methods were inadequate and inefficient, particularly when it came to pattern grading and sizing. At the same time, the viability of a large-size garment sector was also a product of the evolution of the fashionable silhouette. During the second decade of the twentieth century, fitted two-piece ensembles were gradually replaced by more generously cut and easy-to-fit one-piece dresses that, quite literally, created more room for the fat woman in fashion. Within this context, as Claudia Kidwell explains, the financial risk to manufacturers was "reduced to an acceptable level and the mass production of ready-made dresses expanded."[34] Stoutwear, of course, was part of this expansion. Yet, the risk to stoutwear manufacturers was not zero. Indeed, as the above quotations reveal, fit—or rather, achieving a *precise* fit—was a prominent concern even among producers of standard-size garments.

While menswear retailers were more or less confident in their ability to achieve a precise fit for their customers by the 1880s, compulsory alterations were common in womenswear well into the twentieth century. When shopping, rather than choosing a size, a woman would send in her bust and waist measurements and a retailer—each of whom had their own sizing conventions—would then choose the size that most closely corresponded to her measurements, a practice that preceded the industry's adoption of standard sizing by several decades.[35] Yet, for all the promises made about precise fits, there was always an unspoken agreement between the customer and the retailer that the customer would, at the very least, have to bear the costs or labor of hemming a garment.[36] Thus, the goal in womenswear, perhaps more so than in menswear, was to reduce the cost of alterations as much as possible rather than to achieve a perfect fit—a task that was only made all the more difficult by the relentless demands of fashion and the near-constant evolution of the fashionable silhouette. In this moment, the notion of "good fit" was something of a mutable concept.

Even as manufacturers framed aftermarket alterations as a necessary, if somewhat annoying, consequence of the modernization of the garment trade, outside the trade press, poor fit was coming to be regarded as a costly manufacturing error—the root cause of which being inaccurate sizing and grading systems. As one *The New York Times* headline read in 1917, "The nation's bill for correcting manufacturers' errors [is] $300,000,000 annually." *The New York Times* further claimed that female consumers, more so than their male counterparts, bore the brunt of these expenditures:

Not more than 2 per cent of wearers can be fitted accurately without alterations ... [and] not more than 10 to 15 per cent can be fitted even approximately without snipping something here or changing something there. Roughly, this means that 85 to 90 out of every hundred garments sold at retail in this country in the course of a year have to be altered, with the duplication of labor and expense that is entailed.[37]

The enormous cost of secondary alterations, the article goes on to argue, was due to the fact that the womenswear industry based its sizing standards on two false assumptions: "The first of these ... is that a single basic standard measurement for these garments is enough to fit all needs. The second is the assumption that all women are tall."[38] Another article published in *Women's Wear* the same year tackled similar problems, explaining how the standards that manufacturers relied upon in 1915 were based on outdated data: "No one knows where they came from or whether they are typical, or right or wrong; they are merely accepted without further thought, and this is the root of the evil."[39]

As American fashion was turning ever more toward the ready-made, the matter of waste—both of time and money—became a problem of the highest order for profit-hungry clothing manufacturers who struggled even into the second decade of the twentieth century to create well-fitting garments for an ever-growing and increasingly diverse population. Within this context, the old ways of garment cutting and manufacturing were proving themselves obsolete even as consumers were being asked to accept speed and accessibility over good fit. Indeed, with all of the alterations that had to be undertaken after the point of sale, the jury was out on whether or not the technological strides being made in garment manufacturing were actually saving anyone time or money. After the turn of the century, speed had become the defining feature of American ready-to-wear. As with so many other things pertaining to the speeding up of modern life, however, the fat woman would ultimately find herself unable to keep up.

Although a perfect fit off-the-rack would have been out of reach for most American women, perhaps no one was more affected by the inefficiencies of ready-made dress than the fat woman. As early as 1902, Sears Roebuck & Co. offered a range of ready-made garments for standard-size consumers. Even as the company prided itself on its ability to fit everyone, those who were "very tall or very stout," along with those who were "particularly hard to fit for any reason," had to rely upon the services of a mail-order custom tailoring department at an additional expense.[40] Being able to easily order perfectly fitting garments through the mail was a decidedly different practice from the very modern experience of being able to walk into a store and buy a garment off-the-rack, however. By and large, these early attempts to streamline the manufacturing of stoutwear were regarded as unsuccessful, and worse, as an affront to the fat female consumer. As one *The New York Times* article noted, the "made-to-order" business for stout apparel in the 1900s was plagued by "annoying delays, tedious fittings and high prices."[41]

From approximately 1915 onward, the fat woman had therefore increasingly found herself unwittingly at the center of an embattled campaign to reform garment sizing and grading conventions. Amid these efforts, manufacturers and retailers engaged in debates about the relationship between sizing and aesthetics, revealing that the problems in the industry went far beyond fit. In a November 1915 *Women's Wear* piece titled "Revolution in Fitting Stylish Stout Women," the publication argued that there was a "great deal of misconception regarding 'stouts' [within the mainstream apparel industry, with] many figuring the garment must out of necessity be ugly or ill shaped."[42] In a slightly later article, another seller remarked that, beyond being poorly fit, stoutwear garments were also typically "made on a liberally cut pattern with full wide sleeves and skirt" in a "lazy" attempt to accommodate the stout woman's outsize proportions.[43] It was a backward-glancing feature published in the *Dry Goods Economist* in 1921 that perhaps summarized the problem best, and which suggested that the industry had gotten off to a "dismal start" by focusing too much on producing clothes that covered up and hid body rather than on properly grading fashionable styles.[44] What was it about the fat woman's body that made it so difficult to fit?

Beyond the "Perfect 36"

In 1918, a manufacturing group known as the Associated Stylish Stout Wear Makers published an illustrated advertisement featuring two stylishly outfitted stout women standing on a balance with the caption hanging in the white space above them: "Worth Her Weight in Gold to You" (Figure 1.5). In this advertisement, the weight of the stout woman is equated, quite literally, with her value to the industry. Just as the image of a patient on a scale had become synonymous with the modern medical exam, so too was the image of a stout woman on a balance a perfect, but underused, icon for the stoutwear industry: a potent symbol of how the fat woman's bodily excesses could be leveraged for profits.[45] While scales and height and weight charts may have been two of the most ubiquitous tools for quantifying the body in the early twentieth century, another crucial as well as pervasive technology for measuring the body was that of clothing sizing. As Ingrid Jeacle has written, "Standardized clothes sizing is perhaps the ultimate expression of a technology of the body" for the manner it "assigns a statistically generated number to every bodily form" and generates a corpus of "knowledge" or "truth" about the body.[46] Much like the penny scale or height and weight charts, the ostensibly ordinary (but also spectacularly powerful) technology of garment sizing gave form to the ideal body as much as it demarcated otherwise undefinable or unruly bodies. Bodies that did not conform and which flouted the conventions of standard sizing were therefore understood as both deviant and as impediments to mass manufacturing and standardization.

What some in the fashion industry regarded as the sudden and concerning expansion of the American woman's waistline (and what that meant for the industry) was the topic of discussion at a 1916 dinner hosted by the Associated Stylish Stout Wear Makers, which was attended by representatives from national department stores such John Wannamaker's, May and Co., Famous-Barr, and Jordan Marsh, among others. The host of the dinner, Isidor, president of the Associated Stylish Stout Wear Makers, told attendees that while the "propaganda for specialized clothes for stout women" was proving successful in meeting the needs of this "sadly neglected group of women,"

the issue of sizing was still a concern. While Heller acknowledged that new standards needed to be devised, this dinner was more so an occasion to speculate on the reasons why American women were growing so alarmingly fat. As he went on to explain to a crowd of hundreds,

> The general prosperity of the country, the hygienic features of the modern corsets, the labor saving devices in the home that make household duties less laborious than in former years and the almost universal use of the automobile all undoubtedly have made life easier for the American woman, and, in consequence she has taken on weight.... She has, in the majority, outgrown the standard of beauty of figure as accepted in the perfect 36.[47]

In concluding his talk, he remarked that it was now time to abandon the "perfect 36" in order to meet the fit needs of the so-called "perfect 46."

Although the United States excelled in the mass production of garments in many ways, one of the main issues that plagued the ready-to-wear industry from early on was the matter of achieving precise fits for all consumers. The root cause of these difficulties lay in the science of pattern grading, or the process used by manufacturers to produce ready-made garments in a range of reproducible sizes. From the earliest days of the garment industry, there was no single standard for grading and sizing garments, and manufacturers were left to their own devices to establish size specifications through a process of trial and error. As historian Wendy Gamber observes, early sizing systems and proportional techniques "served the few rather than the many" as good fit was highly dependent upon the drafter's understanding of bodily proportions.[48] It wouldn't be until after the Civil War that the process of grading men's garments for different sizes became more precise and the knowledge of how to do so was more widespread. With new data compiled from the chest and height measurements of over one million conscripts, which were used during the war to mass manufacture uniforms, a clearer picture of the "average" build of American men began to emerge, as did early proportional theories.[49] This information was later compiled into tables that were made available to manufacturers of civilian clothing, but which "reinforced and refined what nineteenth-century tailors had long known; that is, that certain sets of measurements tend to recur with predictable regularity."[50] As a nascent form of proportional theory, these tables assumed "human bodies have set proportions and that one body measurement is, therefore, a reliable predictor of other body measurements."[51] While in practice, proportional theories do permit relatively precise fits within large populations, flawed or incomplete data compromise their accuracy. In the case of these early sizing tables, the data reflected the average dimensions of a relatively homogenous population of highly disciplined bodies.[52]

In spite of rampant problems with fit, the industry for ready-made menswear nevertheless preceded that for womenswear by several decades. While menswear statistics were compiled in the 1860s and 1870s, a survey of female bodies was not conducted until 1884 at several American women's colleges, including Smith, the Pratt

Institute, and Vassar.[53] While some effort was made to combine these data with statistics culled from height and weight tables, the standards derived from these surveys were even less comprehensive than those collected for men's sizing and were similarly derived from a rather narrow spectrum of body types: that of young, oftentimes affluent, and, more often than not, slender white women. Because of this, sizes were based on limited range of bust measurements that generally ranged from thirty-two to forty-four inches.[54] Increasingly sophisticated proportional theories—derived from tools and mathematical systems first used by tailors in the 1860s and steeped in Enlightenment ideals of symmetry and proportion—were used to grade sizes up and down from the median size of thirty-six.[55] These systems, however, proved to be quite poor at accounting for the three-dimensional changing shape of the body as it grew larger.[56] As a result, most mass-manufactured garments utilized a standard, intermediate size from which inches were added or removed at the bust, waist, and hips uniformly. For all but the few who were lucky enough to naturally possess these standardized proportions, aftermarket alterations continued to be an inevitability. In this era of increased industrialization and technology, Cookie Woolner argues that "the modern body was more appropriately the thin or the streamlined body, and the fat body was the body that was dragging or slowing the collectivity down."[57] Alongside height and weight charts, sizing systems played a central role in establishing bodily norms, and what was known as the "perfect 36" within fashion industry parlance was the quintessence of this bodily norm.

The perfect 36 referred to the base measurement for women's garments that took thirty-six-inches as its base bust measurement and graded hip and waist measurements based on what was regarded as a "proportioned" or "balanced" figure resembling an hourglass. This was in no way based on the measurements of an actual body but rather was intended to be a statistically generated intermediate size within a target market—that of white, middle-class women.[58] As late as 1899, the perfect 36 was the graded size from which most women's garments were cut so, as Kidwell and Christman observe, "only a small proportion of consumers could obtain anything like a 'fitting garment.'"[59] The problem of the perfect 36 was discussed at length in a 1917 *The New York Times* article in which a manufacturer roundly rejected the logic of prevailing proportional theories:

> [The] "perfect 36" is an idealist's conception of the perfectly formed woman. Whether such women exist doesn't seem to be a factor and whether or not they exist in large numbers to demand garments of the retailer seems not to be a consideration. So the garment manufacturers keep turning out their garments based on the false premise that there are living De Milos to whom to sell perfect 36s.[60]

An article published in *The Dry Goods Economist* echoed these points, explaining how the perfect 36 could not simply be translated to stoutwear due to the fact that "the whole architecture of a stout model was different from the regular sizes."[61]

Proposals for new sizing systems ultimately emerged from insights about the deficiencies inherent in the conceptualization of the perfect 36 and bolstered the notion, circulated within trade publications, that approaches to stoutwear pattern grading needed to be reimagined. As Carmen Keist and Sara Marcketti have observed, the entrance of new conventions for grading stoutwear was symptomatic of a larger drive toward specialization in the ready-to-wear industry during this period.[62] In spite of this push toward greater specialization (and one could argue, inclusivity) in American fashion, a close reading of the trade press reveals that the debates surrounding the veracity of the perfect 36 revolved less around the science and specificities of accurate pattern grading and more so around perceived physical irregularities of the fat female body.

Albert Malsin candidly discussed the "problem" of the fat woman's physique in a 1916 *Richmond Times-Dispatch* article, stating,

> But the problem of clothing the stout woman is only half solved when we succeed in producing a gown all ready to wear that fits her. Many gowns that fit make their wearer look ridiculous because they are all out of harmony with the fashions of the day and because they conceal all the good points of her too generous lines and emphasize the bad ones.[63]

The challenges the fat body posed to the processes of mass manufacturing were discussed in similar terms in a 1922 article appearing in the business section of *The New York Times*, which noted how "many differences in the figures of stout women … leads to manufacturing difficulties."[64] The perfect 36 was therefore something of a scapegoat that industry leaders could blame as the root cause of the difficulties in fitting the stout woman as much as it was a selling point for specialized stoutwear. The real problem for manufacturers, it seemed, was the task of defining the stout body not in relation to an ideal but on its own terms.

This was a difficult, if not impossible, task within an industry that had been built around the pillars of standardization and scientific management famously outlined in F.W. Taylor's 1911 influential *The Scientific Management of the Workplace*. As Caroline Evans has written, the principles of Taylorism "aimed to increase efficiency in the workplace by a sort of mechanical 'divide and rule' whereby each worker was allocated a fixed task and a fixed way of performing it in a fixed place."[65] Henry Ford's assembly line—a system through which workers performed a serialized task with mechanical precision—was a clear manifestation of Taylorist principles. Clothing manufacturing in the early twentieth century was, however, what Nancy L. Green has described as a "flexible industry," that while changed by mechanical production, nevertheless persisted as one underpinned by "hand technology." In other words, it was "a mass-production industry without mass-production methods" for the manner it still relied heavily upon batch production, hand finishing, and piecework in spite of the technological interventions of the sewing machine and batch cutting.[66] In practice, however, the ideologies of Taylorism transformed American industry at all levels in the early twentieth century in the vein of making work more efficient and mechanized—a notion that was reflected in stoutwear manufacturers' preoccupation with waste. More than that, it also affected the aesthetics and form of the products that were being produced within this system. It is no coincidence that Coco Chanel's little black dress was colloquially referred to as the "Ford" for its ubiquity and ease of wear, but also for the serialized and standardized appearance it created for the wearer—or what could be regarded as the "proto-industrial aesthetic" of Taylorism and Fordism.[67] Indeed, as Green argues, the appearance and form of ready-made garments was "defined and defended by American industrial discourse."[68]

Although it had been established that the conventions of ready-to-wear processes were ill-suited to the manufacture of stoutwear, the perception that it was the fat body (rather than the limitations imposed by mass manufacturing) that was inherently problematic was one that was pervasive in fashion industry discourse. Specifically, sizing functioned as a powerful regulatory device that, among consumers, encouraged compliance with bodily norms. Bodies that did not conform to preexisting sizing standards therefore were reflexively "punished" and forced to pay the price, quite literally, of custom tailoring or extensive alterations. A 1927 conducted survey by the Department of Agriculture chronicled the discontents of American women. It found that of 1,368 women surveyed, 31 percent—or roughly the proportion of American women who, it was believed, classified as stout—remarked that they had trouble finding well-fitting garments, while an even higher percentage expressed frustration with the time and expense of altering garments.[69]

As Tim Armstrong has written, the human body is something of a "pressure-point" in modernist discourse. "Modernity," Armstrong writes, "brings forth a fragmentation and augmentation of the body in relation to technology; it offers the body as a lack, at the same time it offers technological compensation."[70] The dissonance that exists between machines and bodies and in the body's failure to conform to the conventions mechanization are particularly manifest on the body of the fat woman within the context of fashion if only because manufacturing systems were not built with her in mind. The fat body was synonymous with failure to the extent that it defied the conventions of standardized sizing, leading to wasted labor and materials, while shouldering manufacturers, retailers, and consumers with costly aftermarket alterations. Beyond the nonstandard proportions of the fat woman's body, however, in professional discourse there also persisted a notion that the stout woman's flesh and the fat residing beneath it possessed qualities that made the task of fitting her all the more challenging.

The Problem with Fat

In the numerous instances in which industry professionals speculated about why large-size dress was so difficult to grade correctly, the peculiar properties of the fat woman's flesh—or the soft, malleable complex of skin and fat that resides between the "natural" or "normative" body and dress—was a recurring topic. In speaking to *Women's Wear* in January 1917, industry consultant Edith M. Burtis advocated for specially designed and graded garments for fat women, arguing that "stoutwear should be bought from stout specialists. There is this to be remembered: the bone structure of the stout woman is not what makes her stout—it's the extra flesh."[71] Here, Burtis draws a crucial distinction between the "natural" frame—or the physical stature of the body as defined by bones and muscle—and the flesh that resides on top of it. Speaking with *The New York Times* a year later, Mrs. S.C. Miller of the Associated Stylish Stout Wear Makers made similar remarks, explaining to the reader,

> Now, in the first place, you have got to have the right kind of clothes for the stout woman, built for her. You can't grade up a suit made for another kind of woman. The frame of the stout woman is individual if she has covered it heavily with flesh.[72]

The idea that fat flesh was something separate from and effectively "worn" on the outside of the body was also pursued by Albert Malsin, who, in an article published in the *Richmond Times-Dispatch* in 1916, argued,

> The layers of flesh which bring stoutness are not added to the human body with anything like mathematical regularity. Sometimes this added flesh appears only in the woman's bust, her hips and abdomen remaining entirely normal. In other cases, it is only the hips or only the abdomen that becomes fleshy. Even when bust, abdomen and hips all take on flesh in about equal amounts, her arms, her lower limbs and other parts of her body may be of normal or possibly of less than normal size.[73]

In these instances, the "layers of flesh" enshrouding the body are regarded as inessential and suggest that, perhaps, beneath all of that excess, there resides a more normative body. In an illustration accompanying the *Richmond Times-Dispatch* article, Malsin underscored this point by exhibiting different ways that fat collects on the "natural" body by superimposing schematic renderings of the three principal "types" of fat women on top of average-sized frames of similar proportions (Figure 1.6). On all three figures, their dress is conflated with the flesh as something that is fundamentally separate from their frames. The frame here is regarded as the rational or "appropriate" foundation for dress, whereas the flesh is rendered ancillary, extra, and deviant.

With the ascendance of the slender feminine ideal, fat had come to be conceived, as Klein writes, as "an excrescence, a corruption of the flesh whose removal left the body intact and in better shape."[74] The problem of excess body fat was considered in a *Harper's Bazaar* article titled "For Women of the Rubens Type" by Jessie Shepherd. In attempting to delineate between desirable and less-than-desirable curves, Shepherd wrote:

> I do not know how many pounds a camel can carry: perhaps two hundred or three hundred; but two hundred pounds of exuberant vitality is a glorious sight for gods and men. Yet it is too often laid upon feminine forms in coarse flabby curves of lifeless fat. Curves to be fine must express joyful, hopeful life…. The globular or spherical curve expresses coarseness, gross heavy selfishness, or sensuality. It is positively repulsive in a human form, and it simply never occurs in health.[75]

The Three Principal Types of "Stout" Women.

1.—The "Full-Busted" Type   2.—The "Stout-All-Over" Type   3.—The "Flat-Busted" Type

Figure 1.6 Detail from "Science At Last Turns Its Attention to 'Stout' People," *Richmond Times-Dispatch* (April 2, 1916), 55. Published with permission from Newspapers.com.

Where the fat body, with its heavy, "globular" curves was "coarse" and "gross," the appropriately slender body was, by contrast, defined by what Schwartz has deemed the "kinesthetic of torque" to the extent that it was light, streamlined, mobile, efficient, and displayed the logic of industrialized society. The ideal body would have been "aerodynamic ... curved but slender, controlled but light," or an ideal perhaps most clearly embodied by the modernist dancer.[76] Rather than being stiff and upright as was the constrained, corseted feminine ideal in the late nineteenth century, this was a naturally slender but physically strong body whose "chief pattern was the spiral; its deepest resource was torsion," and which expressed movement even when in stasis.[77] Above all, however, this was a body that was perfectly slender, if verging on machine-like. Within this context, superfluous flesh existed in industry discourse as something that was effectively "worn" and, likewise, that could be taken off to reveal the "natural," unencumbered body underneath.

More than being a corporeal obstruction to the "natural" frame, however, the flesh of the fat woman was thought to compromise the cut and construction of standard, mass-produced garments. This notion was perhaps most explicitly illustrated in a 1917 *Women's Wear* article titled "Quality as Important as Size in Handling Stouts Trade." In this article, a fashion buyer attempts to explain what he perceives as the peculiarities of the fat woman's flesh:

> Many of the garments brought on for the women in the class we are discussing require alterations. These should, of course, be well made in every case, but they are extremely important where fat women are concerned. They need to be substantially made, as well, for the strain on the garments of the heavyweight is greater than on the average person's clothes. There is a semi-liquid quality about the flesh. It flows. Where draping might answer the purpose on a person of prominent bones, the excess of material anywhere in a garment for a stout person would tend to be bulged out by the flesh which is seeking some place to go.[78]

In the above quotation, the buyer claims that alterations in stoutwear need to be made thoughtfully due to the fact that, on the fat woman, the flesh possesses a "semi-liquid" quality, which permits it to "flow" into and about the garment, causing any excess or draped fabric to bulge unbecomingly. Here again the fat woman's flesh is framed as something unpredictable, excessive, and wholly separate from the body proper. Whereas the body itself is measurable and solid, fat flesh, on the other hand, is rendered a substance that is unstable, and which seeps into the wrinkles and gaps that exist between the "natural" body and dress. Stoutwear garments, perhaps more than their standard-size counterparts, he claimed, had to therefore be made with a great attention to quality because the excessive flesh of the fat woman could compromise their design integrity. A well-made stoutwear garment, by turn, bore in it the capacity to do the job otherwise done by bone and muscle in giving the fat body shape.

The notion that fat possesses a semi-liquid quality, thereby permitting the stout body to "flow" into garments, was also pointedly addressed in a 1915 article in which a stoutwear salesman discussed the challenges of breaking into this niche industry. Commenting specifically on the problem of fit, he explained,

> There is one thing about catering to big women: if you get a garment well made and of the right size, it will fit. These fat women "flow" into their clothes. They are not like the slender ones, and those with pretty figures without an ounce to spare who have to be fitted perfectly. If you give a fat woman a corset that suits her the suit or the blouse or the skirt will do their work.[79]

In this quote, the notion that fat flesh is compositionally different than the flesh of a slender woman is emphasized; however, different from his contemporaries, the salesman frames this as a potential benefit to manufacturers. He argues that the stout woman's fleshiness diminishes the necessity of achieving exact fits. Rather, he poses the idea that her body could potentially "flow" into any gaps—the anthropomorphized flesh, in a sense, doing the work of the tailor or seamstress.

In contrast to the thin, streamlined, and mechanical body of modernity, the fat body is portrayed in these examples in all-too-human terms: as fleshy, flawed, and, perhaps most notably, as *flowing*. Fat, however, was not only problematic within the context of mass manufactured clothing. It was a highly taboo substance within a rapidly modernizing and industrializing America more generally. Ready-made clothing only emphasized the deviance of the fat woman's flesh. The concerns or even anxieties about the excesses of her body so evident within trade publication commentaries recall, in many ways, Mary Douglas' famous reflections on the manner in which pollution and transgression are treated in civil society. In *Purity and Danger* (1966), Douglas explains how all cultural systems are both highly ordered but also highly susceptible to external pressures. Because "society does not exist in a neutral, uncharged vacuum, it is subject to social pressures; that which is not with it, part of it and subject to its laws, is potentially against it."[80] If ready-made dress is understood in these terms— as a cultural system underpinned by a certain logic, and, in the words of Douglas, "laws," determining bodily ideals—then the fat woman's flesh is therefore a form of transgression that places pressure on the margins of the fashion system by undermining its authority to regulate the body. As such, the fat woman was frequently, and quite callously, derided as Other. While *Women's Wear* declared the fat woman "the most important of the special classes of 'freaks' in the ready-to-wear trade" in June 1915,[81] elsewhere stoutwear makers seemed amused by the notion that "even the freaks want to 'look nifty.'"[82] As this pejorative language suggests, this was not a consumer to whom most manufacturers and retailers were eager to cater. Rather, fat women were seen as having "extreme demands," and that the success of a stout department would therein lie in "its ability to meet any test, no matter how severe."[83]

While fat could be understood as something worn on the outside of the body, Douglas provides a lens through which fat may also be seen as an internal threat that pressed at the margins of the rational, streamlined body, displacing the flesh and stretching it to its limits, but also breaching the boundaries of appropriate dress. The "fear" of the fat woman's flesh—itself a form of pollution—is exemplified by the baroque ways that industry leaders spoke about its "flowing" and "liquid" properties and its abilities to seep into the folds and gaps of dresses. Boundaries, Douglas explains, "reward conformity and repulse attack."[84] Such transgressions or "attacks" are therefore subject to forms of "punishment" with the goal of imposing order "on an inherently untidy experience."[85] Indeed, Douglas defines uncleanness as "matter out of place."[86] Stoutwear should thus be understood as regulatory system that put the fat woman's flowing flesh "in its place," as it were, whereas fatness itself became a particularly modern form of pollution—one, somewhat ironically, born from the comforts of modern life.

***

Just as discussions about sizing defined the fat body by its nonconformity to social regulating systems and to the impulse to quantify the body, discussions about the fat woman's flesh similarly defined her as both deficient and excessive in her blatant transgressing of social codes, here materialized through mass-manufactured clothing. The notion that dress can itself be viewed as a social regulating system that punishes bodies that flout these conventions recalls what Peter Corrigan has described as the "natural order of things," or the shape of the natural, unencumbered body, which "is made subordinate to an abstract model that stands outside it."[87] It could therefore be argued that standard-size garments actually give form to a body that is ultimately "subordinate" to the mandates of dress. However, Corrigan also makes another point, noting that real bodies, "made of flesh and blood and not easily moldable plastic," are not ideally suited to mass manufacturing; rather, "ready-made clothing demands ready-made bodies."[88]

As has already been discussed, however, the problems presented by the conventions of ready-to-wear were not necessarily specific to fat women. Regardless of weight, the human body is ill-suited to the conventions and processes of mass manufacturing and exists as a notable pressure point within these systems. Within the context of ready-to-wear as an industry, the very conventions of standard sizing were built upon a flawed foundation, which took as its basis not a real body but a statistical pastiche rooted classical notions of beauty and symmetry. The fat female body, however, stands as an exemplary illustration of how bodies that flout social codes are subject to attempts to control and contain them. It may be said that standardization ultimately creates standard bodies; however, in spite of attempts to create a rational foundation for grading large-size garments, the fat female body ultimately resisted such attempts to define and standardize it. Thus, and somewhat paradoxically, the fat body was one that was defined through the very impossibility of defining it. In the end, what mattered more than weights or measurements was the fact that the fat was beyond or outside of established norms. Even as the fat body resisted clear definition, however, certain "truths" about it were nevertheless established within industry discourse. Discussions about how many fat women there were in the United States and the "flowing" or "liquid" qualities of their flesh established them as Other and thereby laid the groundwork for a more complicated matrix of concerns regarding both the aesthetics and functions of stoutwear.

CHAPTER 2
DESIGNING FOR DISORDER

The story of the founding of the iconic plus-size brand Lane Bryant is the stuff of fashion folklore. In 1900, a recently widowed immigrant named Lena Himmelstein Bryant fell back on her talents as a seamstress within the bustling garment trade of turn-of-the-century New York. With a $300 loan from a family member, she rented a studio apartment on West 112th Street and made a downpayment on a sewing machine.[1] While she first earned a modest living by creating custom lingerie and altering mass-manufactured shirtwaists and skirts, by 1904 she had opened her own storefront at 1489 Fifth Avenue and was beginning to gain a reputation for her superb tailoring.[2] Shortly thereafter, she went on to make fashion history by creating the first mass-market maternity dress, the No. 5 Maternity Gown.[3]

In 1909, Bryant married a fellow immigrant named Albert Malsin.[4] Trained as a mechanical engineer, Malsin saw a more ambitious business opportunity in his wife's innovative maternity dresses into which she integrated adjustable waistbands that permitted the dress to grow with the wearer throughout the duration of her pregnancy. Malsin soon abandoned his own engineering practice and moved their operations to a larger second-floor loft at 19 West 38th Street, in the heart of New York City's Garment District. There, the couple was able to scale their manufacturing by employing high-speed sewing machines and industrial cutting equipment.[5] Not so far away, they also opened up their first dedicated retail store on Fifth Avenue.[6]

While Bryant and Malsin had made a name for themselves with their maternity wear, in 1911 the couple turned their attention to the bourgeoning stoutwear trade. That year, Malsin registered a patent for a garment with an expandable waistband specifically designed for fat women that could "adjust itself easily and naturally to persons of different sizes without the necessity of altering its length or shape."[7] Over the next several years, Malsin authored patents for at least fourteen more garments and foundations that solved a number of problems in large-size garment design and, perhaps more importantly, helped to establish Lane Bryant as an industry leader.[8] By 1915, the company had a robust mail-order division and wholesale business that sold garments to major national department stores such as Macy's and Altman's.[9] In 1916, Lane Bryant went on the New York Stock Exchange, and by 1917 the company's sales had surpassed $1,000,000 for the first time.[10]

Amid this rapid growth, the couple continued to imagine creative solutions to the fat woman's clothing woes. On July 9, 1915, *Women's Wear* published an article titled "Scientific Specialization in Stouts," which discussed a survey Malsin undertook in order to solve problems in large-size garment fit by identifying the points at which bodies exceeding a forty-four-inch-bust measurement deviated from standardized grading and sizing systems (Figure 2.1). In the full-page article, Malsin explained how he took the bust, waist, and hip measurements of 4,500 Lane Bryant customers, which he then cross-referenced with data provided by a large American insurance company of 200,000 female policyholders.[11] Through this study, he arrived at the conclusion that "stout bodies are not simply thin frames plus extra layers of flesh."[12] Rather, as he told *Women's Wear*, the fat woman is "not well proportioned" and that dress, if well-conceived, could be used to mitigate bodily irregularities.[13] He therefore cautioned readers that those seeking to enter the stoutwear trade "bear one thing in mind, above all ... namely that it is impossible to make such garments by the ordinary process of grading."[14]

Reflecting at greater length on his findings, Malsin told the *Richmond Times-Dispatch* in 1916 that "the trouble with the stout woman's clothes in the past has been the utter disregard which their makers have shown for certain well known scientific laws." Continuing, he explained,

> There could be no greater mistake than this. The plainer a stout woman's dress is, the more unrelieved its expanses of fabric, the broader and shorter it makes her look ....
>
> It is surprising to see how much can be accomplished by a proper handling of the most trivial details about a dress.[15]

Speaking about the practice of large-size garment design in terms usually reserved for the applied sciences and engineering, Malsin viewed himself as something of an architect of the body, and in his hands, seemingly superficial design elements like color, line, and pattern became a means to imbue conventional, mass-manufactured garments with the nearly extraordinary power to alter the appearance of the body and, in doing so, to mitigate the growing anxieties about fat in American society.

Malsin's lofty idealism was generally aligned with that of other prominent early twentieth-century designers and industrialists who wanted to apply the tools and technologies of mass manufacturing to bring about social change and to solve problems. In the United States, mass manufacturing is said to have enabled a democratization of aesthetics that transcended class hierarchies, blurred social distinctions, obfuscated ethnic origins, and, arguably, helped everyone to fit in.[16] Such claims, however, have proven to be overstated. Largely unable to purchase well-fitting garments off-the-rack in the first years of the twentieth century, for instance, the fat woman found herself uncomfortably subjected to the limitations of mass manufacturing as the democratic ethos of American ready-made dress ultimately failed to transcend size classifications.

This chapter examines the "design discourses" of stoutwear, or what Lees-Maffei has defined as "writing *about* design ... writing which brings design into being, semantically."[17] As a record of the design process—one that endures even in the absence of a material record, which in the case of stoutwear is largely nonexistent—design discourse reveals the logic, priorities, and values that went into the creation of a designed object. Focusing primarily on articles that discuss the art and science of designing for

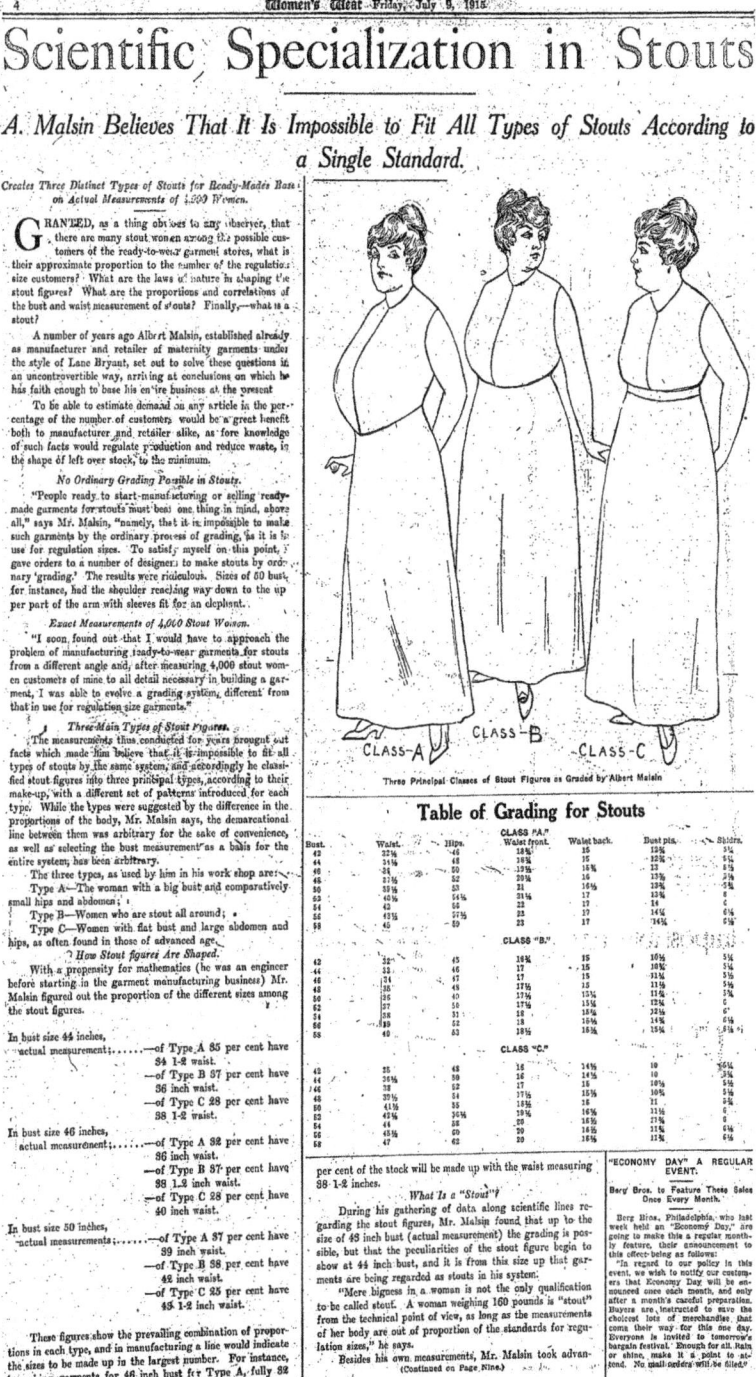

Figure 2.1 "Scientific Specialization in Stouts," *Women's Wear* (July 9, 1915), 4. Published with permission from ProQuest LLC. Further reproduction is prohibited without permission.

the fat body published within the fashion trade press during the first decades of the twentieth century, this chapter reveals how American weight bias dovetailed with the high-minded principles of industrial rationalism, artistic modernism, psychology, and architecture within stoutwear design discourse—all in the vein of eradicating the appearance of overweight. With its broad focus, this chapter seeks to enrich the history of large-size garment design and to broaden the lens through which we view this history by exploring how other figures—among them artists and architects—attempted to solve the "problem" of the fat female body through the medium of dress, but outside of the niche stoutwear sector. Taken together, these discourses reveal how clothing was increasingly being employed alongside a litany of new tools and technologies in the imagined technological utopia of early twentieth-century America to at once solve fat women's dress problems and, to borrow a phrase from Christopher E. Forth, "engineer fat out of existence."[18]

Building Better Bodies

Someday … we may see the designer as the architect and the woman of taste and training as the decorator.

For I think a man has more gift at making the right outline for a tailored suit or dress. It seems to call for a man's handling, according to my judgment.[19]

The above quotation reveals a prominent strain of thought in the discourses of stoutwear design in the early twentieth century—one which equated the practice of designing and manufacturing stoutwear with the more ostensibly masculine, and therefore perhaps more noble, practice of designing built environments. In the article, two stoutwear manufacturers from the New York-based firm Bernstein, Baum, Cravis & Co. were asked by *Women's Wear*, "How do you get your styles?" In their response, they explained how the key was to first find the "right outline" in a suit or dress, after which, "little feminine touches" could be added—a practice which the two argued was best left in the hands of women. Continuing, they suggested that while the subject of decoration has always "troubled" tailors, for "men rarely understand it," women "go to it intuitively and naturally." While in this quotation the manufacturers at once elevate women's work, arguing that it is those "final touches [that] always make or mar a suit,"[20] they also establish a gendered design dichotomy that equated garment design—or, the "right outline of a tailored suit or dress" (i.e., the silhouette)—with the masculine field of architecture and the superficial work of fashion design or "decoration" with women and domesticity.

The sentiments of the manufacturers from Bernstein, Baum, Cravis & Co. found their visual corollary in an advertisement for the New York-based stoutwear firm Baum & Wolff, Inc., which ran in the January 1918 edition of *The Dry Goods Economist* (Figure 2.2). It featured a pen-and-ink illustration of a towering fat woman around whom four comparatively diminutive men donning white artist smocks gather to put the finishing touches on her black dress.[21] The accompanying advertising copy reads as follows:

Figure 2.2 Baum & Wolff advertisement, *Dry Goods Economist* (January 26, 1918), 84. Courtesy the University of Minnesota Libraries & Archives.

Camouflage.

That's the stout dress problem! Make a stout figure appear slim—a curved line straight!

It's just "knowing" that makes our designs flatter the stout figure. Baum & Wolff models don't just fit the figure—they flatter it—change it—give it the youthfulness it needs to answer to style.

Every new silhouette is in Baum & Wolff models—not just "put" there, but built into each model with a thorough knowledge of the stout figure and its needs.[22]

Although perhaps less forceful than the above quotation from the manufacturers at Bernstein, Baum & Cravis who compare the work of the designer to that of the architect, the legitimizing discourses of architecture—and specifically of "building" a better body—are here invoked as a means to elevate the practice of stoutwear design to something higher than "mere" dressmaking or fashion design. Their use of such rhetoric was very much in keeping with a broader shift occurring in fashion manufacturing in the early twentieth century that historian Wendy Gamber describes as the delegitimization of dressmaking as "women's work" and the emergence of "scientific design" as a skill increasingly led and defined by an influx of opportunistic male manufacturers.[23]

With its generally problem-oriented approach to correcting the flaws of the stout body, and its discrete focus on "lines" and "scientific principles," these design discourses more so recalled the utilitarian and rationalizing discourses of early twentieth-century design writ large, rather than that of the more artistically inclined and intuitive language used by French and English couturiers in the late nineteenth and early twentieth centuries to unmoor their practice from mass-market apparel design. As Nancy Troy, Ilya Parkins, Jennifer Craik, and Christopher Breward have each observed, the rarefied language of the couturiers like Paul Poiret and Charles Fredrick Worth was a means to affirm their positions as a singular artistic geniuses.[24] Different from the great couturiers, however, American stoutwear manufacturers were decidedly more embedded in the market, not only as makers of mass-produced clothing but also of mass-produced ideals.

To this end, stoutwear manufacturers' tendency to use scientific and technological rhetoric when describing their design philosophies and practices, rather than notions of beauty or pure aesthetics (i.e., "design for design's sake"), underscored the belief, which was shared by other modernist designers, that "design, if rationally conceived, could help to solve social problems."[25] Thus, even as stoutwear manufacturers invoked some of the more rarefied and emotive language of high fashion in establishing themselves as design innovators in the fashion media, their dual ambition to fit the bodies of fat women and to help them sartorially fit in better aligned them with the democratic ethos of American ready-to-wear.[26] For instance, Baum & Wolff's claims that their garments did not merely "fit the figure … they flatter it … change it" suggest that the practice of stoutwear design emerged from a highly specialized knowledge of "the stout figure and its needs," while the suggestion that "camouflage" is the "stout dress problem" further attests to the problem-oriented nature of stoutwear design and manufacturing.

Rather than designing a fashionable silhouette—a practice with which couturiers were preoccupied—Baum & Wolff, like many other stoutwear manufacturers, aspired to actually alter the physical appearance of women's bodies.

While this manner of equating stoutwear design and manufacturing to architectural practice could be disregarded as mere marketing bluster, it also, and quite importantly, reveals some of the core ideals that underpinned the practice of stoutwear design, such as an overt preoccupation with "the line" and with "camouflage," but also with the nebulous idea of creating garments that are "becoming" on the bodies of fat women. Although mentions of these elements of stoutwear design were widespread across the professional media, perhaps nowhere were they more clearly elucidated than in the design philosophies of Albert Malsin.

In April of 1916, Malsin was invited to, over the course of four weeks, discuss his ideas about stoutwear design within the pages of the *Richmond Times-Dispatch*. In the first of these full-page features (Figure 2.3), Malsin introduced himself and described his particular qualifications for designing women's clothing in the following manner:

I am a mechanical engineer, but instead of designing dynamos or making machinery, I specialize in the design and construction of clothes for stout women.

Doubtless you will think this is a very extraordinary combination. Probably you will be unable to see what connection there can possibly be between engineering and the clothing of a woman whose bust, or waist line, or hips are all out of proportion to the rest of her body. As a matter of fact the two things have a great deal in common. Had I not been trained in engineering and familiar with a number of other scientific branches I should never have been able to do what I have done toward making it possible for stout women to secure clothes that not only fit but make them look less stout. ...

And before you go very far into what I have to say you will agree with me that stout women would have been immeasurably better off in health, peace of mind and good looks if the making of their clothes had been put on a scientific basis long ago.[27]

In the above quotation, Malsin's pedigree in engineering is framed as a sufficient prerequisite for designing so-called scientific stoutwear—a practice that, as he goes onto explain, lies at the intersection of "physics, mathematics, optics, psychology, and other scientific branches," but notably *not* fashion design. In this same article, Malsin derided fashion design and manufacturing practices that invoked "too little science, too much haphazard guess work and rule of thumb."[28] With this comment, Malsin aligned himself with other (mostly male and largely untrained) manufacturers and inventors of the period who, in language that Gamber argues was "condescending at best [and] deprecating at worst," sought to reimagine the "feminine" art of dressmaking as a more scientific, and therefore masculine, pursuit.[29]

In devising what he regarded a more precise, scientific approach to stoutwear design, Malsin's key insight was that larger garments had been improperly graded and

Figure 2.3 "Science at Last Turns Its Attention to 'Stout' People," *Richmond Times-Dispatch* (April 2, 1916), 55. Published with permission from Newspapers.com.

thus the fat woman's sartorial frustrations, above all else, emerged from inconsistent and poor fits. Of equal (or perhaps even greater) importance, however, was his observation that the fat woman's clothes tended to make her "look stout" due to the carelessness with which they were designed. What, however, did it mean for a garment to make a fat woman "look" stout? According to Malsin, "A woman's height should be seven times the height of her head"—an idea steeped in concepts of beauty and symmetry dating back to the Enlightenment—yet stoutwear manufacturers had, by-and-large, failed to acknowledge or respect these universal "laws of growth of the human body and their ramifications." As a result, they designed garments that only exacerbated the fat woman's size rather than creating "an impression of height."[30] To "flatter" the figure was to therefore create the appearance of a body that approximated this ideal by designing garments that visibly compensated for and corrected the fat woman's "odd" proportions. In other words, height was seen as a remedy for stoutness. This, as Malsin told the *Oregon Daily Journal* in 1916, was a design practice "built on the idea of aspiration" toward height, but more importantly, toward slenderness. As lofty as his ambitions might have been, Malsin was careful not to overpromise, noting that "the stout woman cannot expect any more than her slender sister to duplicate the appearance of the distorted, impossible creations which some fashion magazines present as human beings."[31] Even still, Malsin maintained that there existed an inherently "correct" or "true" way to design clothes in order to meet these aspirational ends.

In the second article in the series (Figure 2.4), Malsin discussed this precept in much greater detail, couching it within architectural principles:

The architect knows how to arrange his materials so as to give even a very large building an effect of airy grace, height and slenderness.

I can think of nothing better for the designer of clothing for stout people to keep constantly in mind than one of the great Gothic cathedrals. Aspiration, the reaching for something higher, is the fundamental principal of Gothic architecture, and every line from the cornerstone to the topmost peak of the spire is designed and constructed with this effect in view.

It is exactly the same effect which stout women must constantly strive for in their clothes.[32]

In this text, Malsin argues that designers should "constantly strive" for achieving the appearance of height to compensate for fat and, in doing so, establishes the notion that all stout women are desirous of looking more slender. To the point of architecture, however, Malsin draws one of the clearest parallels between garment design and architectural practice, arguing that stoutwear manufacturers should always keep in mind the "great Gothic cathedrals" and the sense of "airy grace" and weightlessness created by their soaring lines. Continuing, he explained how, "with the right lines rightly applied, [the fat woman] can create as deceptive an illusion of height and slenderness as the architect does with his huge structures of brick and stone."[33]

Even though Malsin was promoting what was, at least in his view, a new and novel approach to fashion design, Patricia Mears observes that a problem-oriented approach to "designing was and remains at the core of American fashion."[34] In his pursuit of fixing the "problem" of the fat female body, however, the familiar and tested ways of designing and

Figure 2.4 "How Science Is Helping 'Stout' People to Look Less 'Stout,'" *Richmond Times-Dispatch* (April 9, 1916). Published with permission from Newspapers.com.

manufacturing clothing proved insufficient. Instead, by couching his design practices within the language of architecture, Malsin was able to tap into a strain of thought that Bradley Quinn has described as fashion's desire to "push forward into the cultural landscape in pursuit of the accomplished forms mastered by art and architecture."[35]

By invoking architectural discourse, stoutwear manufacturers like Albert Malsin were consciously or unconsciously aligning themselves with prominent modernist architects and design thinkers of the period like Adolf Loos and Otto Wegner, who disparaged fashion as "frivolous, functional … wasteful, the antithesis of rationality and simplicity."[36] For Loos, in particular, the ideal in dress was "anonymity" or "simple clothing perfected over time."[37] Within the discourses of modern architecture, naturalistic ornamentation and decorative applications of color and line represented a denial of functionality and were subsequently deemed inessential.[38] Working within this framework, Malsin diminished fashion design as both low skilled and feminine. By turn, the practice of constructing a silhouette, and perhaps more importantly, a silhouette that "flatters" or "changes" a figure, was rendered the more intellectual and exacting task. Indeed, within Malsin's design rhetoric, the discourses of architecture became discourses of mastery.

On the one hand, the prevalence of architectural references within descriptions of stoutwear design practice could be written off as little more than marketing bluster. On the other, they evidence a tendency shared by male designers during this time to make competing statements, each loftier than the next, about having changed the shape of women's bodies—not unlike Poiret's overstated claims, for instance, to have altered the course of fashion in "liberating" women from the confines of their corsets a decade earlier. Even modernist architects who tapped into the rationalizing discourses of the dress reform movement in Germany (and were thus dismissive of fashion) were in this moment making proposals for how to improve upon women's dress, focusing mainly on relaxing the silhouette.[39] This professed preoccupation with essential form (rather than ornamentation) was central to modern architectural and design thinking, but also clearly found resonance within the sphere of fashion and, specifically, within the realm of stoutwear design. Within this context, the silhouette became a means to improve upon the natural and inherently flawed body where the supposed superficiality fashion was believed to have otherwise failed. By invoking these discourses, stoutwear manufacturers thereby became architects not only of garments but of the body itself in a moment in which the bodily ideal, like so much else in American life, was undergoing a dramatic transformation.

Modernist Fashions, Modernist Bodies

While Malsin's and other stoutwear manufacturers' clean and uncluttered silhouettes were being upheld in the fashion media as a more rational approach to solving the fat woman's clothing problems, as the teens bled into the twenties, there occurred a discernable shift in the aesthetics of stoutwear design that was precipitated by changes in fashion more broadly. Rather than any single innovation or breakthrough in stoutwear sizing or pattern cutting, it was the more loosely draped one-piece dresses that fell into vogue in the 1920s, and which were easier to fit to a variety of body shapes, that enabled the fortuitous intersection of standard-size and stoutwear aesthetics. In a 1922 article on the new season's stoutwear styles, *Women's Wear* remarked upon this shift, writing, "There is a certain ease and softness in the line in suits built for stouts this fall. The usual severe effects which were deemed necessary to produce long lines appear to have vanished."[40] Elsewhere, *Women's Wear* described this confluence of fashion and figure flattery as a "happy coincidence," and deemed it "an exceptionally fortunate season for the fat woman. Never before has she been offered so extensive a choice in fabric, color and line and never before has she been able so closely to resemble her slender sister in the way of dress."[41]

Although the silhouette had for some time been growing increasingly relaxed and more youthful, 1922 proved to be a turning point in stoutwear design discourse as the previous decade's rigid silhouettes seemed to suddenly cede to the caprices of fashion. As *Women's Wear* predicted of the coming fashion collections that year,

> It is to be expected that stoutwear designers will give up the attempt to adapt this mode to the stout figure and will concentrate rather on making the most of the novelty in color, lines, fabrics and details, which Paris offers in the new collections.[42]

Within this context, stoutwear garments—having adopted the tubular silhouette that was largely independent from the natural curvature of the body—became something of a blank canvas upon which designers and manufacturers could engage in more "hands off" experimentations in creating the appearance of slenderness as their focus shifted from sizing and construction to the *surfaces* of garments.

As Ilya Parkins observes, fashion somewhat uniquely expresses the dual poles of modernity, which are oftentimes imagined as ideologically opposed: "an ethos of experiment and evolution in the arts on the one hand (modernism), and industrialization and urbanization (modernization) on the other."[43] While this merging of technology and aesthetics is evident within stoutwear design in the 1920s, it perhaps most often associated with the designs of Coco Chanel and Jean Patou, each of whom found inspiration in the functionality of mass-produced sporting attire. Although what was problematically canonized as the "poor look" due to its simplicity was at first only adopted by the leisure class, Chanel's and Patou's simple suits and dresses quickly became oft-imitated stalwarts of the modern woman's wardrobe.[44] Perhaps more importantly, however, their unencumbered silhouettes epitomized a new approach to fashion design that was deeply indebted to the tenets of artistic modernism.[45] Designers like Chanel and Patou, Gilles Lipovetsky writes, effectively "wiped the slate clean" and in the process, engaged in a "desublimation of fashion"—a practice that paralleled movements in modernist art, such as cubism, abstraction, and constructivism.[46]

A number of scholars have noted the exchanges, both conceptual and aesthetic, that were occurring between the worlds of fashion and art in the early twentieth century.[47] For instance, Elizabeth Wilson has observed how fashion in this period was deeply indebted to the modernist rejection of naturalism and the corollary notion that "a painting was just that: a flat representation, not a three-dimensional reflection of the 'real.'"[48] Yet, even as fashion drew upon the language of modernism, it was not "fully modernist since it had hardly begun to question its own terms, nor to question the whole concept of fashion."[49] Even if fashion design lagged somewhat behind other modernist movements, Evans has observed that there was a preoccupation with "designing bodies as modernist" through fashion gestures, sensibilities, and attitudes, or what she describes as "little M modernism."[50] This modernist desire to "intervene in the body" could also be glimpsed in fashion illustration and, increasingly, in photography in the 1920s.[51] In this moment, representations of fashionable dress did not so much demonstrate accurately how clothes were made but rather how the clothed body was *supposed* to look by consolidating modernist design ideals encompassing shape, line, and volume[52] (Figure 2.5). Thus, if the trussed-up, womanly hourglass was the defining silhouette of the late nineteenth century, the abstract, industrial forms of the rectangle (in two dimensions) or the tube (in three) so prevalent in modernist painting were mainstays of the fashionable ideal in the twenties. Within this context, fashionable dress and bodies therefore came to increasingly mirror one another with the modernist lines of the garment determining the contours of the fleshy body underneath.

Throughout the 1920s, American fashion media forcefully underscored this point, as for instance in a 1921 article in which *Vogue* commented on the "engaging youthfulness" of the straight silhouette, describing it as flattering "if one happens to be slim," but "absurd if one's figure is too matronly."[53] A later article titled "The Problem of the Straight Silhouette: Fitting the Flat Back to the Full Figure" went even further, suggesting that only those whose appearance verged on "emaciated" could wear the fashionable "pencil silhouettes,"[54] while another claimed the fact that the straight styles "demand a new figure for many wearers goes without saying"[55] (Figure 2.6). Within these texts, the agency of dress was made manifest: The new styles were said to "demand" a new figure as the straight line became the sole precept that dictated the contours of the fashionable silhouette. As Mark Wigley argues, both in art and fashion, the directness of modernist and industrial aesthetics encouraged the eyes to linger and to contemplate the matter of authenticity.[56] On the body, however, the simplicity of modernist fashions only accentuated the points at which the body deviated from the straight and narrow. While the streamlining of the silhouette may have freed the waistline, it placed new emphasis on the hips—the region that was believed to be first, and most obvious, part of the body at which excess weight showed.[57] Thus, as the voluptuous, mature ideal of the late nineteenth and early twentieth centuries gave way to the mechanical archetype of the 1920s, fatness, by turn, became a visible corruption of modernist ideals and sensibilities.

In response to this new ideal, stoutwear design shifted somewhat in order to enable the fat woman to enclothe herself in the aesthetics of artistic modernism and, in doing so, to inch closer to a bodily ideal that was increasingly unmoored from reality. Whereas mainstream fashion media discourses were more critical of the ability of the fat woman to wear the "pencil silhouette," stoutwear manufacturers saw great potential in its flat, unbroken expanses of fabric, which were coupled with new opportunities in mass garment manufacturing. Sitting at the confluence of modernism and modernization, the new silhouette—simpler in virtually all respects—was also easier to produce and therefore resolved many of the problems in fit that had so plagued the stoutwear industry in its early days. As was reported in a 1922 *Women's Wear* article, for instance,

Figure 2.5 Fall/Winter 1924–1925 Lane Bryant catalog cover.

stoutwear manufacturers were suddenly finding it easier to cut their garments on the same patterns used in the manufacture of higher priced items, while the simplicity of the styles and fabrication, which were made of "poor" fabrics like simple knit jersey and

WORTH

A floating panel is another effective way of concealing pronounced curves. This dress is of black crêpe de Chine with touches of bright blue crêpe, the unusual diagonal line of the panel making it most becoming and dignified to the woman of full figure

JENNY

A full, hanging panel is placed in a strategic position where the tightness begins on a yellow and gold lamé frock, with wide bands embroidered with mother-of-pearl, turquoise beads, and gold thread crossing the plain front and the deep V décolletage

PREMET

In this case, a tunic blouse hanging straight from the shoulders is used to give width to the back of the gown without sacrificing a slender effect. This exceedingly attractive model is of black moire with touches of bright green duvetine at the girdle

These are the frocks from the Paris openings that have lines which help to conceal a too heavy figure

FITTING THE FLAT BACK TO THE FULL FIGURE

Figure 2.6 "The Problem of the Straight Silhouette," *Vogue* (November 15, 1923), 44. Published with permission from *Vogue*, © Condé Nast.

lacked "gaudy trimmings," brought down the cost of production.[58] Running counter to *Vogue*'s assertion that the new styles looked "absurd" on the matronly or stout figure, *Women's Wear* even remarked on the "loose and free" lines of the 1922 collections and provoked the trade journal to declare, "You need not be young, you need not be slim—to wear [the new styles]."[59]

As in the decade prior, the imperative shared by makers of stoutwear throughout the 1920s was to make the stout body appear more slender. With the confluence of the more forgiving straight silhouette and stoutwear design, however, manufacturers proved to be less interested in the "architecture" of the body as they turned their focus to the surfaces of garments. In doing so, they invoked increasingly sophisticated optical theories, borrowed from fields as far flung as Gestalt psychology, in their design discourses—an impulse that was reflected in the writings of members of the European avant-garde as well. Indeed, stoutwear design discourse in the 1920s did not only evidence the impulses of "little M" modernism described by Evans; rather, it emerged as an unlikely site of experimentation for practitioners within the field of "big M" artistic modernism, too.

Body-as-Canvas

In his 1928 book, *Economics of Fashion*, the economist Paul Nystrom reflected on, among other things, the current state of fashion design in the United States.[60] Focusing principally on the intersections of fashion and art, Nystrom drew a number of parallels between the concepts of rhythm, harmony, and balance employed within the realms of interior design and musical composition, and similar principles he observed being applied within the field of fashion design:

> A beautiful style in furniture or garment design illustrates good balance of its parts, harmony, unity and in the detail of its design may even suggest rhythm.
>
> One of the major purposes of art as at present conceived is to make the best effect possible from the means at hand both from the standpoint of fashion and good taste. Apparel art is intended to make the wearer look as pleasing as possible. ... Lines, masses and colors are skillfully manipulated to create illusion or to make impressions which, without art, would be completely lost.
>
> Perhaps the most commonly used are the line illusions. By clever use of line, short persons are made to look tall, tall persons to look shorter, and stout persons slimmer. Individual defects are minimized and good points are strengthened by the same method. Many of these illusions are described in books on design or psychology.[61]

In the above excerpt, Nystrom explains how one of the core tenets of "apparel art" was to "make the best effect possible," which in the case of fashion specifically amounted to making "short persons ... look tall, tall persons to look shorter," and, perhaps most notably, to make "stout persons slimmer." Rather than by means of physically reshaping the body, as for instance with corsets and other constraining undergarments, Nystrom wrote that the principal tactic for meeting this end was through so-called "line illusions." Continuing, Nystrom explained how these design techniques had been derived from "familiar ... illustrations of squares divided by widely spaced horizontal and vertical lines" that, when applied to dress in various ways, functioned to "add height" and thereby reduce apparent width in the wearer.[62] Describing what he referred to as "mass illusions," which pertained either to increasing or decreasing the apparent weight of an object, Nystrom argued that a space divided looks larger than an unbroken space, and thus a plain dress had the effect of making a "large person appear smaller."[63] Breaking with stoutwear design discourses that stressed the importance of firm foundations and severe tailoring in redefining the contours of the stout body, Nystrom also posited that one effective way to achieve this was through "soft drapey materials [that] are, as a rule, more becoming to a large person than are stiffer materials which make angular lines."[64] Invoking similar language, he also suggested that "large persons should also avoid brilliant or very light colors as an area of black or of dark color looks smaller than an equal area of brilliant or light color."[65] Above all, however, Nystrom stressed the prevalence of the scientific use of lines in garment design that had a "distracting influence" from "marked irregularities in the figure," and which, he noted, were derived from "modernistic design."[66]

Writing during the latter years of the 1920s, and therefore with the benefit of hindsight, Nystrom had indeed picked up on a prominent ideological current within stoutwear design discourse that tapped into scientific and artistic themes, and specifically the principles of optical illusion. The preoccupation with creating the mere *illusion* of slenderness cropped up in numerous articles discussing stoutwear design in the 1920s as, for instance, in an article claiming that the design of stoutwear was "governed to a great extent by the necessity of creating an illusion of slenderness."[67] This was a stark departure from the ways about which slenderizing the fat body was discussed only a decade prior, and which focused on altering the physique through a firm foundation of corsetry.[68] A 1926 *Women's Wear* feature titled "The Selling Points of Your Merchandise" visualized this new, more hands-off approach in a series of sketches that highlighted the specific features that fulfilled the fat woman's perceived "desire to attain the appearance of slenderness." Emphasizing the importance of creating visual interest near the waistline, for example, the feature explained how many of the pictured garments "place the chief details of construction and trimming near the center of the figure, keeping the outlines subdued and devoid of emphasis [so as to create] an impression of slimness."[69] Similar optical effects were discussed in an August 1922 *Women's Wear* feature that celebrated the diversity of the new stoutwear offerings while at the same time stressing the effectiveness of straight lines to "break up the width [of the fat woman's] back" and circular arm treatments that "carry the eye across instead of up and down … [causing] the eye to waver and suggest confusion to the beholder."[70]

Even as the slenderizing effects of these various design features were detailed at great length throughout the professional media, rarely were these discussions embedded within a more thorough exploration of the optical theories referenced. A notable exception came in the form of a twelve-part series of instructive articles titled "Selling the Customer Smartness through Basic Art Principles," written by Carl N. Werntz, an instructor at the Chicago Academy of Fine Arts, and published in *Women's Wear* between June and September 1924. The stated aim of the twelve-part series was to delimit the so-called "psychology of line" and to unravel the popular notion that there was a single "good line" upon which all dresses should be built.[71] Rather, Werntz, like his contemporaries, was a proponent of the idea that dresses should be designed with the aim of creating a "pleasant sensation," rather than with fashion in mind. Focusing on the psychological principles underlying what made a line "good" versus what made a line "bad," Werntz discussed an effect known as the Müller-Lyer illusion,[72] which theorized how line segments of equal length can be made to look shorter or longer depending upon which way the arrowheads appearing at either end of the line segment are facing (Figure 2.7). Within the realm of fashion he argued that this principle could be fruitfully applied to "adapt selected models to suit abnormal figures."[73] In the following week's feature, Werntz further argued that

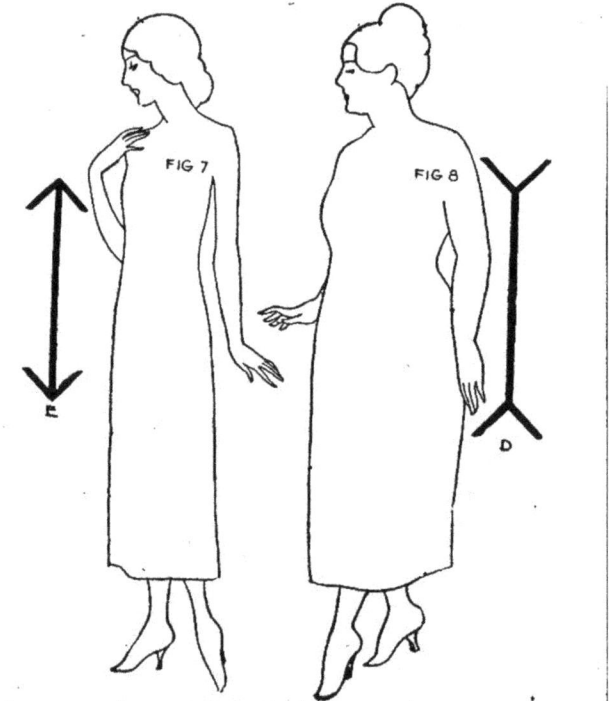

Selling the Customer Smartness Through Basic Art Principles

Illustrated Demonstrations on Charm and Artistry in Appearance Related to the Problems of Manufacturers, Buyers and Salespersons

Originated and Copyrighted by CARL N. WERNTZ,
Director the Chicago Academy Fine Arts

NO. 5   ADAPTING A MODEL TO DIFFERENT FIGURES

DO THE vertical lines (D and E) at the sides of the picture seem to be of different length?

You know they are the same, of course, but though I have seen this drawing for years, "E" still looks the shorter.

Through this simple diagram I will show you a principle in the psychology of line—that is, the general effect lines have upon the brain when their forms are transmitted through the nerves of the eye—which is one of the most important basic principles of appearance. Besides being of use in designing new gowns to suit normal figures to best advantage, it is of wonderful help in adapting selected models to suit abnormal figures.

Carefully examine the little diagrams referred to. Notice that the vertical line of D seems much longer than that of E. Measure and you will find they are just the same. This, of course, is the old optical illusion.

When applied to raiment, this simple diagram shows you the only sure way of making the short woman seem taller, the tall woman less noticeable, the fat woman less wide and the thin woman seem to have a plumper figure.

To be sure you understand this valuable appearance aid, experiment on tracings of these figures as you were requested in the previous lesson on sketching.

Figure 2.7 Carl N. Werntz, "Selling the Customer Smartness through Basic Art Principles," *Women's Wear* (July 19, 1924), 14. Published with permission from Proquest LLC. Further reproduction is prohibited without permission.

the illusion, while little understood, had long been used by dressmakers to adapt dresses for "normal figures," but could specifically "do much for the heavy figure to add apparent height and correct unbecoming proportions."[74]

Throughout the series, Werntz discussed not just clever dressmaking techniques but also how fatness had come to be regarded as an abomination of modernity and, specifically, of the modernist body. This manifested in the visceral language he used to describe, on the one hand, dress as an expression of the modernist desire to intervene in the body and, on the other, the fleshy imperfection of the fat body. If artistic lines were "straight" and "strong," the fat female body, on the other hand, was deemed "sagging" and "unbalanced." Despite the desultory language with which he spoke about the fat woman's body, Werntz offered her a minor concession, arguing that "the artistic difference between the normal, fat and thin figures, is not entirely a matter of size" but rather could at least partially be attributed to the careless application of "weak" lines in her dress.[75] By referring to the fat body as "artistically undesirable," Werntz did not, however, speak to an eternal or absolute conception of beauty but rather to the modernist sensibilities of mechanical simplicity, straightness, and flatness. Werntz, not unlike his contemporaries, effectively viewed the surface of the fashionably tubular silhouette—made all the more expansive by the fat woman's proportions—as a blank canvas, ripe with potential to transform the body without resorting to more drastic means, such as diets, exercise, or weight-loss gimmicks. Even beyond the specific remit of stoutwear manufacturing, however, the tubular silhouette proved to be an enticing canvas for established artists and couturiers to engage in further experimentations in visual perception. The fat woman's dress therefore became an unlikely site upon which art, fashion, and science converged in the pursuit of solving the problem of the fat woman's figure.

The Art and Science of Looking Slender

Within the wider field of fashion, the modernist impulse within 1920s stoutwear design discourse was more generally characterized by a desire, shared by designers, to make the invisible logic of science visible—a desire that Wilson argues was precipitated with a deeper need to "come to grips with the nature of human experience in a mechanized, 'unnatural' world."[76] Stoutwear designers' preoccupation with optical illusions was a clear manifestation of this impulse in their borrowing of optical theories from the field of Gestalt psychology. Born from a growing interest in the laws of perception among scholars working in the adjacent fields of physics, psychology, and philosophy in mid-nineteenth-century Europe, the underlying concern of the German school of Gestalt psychology was the question, "How do we see?"—a question which sought to probe the relationship between the eye, as an organ, and the cognitive functioning of the brain.[77] Although a number of paradigms were conceived to answer this complicated question, members of the Gestalt school departed from other schools of thought in their interest in the individual components of perception, and the idea that the brain tends to group discrete elements (i.e., dots, lines, voids, etc.) in order to create a complete picture—the platitude, "The whole is greater than the sum of its parts," forming the cornerstone of their practice.[78] In order to visualize their theories, the Gestalt psychologists conceived a number of optical illusions such as the aforementioned Müller-Lyer illusion, which came to be well known not only in Europe but also in the United States, where a number of prominent members of the school had sought political asylum in the 1920s.[79] Even beyond the remit of psychology, their theories proved highly impactful—inspiring early modernists like Paul Klee and Wassily Kandinsky, and undergirding modernist movements like De Stijl.[80]

Working somewhat closer to the field of fashion, Sonia Delaunay's modernist robes and dresses expressed a similar preoccupation with the Gestalt school's theories of perception. In applying the principles of Simultanism to fashion, the Ukrainian-born French artist—not unlike stoutwear manufacturers during this period—was expressly uninterested in the cut of garments and instead focused on how color and texture could work together to destroy the illusion of a well-defined silhouette[81] (Figure 2.8). For her, a dress was little more than a wearable painting animated by the kinetic movements of the body—the contrasts of color used to "fuse the wearer's body with the dress."[82] As in her paintings in which she fractured shapes into cubist planes of color that permitted multiple views of an object simultaneously, in her dresses and robes, Delaunay sought to create unity between the disparate planes of the body and those of the garment to create a single, uniform impression.[83]

For members of the European avant-garde, dress was not just a fashionable covering for the body; rather they believed in the potential for clothing to be a conduit or mediator of modernity rather than just a reflection of it.[84] Just as the body figured centrally in the changes that were occurring within Western culture at large, however, so too did the body figure centrally in their proposals. A defining characteristic of the sartorial experimentations of artist-designers like Sonia Delaunay was the manner in which straight-cut dresses that "liberated" the body were treated as blank canvasses. Upon them, they could explore the relationships between silhouette, color, and line as they attempted to create harmony between dress, the body, and its environment. Modernists held contempt for the ornate, superfluous curves of the fat body, which harkened back to an earlier, preindustrial time. In their hands, however, dress became a medium to streamline or reengineer the body to maximize efficiency and beauty. Although these proposals took many forms, as a whole they were strikingly similar to the period's stoutwear design discourses—namely in their preoccupation with the surface of garments and with creating the impression of a rational, streamlined silhouette—while more broadly sharing a pronounced rejection of fashion's tendency to treat surface decoration as subservient to silhouette.

Although it is difficult to trace the seemingly unlikely channels through which these high-minded ideals emerging from the European avant-garde came to infiltrate the design discourses of American stoutwear manufacturers, Richard Martin has helpfully argued that when thinking about the parallels between modernism and fashion during this period, which are so visibly and obviously apparent, if impossible to pin down, it is permissible to view this relationship as "openly and as broadly applicable," for it was

Figure 2.8 Sonia Delaunay in her studio, 1924. Heritage Images via Getty.

"almost inevitable that the planes, cylinders, mutable optics and dynamic motion of [modern] art would engage fashion."[85] More specifically, Martin contends that it was not so much a specific and codified set of modernist principles or aesthetics that changed the world of fashion in the early twentieth century but rather a more transient "culture" of modernism that infiltrated all facets of visual culture.[86] Valerie Steele echoes this point when she explains how, not unlike "the new painting, the new music and the new literature," fashion during the 1920s was inevitably bound to undergo its own "internal stylistic revolution."[87] Namely, it would be the modernist interest in visual perception that trickled down to the manufacture of everyday dress, and specifically, to the practice of designing slenderizing dresses. As Martin explains, the greatest contribution modernism made to fashion was its disintegration of the "obdurate silhouette" into something more visibly modern, and which allowed for "multiple readings and ambiguities" both of garments and of the body—a notion that was mirrored in stoutwear manufacturers' preoccupation with slenderness.[88]

At the same time, however, it may be argued that the intense interest in perception that manifested in the work of the Impressionists, Cubists, and Surrealists, and which trickled down to fashion, was less of an inevitability, as Martin suggests, than it was a response to the massive convulsions in knowledge that occurred in the nineteenth century. New discoveries in the natural sciences, for instance, revealed the underlying logic of the field of vision. Even early experimentations in chronophotography by Muybridge and Marey revealed that human and animal locomotion was mechanized and rational, but also highly abstract.[89] This evolution in scientific discourse and visual literacy had ramifications across culture, but its effects could very clearly be glimpsed in the fine arts as well as in fashion.[90] Indeed, as Jonathan Crary writes, in many ways, "art and science were both part of a single interlocking field of knowledge and practice."[91] To this list, however, we might also add fashion.

Although there are multiple sites within the field of fashion during this period in which the close associations between art and science could be observed, stoutwear is one (albeit somewhat improbable) arena in which these ideals that were often limited to mere sketches and prototypes came to fruition. Even at a more conceptual level, however, the potential for fashion to be utilized to specifically bring the fat body more in line with the modernist body was not entirely lost on the artistic avant-garde. As the Russian Constructivist designer Nadezhda Lamanova explained in her 1923 essay, "Concerning Contemporary Dress,"

> It was thought possible, for example, to fight a massive figure by lacing it tightly in a corset or in narrow clothes; in fact, this had the opposite effect, emphasizing even more the lack of proportion between the parts. The fight against a corpulent body has to take a different direction; a silhouette cannot be slimmed except by hiding disproportions, breaking them into planes of a different shape.[92]

Similarly, the painter Leon Bakst—whose experimentations in fashion and dress were only limited to stage costumes, but which suffused into mainstream fashion discourse in multiple sites by way of a series of public lectures that detailed his theories of color harmony and line illusions—wrote in a *Vogue* article about how he had come to appreciate the more "serious ramifications" of the "art of costuming," and specifically the ability of dress to "hide imperfections" without "[correcting] the incorrigible."[93] In an illustration that accompanied the editorial, Bakst demonstrated this notion through side-by-side illustrations that showed the slimming effects of vertical lines and the "disastrous" effect of horizontal ones on the stout body (Figure 2.9). Bakst proffered similar advice during lectures in Toronto in New York that same year, arguing in one that women should "correct what [is] correctable but do not touch anything that is not correctable,"[94] and in another, offering the platitude, "What one cannot see, one imagines to be beautiful."[95]

Working more explicitly within the field of fashion, the so-called "kinetic designs" of the French couturier Lucien Lelong were another expression of this modernist design ethos, which had somewhat unlikely connections to stoutwear design discourse. As reported by *Women's Wear* in August 1925, Lelong had come to be considered a disciple of what was described as the "modern school" of haute couture due to the fact that he was an active exponent "of the present era of high powered motor cars, outdoor sports and informal social creeds," which culminated in his "emancipatory" designs.[96] On the occasion of the first presentation of his kinetic designs in Paris, *Women's Wear* reported that Lelong's new dresses embodied "the fundamental spirit of modern times" and rejected the old ways of designing garments "statically."[97] Lelong's imperative to make the tenets of modernism visible perhaps manifested most clearly, however, in his own discussion of the suitability of his designs for fat women. In speaking with *Women's Wear* about their sartorial plight, Lelong explained,

> Last season I emphasized the point that the present silhouette is particularly well adapted to the stout figure. Kinetic design has only enhanced this quality of the modern line to impart slenderness and the look of youth to its wearer. I feel sure that the woman whose figure is not so youthful as it once was will find consolation when she puts on these gowns.[98]

Lelong was again quoted in *Women's Wear*'s "Styles for Larger Women" section in October 1925 wherein the couturier spoke in more detail about which features of his

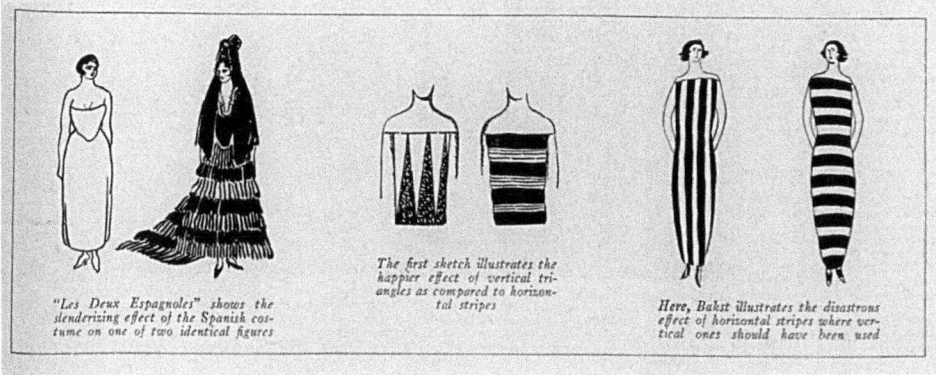

"Les Deux Espagnoles" shows the slenderizing effect of the Spanish costume on one of two identical figures

The first sketch illustrates the happier effect of vertical triangles as compared to horizontal stripes

Here, Bakst illustrates the disastrous effect of horizontal stripes where vertical ones should have been used

Figure 2.9 "Bakst: A Famous Artist Analyses the Slim Silhouette," *Vogue* (December 1, 1923), 61. Published with permission from *Vogue*, © Condé Nast.

designs were specifically becoming on the fat woman, suggesting, for instance, that "by commencing at a point slightly above the normal waistline in the front, gradually flaring until the hemline fullness is contrived … the effect of a gradual circular flare" is created on the wearer.[99] While elsewhere in the fashion media, Lelong spoke about the suitability of his kinetic designs for the circumstances of modernity,[100] in the above quotations Lelong more explicitly describes the power of the fashionable silhouette to "impart slenderness and the look of youth to its wearer"—qualities that were synonymous with the construct of the modernist body. Emerging from the discourses of "mathematics, logic and art," or what Lelong himself declared "logic in design,"[101] the rhetoric of kinetic design was said to bear in it the capacity to imbue not only garments but also the wearer's figure "with the characteristic dynamism of the age."[102]

In spite of the appeal of Lelong's rhetoric, his designs were actually more in keeping with the styles promoted during these years by both Vionnet and Doucet, among others.[103] The general consensus was that the looser, sportswear-inspired mode of the early to mid-1920s, which, quite notably, was cut generously around the waistline to permit freedom of movement, also happened to do a better job of concealing excess flesh than the more waist-conscious silhouettes popular in previous years. This fact, however, did not stop stoutwear manufacturers and retailers from invoking the highbrow discourses of artistic modernism to market their wares as new and innovative, nor did it deter modernist artists and fashion designers from explicitly framing the fat body as a site of modernist speculation and experimentation—or, more bluntly, as a business opportunity. Indeed, in the hands of these designers, the discourses of modernism became potent rhetorical tools that enabled them to secure their positions as design innovators.

***

Although the fat female body was, in many ways, an embodied rejection of modernist ideals, fashion design was nevertheless regarded as a powerfully effective way to correct its flaws. In the hands of manufacturers, a tubular dress, with its uninterrupted expanses of fabric, was not just a way to cover up and conceal fat; it was quite literally a blank canvas upon which the laws of perception could be tested in an effort to create the appearance of the flesh transformed.

Stoutwear manufacturers engaged in a delicate balancing act by both tapping into and negating the mandates of fashion, which largely manifested in adapting the silhouette to make the fat female body aesthetically acceptable within an increasingly fat phobic society. Within this context, the design discourses of stoutwear ultimately reflected the values of appropriate and fashionable femininity, which, in the early twentieth century, was something of a moving target. As the teens bled into the twenties, for instance, the conservative appearance of stoutwear superseded its capacities to slenderize. Stoutwear had itself become a design cliché, known for its conservative lines and drab color schemes. In early 1920s, however, fashion suddenly became more accommodating of the fat body—the straight lines and simple construction of the tubular silhouette having proved to be an effective way to create a slender, streamlined appearance, even on larger bodies. For a fleeting moment, there was more space, both literally and figuratively, for the fat body in fashion.

The design discourses of stoutwear did not, however, exist in or emerge from a vacuum. Rather, they were bolstered by a network of advertisers and retailers whose job it was to convince consumers of the transformative capacities of stoutwear. Given the largely conservative or at least unremarkable appearance of most stoutwear garments, which did not forthrightly reveal the sophisticated scientific principles that underpinned their making, advertising was a necessary addendum to stoutwear design discourse.

CHAPTER 3
FITTING THE MIND

In a 1922 interview with the *American Cloak and Suit Review*, Charles May of the Associated Stylish Stout Wear Makers explained to the trade journal that "fitting the body" of the fat woman was but one-half of the retailer's job—and perhaps the easier half. "Fitting her mind," May went on to argue, "is an entirely different part of the task … The woman must be studied carefully and the selling must be done on something which almost approaches a scientific scale." Continuing, he explained,

> I cannot impress too strongly upon the mind of the buyer that he must buy for an unknown market. Strange as this may sound it points the way to the most successful policy. The retailer cannot guess anything as far as stoutwear is concerned. It is not a case of gambling—a plain and simple hazard for what some merchants have found to be big stakes.[1]

With the phrase "fitting the mind," May obliquely refers to the process of earning the fat woman's trust and therefore her patronage. Through his own experience, May had found that "argument will not bring the desired results …. She must be assured that it is a simple matter of fit for her." As May argues, looming large over the task of selling stoutwear was the complicated matter of the fat woman's unpredictable temperament. Unlike her standard-size counterpart who was in many ways more "knowable," the fat woman was, at least for May, a confounding, if not difficult, figure. Ostensibly, a disorderly mind accompanied a disorderly body and thus rather than being a "sure bet," she was a "gamble." However, even as stoutwear manufacturers conceived of ways to remedy the fat woman's sartorial grievances, garment fit, it seems, was only one half of the problem. The problem of "fitting" the fat woman's mind seemed to be an equally urgent one.

Together with the scaling of stoutwear manufacturing, a secondary but critically important task was that of generating a steady stream of demand. Although a perennial topic of debate within the trade press, an overt concern with inciting consumer demand was not unique to the stoutwear industry. Industrialists across the spectrum of American manufacturing had by the 1910s come to realize that advertising was an essential part of mass distribution and was thus an important, if not critical, investment. Beyond just developing approaches and pitches that appealed to the widest swath of consumers, however, advertisers were becoming increasingly preoccupied with demystifying the inner life of the consumer in order to arouse their most basal human instincts—among them, beauty, respect, and belonging. By the 1920s, the field of modern advertising had come into its own, supported a robust trade press in which "experts" opined on consumer psychology and the science of manufacturing desire. According to Jackson

Lears, it was through the professionalization of the field that advertisers had become convinced of the fact "that human minds were not only malleable but manipulable," and the most potent manipulation was that which leveraged a perceived (or manufactured) shortcoming into a sale.[2]

This chapter explores these "manipulations"—as well as their underlying assumptions—and considers the possibilities and opportunities afforded to fat women through the act of consumption. Specifically, it investigates advertisers' attempts to translate the fat woman's perceived desires, as well as her insecurities, into sales and how in the process they "tailored" or "fit" their sales pitches to her mind. In doing so, it first situates the fat woman within the broader context of the burgeoning field of consumer psychology in the early twentieth century by showing how within fashion media discourses her disorderly outward appearance was used as an indicator of her tumultuous inner world. Phrased another way, this chapter explores how weight bias, including damaging assumptions and stereotypes about fat women, informed and gave shape to advertising practice. It then takes a step back to consider the etymology of the term "stout" and how it was reluctantly chosen as a substitute for "fat" in advertising copy. The chapter then concludes by examining how this complex of ideas manifested in printed advertisements that promised to help the fat woman circumvent the personal failure of her weight through the practice of fashionable consumption. In its entirety, this chapter demonstrates the key role that stoutwear advertising played in perpetuating weight bias and in mediating the conditions of fat female embodiment while also questioning the possibilities and limitations of consumer citizenship.

The Psychology of Selling

Beginning in the late nineteenth century there emerged a capitalist culture that, as William Leach writes, was "forged by merchants in the company of enthusiastic politicians, reformers, educators and artists ... so powerful as nearly to dwarf all alternative cultures."[3] This confluence of circumstances gave rise to the birth of "consumer culture," or "a culture of the use of appropriation of objects or things."[4] While an influx of new things formed the material foundations of the new consumer culture, advertising served as a vital medium for the creation of a desiring buying public and as a means of controlling demand.[5] During this time, the business of advertising began to evolve beyond catchy slogans to a more complex approach of presenting aspirational visions of everyday life not as it was but as it *could* be.[6] Many early twentieth-century advertisements utilized a predictable but effective formula in which a previously unknown lack or shortcoming, or a deeply engrained insecurity, was presented to the consumer. The advertiser would then helpfully intervene in with a cheap and easy remedy (usually a good or service) that either improved the consumer's physical or emotional state or provided a solution to the complexities of modern life.

Underpinning the practice of modern advertising was a discernible current of psychoanalytical thinking as retailers and advertisers strove to better understand the

American consumer. Walter Dill Scott, author of a popular advertising manual titled *The Psychology of Advertising* (1903), provocatively suggested that advertisers must not merely think like but *be* psychologists:

> Ordinarily the business man does not realize that he means psychology when he says that he "must know his customers wants—what will catch their attention, what will impress them and lead them to buy," etc. In all these expressions he is saying that he must be a psychologist. He is talking about the minds of his customers, and psychology is nothing but a stubborn and systematic attempt to understand and explain the workings in the minds of these very people.[7]

Beyond just "knowing" their customers, Scott suggests that advertisers should leverage psychosocial insights to the singular end of making sales. Within this context, observed weaknesses and social and physical shortcomings became potential boons to sales. Advertisements, in a sense, had become sites of alternative identity construction in which consumers could glimpse newer and better versions of themselves enhanced by a vast array of new and spectacular products and services.

As advertisers came to more intimately understand the American buying public, however, they also came to view a single national market as increasingly inefficient and unpredictable. Guided by advice from experts like Walter Dill Scott, advertisers turned their attention to identifying more localized and previously underserved consumer groups.[8] In a chapter that focused on advertisements directed toward fat people, for instance, Scott spoke about the importance of depicting fat people in a manner that would inspire feelings of sympathy and admiration from the reader, rather than the more "familiar" feelings of pity and disgust. Comparing two advertisements for fat-reducing compounds, Scott argued that one portraying an unfashionable fat lady, "dress[ed] in plaids, which, as every corpulent person knows serve but to increase the apparent size," is "ridiculous" (Figure 3.1). By contrast, an advertisement for a fat-reducing ointment featuring a photograph of a fat woman possessing a more evidently fashionable S-curve silhouette—her hair piled high and her posture demure—is deemed more sympathetic (Figure 3.2). He writes,

> She is apparently making the best of a bad condition. If she is going to use the Howard Obesity Ointment, it certainly must be worth considering. I feel sorry for her and sympathize with her in her affliction. She certainly feels about the matter just as I should, and consequently it is easy for me to imagine myself in her stead and to feel the need for relief from obesity and to take the necessary steps to secure such relief.[9]

According to Scott, advertisements were successful when consumers were able to identify a solution to a problem, be it psychological or, as in this case, physical. With the insight that everyone aspires toward a more improved version of themselves, however, Scott argued that consumers feel most sympathetic "for those whom [they] might call [their]

Figure 3.1 Advertisement from *The Psychology of Advertising* (Boston: Small, Maynard & Company, 1921), 42.

ideals," or those who appear prosperous, well-dressed, and happy rather than confined to a less-than-desirable way of existing in the world.[10]

While Scott and his contemporaries regarded this approach as simply the most effective way to make a sale, Stuart Ewen has gone so far as to describe early twentieth-century advertising as a "civilizing processes," or as "productive of a homogenous national character" within the context of advanced capitalist mass production.[11] If mass manufacturing created standardized bodies, then it was advertising that both democratized and standardized desire across a heterogeneous population. Yet, even as "consumer" came to be what Celia Lury has aptly described as a "master category of identity" in the United States,[12] this did not mean that all Americans were necessarily "ideal" or "desirable" consumers. Under the ideological framework of "consumer citizenship," dollars are synonymous with votes. Individuals whose income or racial or ethnic identity prohibited them from voting with their dollars did not, at least in the minds of advertisers, count as citizens at all.[13] In early twentieth-century

No. 4.— She begets my sympathy.

Figure 3.2 Advertisement from *The Psychology of Advertising* (Boston: Small, Maynard & Company, 1921), 44.

America, the 30 percent (or more) of Americans who were disenfranchised from the market therefore included recent immigrants and racial and ethnic minorities, and particularly African Americans.[14] As a result, these groups were not targeted with any particular zeal, nor would they have seen their likenesses represented in advertising imagery.

Although a reviled figure in American society, different from racial and ethnic "non-consumer citizens," the fat woman was acknowledged to possess buying power and therefore had the potential to be a "good" consumer. This was due to the fact that, by the 1920s, advertisers had acknowledged that women—many of whom oversaw their household economies—were a particularly powerful consumer group.[15] Yet, even as the female consumer became the object of intense interest among advertisers, she was nevertheless enduringly linked with the damaging stereotypes of being emotional, fickle, and vice-prone.[16] This would have a significant impact on the tone of early twentieth-century advertising, which was "committed to a view of 'consumer citizens' as an emotional, feminized mass, characterized by mental lethargy, bad taste and ignorance."[17] Even more so than the "average" woman, however, the fat woman was believed to be particularly impulsive, unintelligent, and emotionally maladjusted, but also full of latent desire.

In many ways, the fat woman's ability to consume was embodied by her corporeal excesses—her insatiable hunger for food lazily equated with other forms of consumption. In a society still governed by the Protestant ethos of sacrifice and restraint, maintaining a trim physique was regarded as a compensatory strategy for other "temptations of the flesh," including overconsumption.[18] The crucial difference between ascetism as a route to moral salvation and modern dieting and exercise as practices that compensated for anxieties about overconsumption, however, could be located in the fact that the body itself had increasingly come to function as a vehicle of self-expression. No longer were weight-loss regimens pursued in order to attain spiritual catharsis; rather, outer appearances were managed in order to give the mere impression of strong character. Indeed, in the 1920s, bodily discipline and other indulgences of the flesh were no longer mutually exclusive. Rather, as Featherstone suggests, "Within consumer culture, the inner and the outer body [became] conjoined: the prime purpose of the maintenance of the inner body [was] the enhancement of the appearance of the outer body."[19] Whereas excess in previous decades would have been written off as merely unfashionable or unbecoming, the moral mobilization against fat that occurred during the interwar years all but ensured the fat woman's social decline.

Despite society's low opinion of the fat woman, the difficult truth was that her patronage was necessary to ensure the continued growth of the American fashion industry. Just as the automobile industrialist could not rely upon a narrow swath of the moneyed elite to match his production capacity, American garment manufacturers could not expect standard-sized women to prop up the burgeoning market for ready-made clothing on their backs alone. In other words, the fat woman was, quite literally, a massive opportunity; however, in order for stoutwear to be profitable, women had to remain both fat *and* discontent. In addition to navigating this paradox, advertisers identified other challenges that came with selling to fat the fat woman. Because she was in the minds of advertisers less acquainted with the norms of fashion consumption, they believed that she required singular appeals, strategic keywords, and an all-around different approach to selling. Thus, before implementing such strategies, advertisers had to better understand with whom, exactly, they were dealing.

Fat Bodies, Thin Skin

Second only to the issue of fit, the matter of the fat woman's inner life—and specifically her drives, desires, and insecurities—was a prominent one in professional media as advertisers and retailers attempted to construct a composite picture of the "typical" fat American woman. This struggle to qualify her peculiar disposition can be glimpsed in an article titled "Quality as Important as Size in Handling Stouts Trade," published in

Women's Wear in January of 1917, in which a retail manager attempted to sketch out a psychological profile of his consumer:

> The fat woman is extremely sensitive about her proportions. She herself may make a joke about her dimensions when among her best friends, but nobody else should try making the joke unless he wishes to lose his popularity. One of the reasons why the "hefties" are touchy on the subject of their weight is that they have a guilty conscience. Their flesh is usually the price they pay for indulging themselves in the way of eats, and they know it.
>
> … Our fat sisters are mostly as sensitive as they are fat. Everybody knows the habitual hurt looks that the big women wear. Quizzical looks and open ridicule does it. Before one of these nerves herself to enter the department where "stouts" are to be had, she has hesitated many a time. So when at length she does come into the department, its force is in duty bound to put her at ease, which is best done by a judicious use of compliments.[20]

In the above quotation, the retail manager draws an important parallel between fat women's size and their feelings of unease within retail spaces, arguing that they are "as sensitive as they are fat." Continuing, he claims that this sensitivity is an embodied manifestation of their guilt, framed here as the price paid for "indulging themselves in the way of eats." Even while discussing the possible rewards of their patronage, the retail manager's contempt for fat women is thinly veiled. Not only were they deemed guilty, they were also pathetic, variously and derogatorily referred to as "hefties" and elsewhere as "freaks," and perceived as being totally unacquainted with the norms of appropriate, measured consumption. Wracked with guilt over their own gluttony, they were regarded as emotionally fragile individuals, and salespeople were instructed to treat them with care, putting them at ease by masking any prejudices and feigning compliments.

Behind the scenes, advertisers and retailers did not mince words, showing little pity for the plight of the fat woman at the same time they debated about how best to curry her favor. Attacks such as these, however, did not acknowledge how the retailers' and advertisers' own biases and practices may have been complicit in contributing to her grim disposition. Indeed, as Stearns writes, American opinion had shifted to such an extent that it was taken for granted that fat people were emotionally and physically flawed and thus "no explanation for criticism seemed necessary."[21] Said so, it must nevertheless be asked: How did fat women, rather than men, become target of such vicious attacks?

In the early twentieth century, American weight bias sat at the confluence of a number of different factors—cultural, technological, and medical. Chief among them, however, was the fact that, even as fatness was increasingly being medicalized, or perceived by doctors as an illness, it was not treated in the same way as congenital diseases. Instead, fat was regarded as being a malady of the body, but also a uniquely pathological disorder that manifested in one's lack of willpower and impulse control. The imperative to manage one's weight therefore had less to do with health and was more so a matter of exhibiting restraint in an age of excess. With weight bias functioning as a deeply engrained reaction to the overabundance of modern life, the fat person existed as an object of derision and disgust, rather than of empathy or compassion the same way a "genuinely" sick person was. Yet, even as men and women were in some ways equal targets, the cultural stigma against fat women was far more pronounced and much more deeply entrenched in the American imaginary. This was due to the fact that fat was read differently on the bodies of men and women. While a degree of fat in boys and men could connote strength, power, wealth, or prestige, for women it almost always symbolized failure.

The physical and psychological shortcomings of the fat woman reached levels of hyperbole in turn-of-the-century carnivals. This was the era of the "fat lady" as a ubiquitous freak show spectacle. Fat ladies—alongside thin men, bearded ladies, dwarves, and conjoined twins—were sources of morbid entertainment for audiences curious about exotic and unfamiliar bodies. The freak show was a space in which middle-class Americans could enjoy carnivalesque humor in a culture that increasingly required the careful maintenance and self-regulation of the body.[22] However, these everyday spectacles were not mere entertainment; they also reinforced and, perhaps more importantly, normalized biases against fat people. In their shows, fat ladies performed exaggerated stereotypes for their paying audiences in order to realize preconceived notions about the behaviors and dispositions of fat women, thereby not only revealing but also cementing prejudices against and fears of female overweight. One such fat lady who went by the stage name "Jolly Mabel" was described in a 1913 The New York Times article as weighing over 600 pounds and as having a mean temperament. Jolly Mabel, who yelled at everyone around her with "a voice that could make the mountains to rock," was, ironically, not so jolly.[23] Carnival "freaks" like Jolly Mabel performed in the aggrandized mode whereby they enhanced stereotypical character traits and bodily features to heighten the entertainment value of their performances.[24] Mabel's outbursts would have therefore been perceived as going hand-in-hand with her grotesque size. Not unlike Jolly Mabel, fat women were seen as emotionally unstable, pitiable figures who ate to excess in order to mask or remedy other problems.

In the eyes of stoutwear manufacturers and advertising executives, the fat woman's unpredictable and fragile temperament was only exacerbated fashion's mandates. While standardized sizing laid bare the fat woman's physical excesses, changes to the fashionable silhouette put more of her body on display, giving onlookers more to analyze and critique. Underscoring this point, the trade press was littered with sensationalized anecdotes about temperamental consumers as, for instance, a 1915 Women's Wear article that described an encounter between two sales associates and a difficult-to-fit consumer:

The two stood back to watch what happened as a bulging matron approached laboriously and asked with a belligerent laugh-if-you-dare expression: Can you fit me in a wash skirt? I saw your ad.

The salesgirl took the lady's measurements and responded pleasantly with no sign of amusement, that she certainly could and proceeded to do it …. Her doubt and resentment gave way to hope and then to delight and instead of buying one, she bought three, the first, she said, she had ever bought ready-made in her life.[25]

Within retail spaces, the issues surrounding the fat woman's emotional shortcomings were discussed with little reflection on the seller's role in provoking her self-conscious distress; however, none was really needed. It was taken as fact (if not for granted) that the fat woman was difficult, temperamental, and emotional—the carnival fat lady functioning as a hyperbolic archetype of the "typical" fat woman. The professional fashion media therefore served as yet another space in which negative stereotypes about fat women were propagated and given nuance.

In many ways, fatness had by the second decade of the twentieth century come to be widely lamented as what Stearns has described as "a badge of irretrievable personal shame" that was only exacerbated within the context of consumer culture, and especially within the spaces and places of fashionable consumption.[26] During this period, individuals who did not meet the sartorial and aesthetic norms of consumer culture were branded as social outcasts.[27] For the fat woman, her marginal status was affirmed by her literal inability to wear mass-manufactured garments. In some instances, however, it was acknowledged that the garment industry—and the sense of guilt it engendered in women who could not approximate contemporary beauty ideals, nor wear standardized clothing off-the-rack—likely had something to do with the fat woman's low self-esteem and fragile character. In a rare bout of introspection, the *Dry Goods Economist* advised buyers,

If you want the stout trade, you must not "rub it in" by insinuating that women of over 42 in. busts are abnormalities, requiring specially designed clothes …

She knows that nobody loves the fat lady who *looks* fat. She knows, moreover, that the general public's ideal figure, at least for some years past, has been that of a sort of enlarged and animated clothespin.[28]

In this quotation, the trade journal advises stoutwear retailers and salespeople to avoid any actions that might lead fat women to believe that they are in any way a challenge to fit. Moreover, it suggests that the fat woman's emotional shortcomings could at least partly be blamed on the prevalence of fashionably slender silhouette, humorously described here as looking like an "enlarged and animated clothespin."

With these facts in place, the stoutwear industry turned its attention away from the matter of fitting the customer's body to, in the words of Charles May, "fitting her mind."[29] Through this process, advertisers and retailers had come to believe that the fat woman had grown reticent to identify as such, and understandably so. Many questions remained, however. Among them, how were advertisers and retailers supposed to apply this knowledge to selling and advertising practices? What was the best way to stoke the fat woman's anxieties without alienating her? And perhaps more importantly, how were they to address her without causing offense? As one retailer had suggested, the stoutwear maker couldn't simply emblazon his storefront with the word "stout" in big letters.[30] Beyond understanding the total world of the fat woman, advertisers and retailers therefore had to accomplish the deceptively difficult task of figuring out how, exactly, to refer to her.

Fat, Large, or Stout?

Although the curvaceous silhouette is oftentimes conflated with the fat body, as discussed previously, there are exceedingly few moments in the history of the modern West during which fatness has been idealized. As such, there has been no shortage of words throughout history that have been variously employed to deride or diminish the fat person. As early as the sixteenth century, a variety of terms began to emerge that formalized different types or stages of fatness and which, as Vigarello suggests, "testified to the increasing discrimination of the eye."[31] By the late nineteenth century, "dumpy," "pudgy," and "tubby," "sodpacker," "butterball," "jumbo," and "porky" had all entered the American lexicon as the social stigma of fatness increasingly "blushed from language itself."[32] Within fashion advertising—a space in which advertisers wove dreams, promised fantastic transformations, and conjured images of beautiful, idealized bodies—the desultory and frequently crass language used to refer to fat people was off limits. In its place merged euphemisms like "matronly," "generous," "odd sized," "large," and, of course, "stout," which were variously invoked to refer to both women and to large-size dress from the second decade of the twentieth century onward.[33] They were not used interchangeably, however, for they all carried with them different discursive baggage. Matronly, for instance, connoted both a manner of dressing and a body that were closely associated with old age. Conversely, the term "odd sized" was invoked most frequently to refer to women who were both short and somewhat overweight, but was a term that predated stout by a decade or more.[34] Although each term connoted a different type or degree of female corpulence, each emphasized the fat woman's embodied departures from beauty ideals by framing her body as a problem—a notion that is particularly evident in the case of the term "odd sized," which forcefully underscored the fat woman's "odd" proportions beyond the spectrum of standard or normal sizes.

Within this constellation of terms, however, "embonpoint" and "avoirdupois," which were occasionally invoked within fashion discourse to euphemistically refer to women of larger proportions, were singular outliers. The term "embonpoint," for instance, originated in France in the late eighteenth century as a complimentary but infrequently used term that referred to a person who was plump, but who had a generally "well-nourished" appearance. It would not enter the English lexicon, however, until the early nineteenth century when the spelling was anglicized, even as the positivistic connotations remained. Derived from the old French, the term "avoirdupois," by contrast, was a much older term and was used throughout the duration of the fifteenth and sixteenth centuries to refer to a standard unit of weight used in Great Britain, and only came to be an uncommonly used adjective to describe bodily heaviness in the mid-nineteenth century. When invoked within fashion discourse in the early twentieth century—as in utterances like, "those with only a tendency to avoirdupois"[35]—the usage of such terms, albeit infrequent, tapped into a broader tendency within the discourses of fashion to borrow terms and phrasings from French (e.g., "mode," "vogue," "camisole," "boutique," etc.) as a means to create an aura of desirability and fascination around an object (or in this case, a body) by tapping into the allure and heritage of French fashion. When applied to the fat female body, the terms thus lent a momentary sense of fashionability or even beauty to bodily corpulence. On the whole, however, the many euphemisms for referring to fat women operated within a framework that effectively Othered them. Among them, however, no term was deemed as universally problematic as "fat."

Although the term "fat" was used liberally within professional media, it was widely acknowledged that advertisers and salespeople should avoid publicly invoking the term or risk offending and isolating the consumer. For instance, in a *Women's Wear* feature about the practice of writing "sensitive advertising," the trade journal explained how

> Advertising to fat women is a very delicate matter indeed. While excess flesh is not exactly an infirmity, it comes very near to it in the feelings of its possessor. It is a close approach to calling attention to a person's age or his deafness, or some other defect of which he has not, or thinks he has not the mastery ....
>
> Nearly all of the advertisements carefully sidestep the word "Fat."... "Fat" pictures a sad state.[36]

With the term "fat" deemed inappropriate, salespeople and advertisers were therefore advised to, as one article suggested, rely heavily on their thesauruses to find suitable and positivistic synonyms:

> [When] the buyer who is catering to the business of the stouts desires to interest them in his line, he will find that it pays to get him a book of synonyms and use all the euphemistic words in the list instead of making a straightforward, frank appeal to the fat woman. Speak of "women with dress requirements out of the ordinary," or of "women who have difficulty in getting fitted in ready-to-wear garments of usual sizes" or sometimes the word "stout" may be used to advantage. Another good way to reach the "cornfed" is to put the emphasis on the "sizes in stock" and mention them in connection with the statement in some pretty language that any stout in town can find something that will fit her.[37]

The ultimate resolution for the problem of how to speak about and how to advertise to women whose bodies fell outside of the spectrum of standard sizes without calling them fat, or any other term that might cause offense, was to engage in a delicate game of word play—one in which the emphasis was placed on garment fit and the availability of so-called extended size ranges, rather than on women's bodies. Even in this passage, however, the salesman grapples with how to refer to the fat woman herself, even derogatorily referring to her at one point as "cornfed." The general consensus, however, was that any familiar terms for corpulence were to be avoided.

Within this context, "stout," an old term, found new usefulness in fashion advertising beginning in about 1915. According to the *Oxford English Dictionary*, the earliest uses of the term "stout," which derives from the French *estout*, may be located in the early fourteenth century when it described an individual who was "proud, haughty or arrogant." Through the fourteenth and fifteenth centuries, it enjoyed similarly positivistic usage, connoting objects (e.g., ships), animals (e.g., horses), or persons who were "sturdy" or "resolute." Notably, when stout entered the American English lexicon in the late eighteenth century, it connoted an individual "of strong body" or with a "powerful build." By 1860, however, its meaning had become more ambiguous if not uncomplimentary. Perceived as a by-product of the aging process and as a malady suffered by women almost exclusively, stoutness had become synonymous with a "matronly" appearance.

This gendered discrepancy was addressed in a column titled "Between the Lines with the Ad Men" that ran in a May 1922 issue of *Women's Wear*, which juxtaposed the terms used by advertisers and retailers to refer to fat men versus those used for fat women. In it, *Women's Wear* describes how R. H. Macy & Co. had

> hit upon a merry and yet unoffending name for the man of "heroic proportions," "Mr. Avoirdupois" is pitied for the trouble he is put to in shopping for his own apparel, unless at Macy's where "A physique of robust proportions may be clothed from head to foot as quickly and as satisfactorily as one of regular dimensions and at lowest-in-the-city prices.[38]

While men of larger proportions are here described as "heroic" and "robust" with Macy's promising to outfit him "head to foot" as quickly as slender men, in stark contrast, stoutness in women connoted that she need no longer "worry about the matters that once concerned her, and she can accept reality."[39] When invoked in reference to a body (as opposed to dress), stout had come to denote a silhouette that was generally undefined, big all over, less than feminine, out of fashion, and, as some believed, distinctly American.[40] Advertising executives therefore warned that "the subject [of stoutwear] is one which has dynamite in it and will explode if handled clumsily."[41] However, the matter of choosing a neutral term was one of the utmost importance for advertisers and manufacturers. Indeed, as one advertising expert remarked to *Women's Wear*, "Of course the first problem in advertising to fat women is to let them know that they can get their sizes."[42] Within this discursive minefield, "stout," an ambivalent term, was adopted as a standard by retailers and advertisers, but only reluctantly. The second, and perhaps more challenging problem was that of how to make (or at least feign) an earnest appeal to fat women in order to earn their trust and, with it, their patronage.

Small Advertisements for Large Sizes[43]

The fashions are all for the slender.
The models displayed are all small.
From the pictures I judge the creations
Aren't made for the obese at all.
The counters are crowded with women
Who look at the book plates thereon
And think that they will resemble
The prints in the latest *Bon Ton*.
Oh, why doesn't someone in Paris
Successfully launch a campaign
To glorify embonpoint beauty,
And comfort the "stylish stout's" bane?[44]

The above poem appeared in a Lane Bryant advertisement published in the June 26, 1927, edition of the *Brooklyn Daily Eagle*. Titled "Song," it is said to have been written by a woman named Eleanor Alletta Chaffee and sent to the *New York Sun* where it was published on the "Women's" page as an op-ed. Bemoaning the prevailing fashion for the "boyish" silhouette, Chaffee's "Song" critiques narrow beauty norms, but also French designers for failing to provide "creations" for the "obese." Although critical of the limited options for fat women desiring stylish clothes, the poem, when co-opted by Lane Bryant, became fodder for the company to situate itself as a sympathetic intermediary in a hostile consumer landscape—one uniquely attuned to the plight of the fat woman:

There is no other comparable feminine beauty. Sixty out of every hundred American women have embonpoint beauty, in more or less degree. And since, according to *Worth*, the great couturier of Paris, woman herself is the final arbiter of Fashion, these sixty will dictate the normal trend of Fashion ... and Paris will express that trend in *Styles* ... But—

... "*The models displayed are all small.*" They ARE—except in the Lane Bryant shops, where you may see the same, current Paris styles in LARGER models.

Had you known this, it never would have occurred to you to write your song.[45]

Among stoutwear advertisements, this one is remarkable for a number of reasons, not least of which being the way it so directly speaks to the plight of fat women for whom Chaffee serves as a kind of surrogate. Also of note is the frankness with which it remarks upon the fashion industry's role in dictating beauty norms and American garment manufacturers' blind adherence to the edicts trickling down from Paris. More clearly (and in more words) than other stoutwear advertisements, "Lane Bryant's Reply," as it is called, lays bare the constructedness of the slender ideal while at the same time promoting the notion that "embonpoint beauty" is the most essential and truest form of beauty. In its final lines, the advertisement—which is signed off by Lane

Bryant herself—notes, "Paris creates the styles … Lane Bryant fits them to your figure. *That sums it up.*"[46]

This advertisement was the subject of analysis in an article that appeared in the "Merchandising and Promotion" section of *Women's Wear* a week after it was originally published in *The Brooklyn Daily Eagle*. Commending the company for its decision to reproduce the poem in full, *Women's Wear* noted that the sincere appeal would surely resonate with women of standard proportions as much as it would fat women.[47] Touching upon several universals, the advertisement also critiques the continued hegemony of Parisian fashions, as well as the contentiousness of the boyish silhouette.[48] In addition to provoking feelings of sympathy for the fat woman, it also tapped into certain nationalist discourses by juxtaposing impractical and unaccommodating French fashions with their more democratic American counterparts. Within this hostile landscape, Lane Bryant stepped forward, presenting herself as an ally and friend to the fat woman—one who offered simple, straightforward solutions to complicated structural and endemic problems. In short, Lane Bryant's message is that it is not the fat woman's body that is the problem, but rather the industry and the matrix of ideals that it perpetuates. Thus, the solution to the persistence of the slender ideal was to shop at Lane Bryant Stores, or spaces in which the fat woman had equal footing and "the youthful styles of Paris [are sold] in *Lane Bryant Sizes 18+ to 28+*".[49]

This advertisement is an example of what Roland Marchand has described as the "side-by-side" approach, which was in ascendance during the interwar period. Marchand explains how this new manner of writing advertising copy "set forward a model of life's struggles that was well-tailored to strike a responsive chord among people conscious of the increasing dependence of their life ambitions on large organizations and impersonal judgements."[50] Tapping into and exploiting the consumer's insecurities, this new approach was a direct consequence of the psychological bent of modern advertising and its concern with the inner life of the consumer: "As society's increasing pressures and complexities made the consumer uneasy, the advertiser intervened with sympathetic advice on how to triumph over the impersonal judgements of the modern world."[51] In this example, Lane Bryant identifies the oppressive system or institution (Parisian fashion), the problems (narrow beauty standards and a lack of choice) and the solution (Lane Bryant's fashionable large-size garments). Signed off by Lane Bryant, the advertisement was intended to strike a personal and emotional chord with the consumer, not unlike a letter to a friend.

With this advertisement—one that was deemed successful by *Women's Wear's* advertising experts—Lane Bryant offers the fat woman more than just sartorial salvation. By providing her access to a market that had previously excluded her, the brand is also selling the promise of full citizenship by habituating her to the idea that consumption was a cornerstone of civilized society and a pathway to social progress. One of the traits of this style of advertising was, as Ewen writes, offering a "mass produced solution … to the ills of mass society."[52] This approach was mirrored across Lane Bryant advertisements as, for instance, in an example published in the pages of *The Ladies' Home Journal* in September 1923 (Figure 3.3). Appearing underneath an illustration of two fashionably

Stout Women

Dress Fashionably ~ Look Slender

"WHY, I hardly knew you! What a difference the lines of that dress make in your figure! You look so nice and slender!" Thus your friends will greet you when you wear clothes designed to give straight slender lines to your figure.

Time was when the woman of fuller proportions had to be content with almost anything that would go on at all. It was so discouraging! Her choice was limited. Her size was difficult to find and never was found in the newest style garments—until Lane Bryant solved her problems for her.

Now, the stout woman need no longer envy her slender sister the fashionable clothes she wears so well. She, too, can dress as fashionably. No more shopping everywhere in vain for a size that will fit—Lane Bryant has garments for every type of stout figure, ready to put on and wear, in every size up to 58 bust.

Following the dictates of Paris and their acceptance by smartly dressed New York women, Lane Bryant interprets each new mode into garments of fuller proportions with pleatings here, and flounces there—with panels and draperies that effect longer lines, concealing too much fulness where concealment is required or adding fulness where fulness is needed for correct proportion.

Always, though, featuring the newest style details, as created for the average figure, building them into garments made large enough to fit and become the woman of fuller figure.

Send For Your Book Today

The garments pictured here are typical of the hundreds shown in the Lane Bryant Style Book for Fall and Winter. Extra large sizes in Coats, Suits, Dresses, Blouses, Skirts, Corsets, Underwear. Full, roomy sizes—38 to 58 bust.

Style Book FREE

88 pages, many in colors, picturing newest styles in Coats, Suits, Dresses and other apparel just for Stout Women. Sent free. Ask for it TODAY.

Stores: New York   Chicago
Brooklyn   Detroit

38th Street at Fifth Avenue

Lane Bryant
NEW YORK

This Style Book is Free
Write for your copy today

Address Dept. 52

Figure 3.3 Lane Bryant advertisement, *The Ladies' Home Journal* (September 1923), 151.

dressed fat women, the advertising copy recounts what, for some readers, would have been a welcome social interaction:

> "Why, I hardly knew you! What a difference the lines of that dress make in your figure! You look so nice and slender!" Thus your friends will greet you when you wear clothes designed to give straight slender lines to your figure.
>
> Time was when the woman of fuller proportions had to be content with almost anything that would go on at all. It was so discouraging! Her choice was limited. Her size was difficult to find and never was found in the newest style garments—until Lane Bryant solved her problems for her.[53]

In so many words, by producing fashionable stoutwear, Lane Bryant promised to help fat women to find acceptance in an increasingly fatphobic society. At the same time, and quite importantly, it also indebted consumers to Lane Bryant, which in this advertisement situates itself as a singular outlier in the stoutwear landscape uniquely positioned to fulfill fat woman's needs and desires. In the above text, Lane Bryant assumes the fat woman's burden by "solving her problems for her." Indeed, as Keist argues, advertisers' use of terms such as "specialized" and "scientific" in advertising copy may have even been strategically deployed in order to exploit consumers' lack of confidence in both dressing themselves and navigating sellers' increasingly grandiose claims.[54]

Also of note, however, is the manner in which advertisements such as these so delicately navigate the issue of how to refer to the consumer by using a host of euphemisms and turns of phrase to artfully avoid invoking the terms "fat" or "stout." Throughout the aforementioned advertisements, the phrases "embonpoint beauty," "women like you," "woman of fuller proportions," "correctly proportioned larger sizes," "not slender," "larger models," and "Lane Bryant Sizes" are used in lieu of more blatantly offensive alternatives. While it is likely that the Lane Bryant brand had become more or less synonymous with stoutwear by this time—therefore obviating the need to provide further clarification about the type of garments being promoted—the company's omission of these terms is nevertheless in keeping with conventions in stoutwear advertising in the mid- to late 1920s, and specifically the practice of avoiding "explosive" terms when speaking to and about fat women.

Women's Wear's analyses of Lane Bryant's advertisements were, in many ways, aligned with the self-reflexive tendencies of advertising from the 1920s onward. Similar commentaries, in which advertisements of all kinds were carefully studied by "experts" to assess their persuasiveness, were a mainstay in the pages of *Women's Wear*, but also in advertising and clothing trade journals like *Printers' Ink*, *Dry Goods Merchants Trade Journal*, and *Dry Goods Economist* during this time.[55] Given the potentially volatile nature of stoutwear advertisements, however, it is not surprising that there were so many words dedicated to the issue of selling to the fat woman. While such close readings of stoutwear advertisements reveal much about how advertisers dealt with the problem of terminology, they somewhat obscure the important role that images played in selling stoutwear, too.

While text was frequently employed to reassure the fat woman that she was the rule, rather than the exception, advertising imagery functioned to reinforce the sophisticated philosophies that underpinned stoutwear design, and specifically its capacity to effect the appearance of slenderness. Different from trade articles that breathlessly described the profitable future of stoutwear, and which frequently featured grotesque caricatures of fat embodiment, consumer-facing stoutwear advertisements were more in keeping with broader shifts in advertising aesthetics that reflected the gradual whittling away of the feminine bodily ideal. As Lears writes, the advent of national, mass advertising in the early twentieth century brought about a "bureaucratic rationality to the iconography of the body," one in which the body "began to be sterilized and submitted to the ethos of rationalization."[56] The period between 1910 and 1920—a decade largely defined by the tenets and aesthetics of Taylorism, Fordism, and artistic modernism—was the proverbial tipping point during which realistic depictions were superseded by more stylized archetypes of youthful beauty.[57] While this affected the manner in which both sexes were depicted, it was particularly evident in representations of women, who, along with their corsets, "shed their voluptuous and maternal connotations and began to look (as well as behave) more like girls."[58]

This shift from the more mature, maternal body to a more youthful ideal is clearly glimpsed within stoutwear advertisements, which, as the 1920s wore on, depicted increasingly unrecognizable depictions of fat embodiment. Most of the time, the only cue that a reader would have had that the women depicted were stout would have come from the accompanying advertising copy. Unmoored from the cultural stigma of overweight in interwar America, the unbelievable transformations depicted stoutwear advertisements ran parallel to a broader shifts that were occurring in the field of fashion illustration at the time. Whereas fashion photography in the first decade of the twentieth century favored realism, fashion illustration during the interwar period became flagrantly stylized and, as Buckley and Fawcett point out, "had no purchase on what was 'real.'"[59] This was due in no small measure to the growing influence of art deco motifs within the fashion media during this period and the gradual, if temporary, turn away from photography.[60] Breward attributes this shift during the interwar years to a growing interest in the symbolism of fashion and its capacity to communicate moral and aesthetic values, rather than the material qualities of dress as a commodity.[61] In many ways, illustrations were deemed a better illuminator of these ideas than were photographs, which were perhaps viewed as too indexical. Amid this shift, advertisements came to function less as mirrors than as arenas for navigating the competing standards and contradictions inherent in feminine identity construction during the First World War and after.

A Lane Bryant advertisement published in the *Brooklyn Daily Eagle* in April 1924 reveals how some of the particular contradictions that were so central to fat embodiment were negotiated within stoutwear advertisements (Figure 3.4). Donning streamlined day dresses cut along the lines of the fashionable tubular silhouette of the mid-1920s, the four figures pictured in the ad are elongated to such an extreme that they appear at once fashionably slender but Amazonian in proportion. While lacking any of the obvious visual hallmarks of overweight, they nevertheless tower over a roughly sketched city

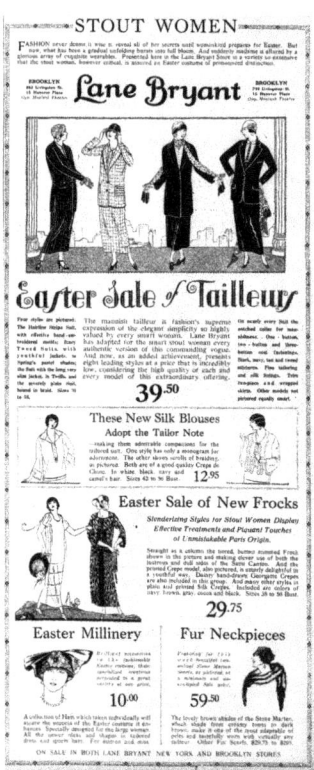

Figure 3.4 Lane Bryant advertisement, *Brooklyn Daily Eagle* (August 15, 1917), 24. Published with permission from Newspapers.com.

skyline in the far background. Perhaps the most obvious contradiction in the manner they are physically depicted, however, lies in the fact that they are rendered so slender by a company that dealt in stoutwear, and thus for whom it was in the best interests that fat women remain so.

A further contradiction lies in the way their cropped haircuts and youthful features stand somewhat at odds with the conservatism of their dress, but their look, in totality, nevertheless reads as modern. Perhaps most notably, however, the women are shown at ease and at one with their surroundings—their modern posture and styling creating a harmony that belies the fact that stout women were regarded within American society as being so totally out of sync with the architectures and rhythms of modern life. Absent here is the disapproving, withering gaze of fat stigma. Instead, the reader sees only the physically—and socially—transformative capacities of stoutwear. Not only do Lane Bryant's "scientific" garments slenderize the fat woman's body, they purport to alter her total world, permitting her not only to fit her garments but to also *fit in*.

Different from earlier examples, which utilized photographs solely for the purposes of illustration (Figure 3.5), these advertisements are patently more preoccupied with the symbolism of stoutwear and the particular moral and aesthetic values embedded

Figure 3.5 Sveltline advertisement, *Brooklyn Daily Eagle* (August 15, 1917), 24. Published with permission from Newspapers.com.

within it. Whereas fat women appeared in stoutwear advertisements floating in open space and without context so that the focus was solely on the construction and fabrication of their garments, here, the women are shown at ease, engaging in leisure activities and emancipated from their tailors and dressmakers to whom they were previously beholden. Even if the style of the illustrations—which, with their sinuous lines and flat expanses of pattern, were clearly (albeit reductively) inspired by those of Georges Lepape and Paul Iribe, and popularized by Paul Poiret during this period—reveals little detailed knowledge about the "real" garments, the illustrations better exude what is described in both advertisements as the "smart," "youthful," and "simple" style of Lane Bryant's "specially designed" apparel.

The dissonance between what was represented and what was written in the pursuit of depicting increasingly stylized and idealized representations of stoutness, however, became even more flagrant as the 1920s bled into the 1930s. In one Lane Bryant advertisement that appeared in the *Brooklyn Daily Eagle* in August 1930, for example, the figures, with their fashionable Eton crops framed by exaggeratedly large collars, look scarcely different in size from a standard-size figure depicted in an adjacent Martin's advertisement (Figure 3.6). Notably absent in this example is any use of the word "stout"—the phrase "larger woman" being invoked only in the fine print in the

Figure 3.6 Lane Bryant and Martin's advertisements, *Brooklyn Daily Eagle* (August 3, 1930), 8. Published with permission from Newspapers.com.

bottommost register. On the one hand, the similarity of the two illustrations stands as a testament to the pervasiveness of the youthfully slender ideal that, in this moment, was reaching its apogee. On the other, these highly stylized illustrations also seem to depict the truly transformative capacities of stoutwear. Although the illustrations are strikingly similar, they convey two distinct kinds of knowledge for two very different readers. In the Martin's advertisement, the slender ideal is merely reinforced; in the Lane Bryant advertisement, however, a new possibility for fat embodiment is put forth—one in which the practice of slenderizing the body becomes the primary objective of dressing as a fat woman.

Although in many ways, the visual tropes of stoutwear advertising were merely in keeping with the visual conventions of fashion illustration at the time, the evolution (or gradual whittling away) of the fat female body within these spaces was also informed by modern advertising theory. According to advertising experts such as Walter Dill Scott, advertisements were successful when consumers were able to glimpse a more improved version of themselves through the product offering—someone with whom they not only empathized but who they also admired. With slenderness elevated as the feminine ideal, a successful stoutwear advertisement would enable the reader to imagine herself as slender—her aberrant curves and generous proportions elegantly whittled down to a silhouette more in keeping with the prevailing ideal. Yet, as representations of stoutness were slimmed down, they also became increasingly unmoored from the realities of fat embodiment to the point that, in some examples, they looked scarcely different from the slender women they appeared alongside in the fashion media. As exaggerated as they were, however, such advertisements provided a resounding affirmation of the transformative capacities of stoutwear, while at the same time revealing the limitations of consumer citizenship.

**

In the bourgeoning consumer landscape of early twentieth-century America—one in which the category of "consumer" was itself expanding with the discovery of new markets—the fat woman occupied an ambivalent position. Different from other "non-consumers," such as racial and ethnic minorities, the fat woman, although a reviled figure in society at large, was nevertheless deemed a potentially "good" consumer. The reason for this was twofold. First, as a (presumed) wife and mother, she was recognized as being the principal overseer of her household economy. Second, she was recognized to possess a great deal of pent-up demand due to the fashion industry's long-time neglect of her. These facts, however, did not make the task of selling to the fat woman an easy or straightforward one.

In the minds of advertising experts, the fat woman's disorderly body was a physical manifestation of her tumultuous inner world. Because she was believed to be plagued by bouts of impulsivity, irrationality, and self-loathing, advertisers believed she required different, verging on scientific, selling strategies, which were exhaustively detailed and debated in the advertising and fashion trade press. The challenges of selling stoutwear were further compounded by the inherent contradiction that the success of the market rested on a steady stream of demand, even though stoutwear was underpinned by the logic of designing fat out of existence. Advertisers therefore had to toe a fine line in selling the fat woman on the slenderizing capacities of stoutwear without alienating her. In practice, this ultimately boiled down to selling the idea that stoutwear was a more modern and expedient means of attaining a slender appearance than permanent weight loss methods.

Within stoutwear advertisements, this complex of ideals manifested in the creation of a "stout ideal"—one in which the deviant fat body was subjected to the aesthetics and logic of mass manufacturing, but also to the streamlined, serialized images of modernist bodies that pervaded the fashion media during this time. The advertising copy, however, betrayed the idealized illustrations by revealing that the body underneath was unruly and therefore in need of a design intervention. Within this context, mass-manufactured stoutwear was upheld as crucial technology that not only fit the fat woman's non-normative frame but which also helped her to socially and aesthetically *fit in*. According to this new model of fat embodiment, a woman could be overweight and evade criticism and censure as long as she selected garments that helped her inch closer to the fashionable ideal. Far from emancipating the fat woman, however, it could be argued that stoutwear and stoutwear advertising actually functioned as civilizing mediums, thinly veiled in the liberationist discourses of the transformative power of mass consumption.

As the line between citizen and consumer grew increasingly blurred, access to the marketplace became a necessary requirement to achieve full personhood in the United States; however, stoutwear advertising reveals just how tenuous this form of citizenship was. A fat woman's fall from grace could come in the form of an ill-fitting skirt, a poorly placed ruffle, or any other design element that accentuated, rather than diminished, her size. Stoutwear advertising functioned to remind fat women of this fact while also promising them their sartorial salvation—a tactic that indebted fat women to stoutwear retailers while also more deeply entrenching the cultural consensus that fatness was a personal failing. To be a fat woman in early twentieth-century America therefore required constant vigilance and the acquisition of various consumer goods—from beauty products to slenderizing stoutwear—to mitigate the stigma of overweight. Indeed, in the world of advertisements, social acceptance was always just one purchase away.

Stoutwear advertisements did not, however, exist in a vacuum. Rather, they were but one thread in the tapestry that was American visual culture and popular media. The following chapter will investigate another thread—the American women's and fashion press—in exploring the wider visual, discursive, and cultural contexts in which the discourses of weight bias circulated.

CHAPTER 4
PARABLES OF OVERWEIGHT

While the slender ideal had been in ascendance since at least the 1890s, by the 1920s it had all but cemented itself within American life and visual culture. It is in this moment that the streamlined, youthful, bordering on *weightless* bodies became a potent symbol of what Christopher Forth has referred to as "corporeal utopianism" and could be seen leaping and bounding from the pages of fashion magazines and advertisements for consumer goods of all kinds. These slender bodies "[rose] above all manner of constraints … tradition, history, ageing and even death itself" and, in doing so, "fueled the bodily dreams and ideals of a modern world."[1] While the "flapper" archetype was variously described in the fashion media as "a sort of enlarged animated clothespin" and a "pencil," the feminine ideal of the 1920s was rather more complex.[2] As discussed in previous chapters, the streamlined body animated by what Hillel Schwartz refers to as the "kinesthetic of torque" possessed a host of traits informed by machine age aesthetics. The ideal body was one that was slender, but it was also smooth and efficient and, most importantly, expressed a sense of movement even when in stasis.[3] New trends in fashion merely served to emphasize this bodily ideal. While the relaxed, tubular silhouette permitted maximum freedom of movement, tanned, toned legs—revealed by shorter hemlines and sleek silk stockings—recalled the aerodynamic forms of new modes of transportation, such as airplanes and automobiles.

The modernist dancer, perhaps more than any other figure, best embodied this ideal. In the fashion media, it was not uncommon for dancers to be elevated as exemplars of feminine beauty, nor for dance to be presented as an effective and pleasurable means of ridding the body of excess weight.[4] As a 1924 *Vogue* article entitled, "The Importance of Being Beautiful" suggested, beauty went far beyond having a pretty complexion and trim waist. Using language that conveyed a sense of bodily dynamism, the magazine argued that a woman's beauty was expressed in "the buoyant set of her shoulders, in the flexible curve of her back [and] in the spontaneity of the whole."[5] Illustrated by line drawings and photographs of women engaging in floor exercises inspired by the methods of the English dancer Margaret Morris, the article promised that with daily practice the assiduous woman could attain a "graceful carriage … the fundamental principle of beauty"[6] (Figure 4.1). Similar advice was proffered in *Harper's Bazaar*, where in an October 1923 beauty column, Helen Bullitt Lowry touted the benefits of "getting thin to music," writing, "The phonograph, which in its day was a proletariat instrument of torture, has at last been hitched to a mighty new art purpose—to restore to the thirties and forties the lithe hips and tummies of the twenties."[7] While such articles offered advice and instruction in how to attain a slender physique, they also provided women with a standard against which they could compare their own imperfect bodies. It is within

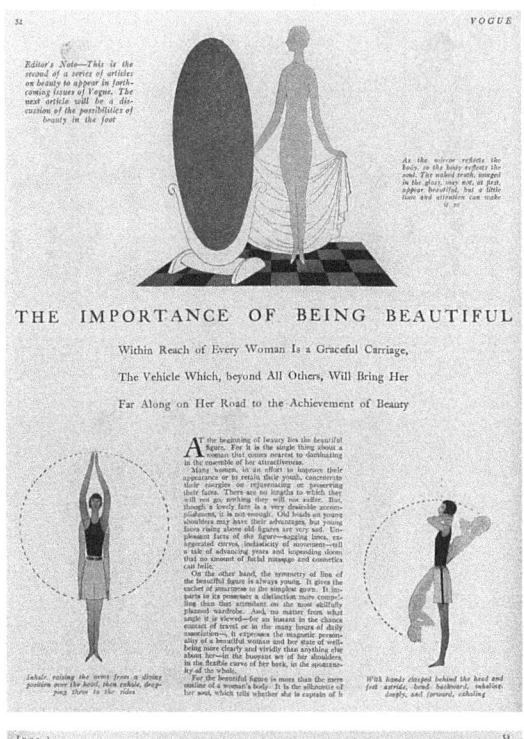

Figure 4.1 "The Importance of Being Beautiful," *Vogue* (June 1, 1924), 52–53. Published with permission from *Vogue*, © Condé Nast.

this context that exercise and other acts of self-surveillance became indispensable parts of the modern woman's beauty regimen and central concerns in women's and fashion magazines. While articles like those touting Margaret Morris' fitness routine were wedged between glossy fashion editorials, less glamorous advertisements for commercial weight-loss programs employed similar imagery and language (Figure 4.2) Although a far cry from nineteenth-century beauty culture, which privileged natural products and light-handed remedies that would *assist* rather than *alter* a woman's appearance, beauty culture in the 1920s furthered the powerful notion that ascribed bodily features—namely body mass and shape—could be transformed with diligence and hard work.[8]

Figure 4.2 Susanna Cocroft Advertisement, *The Ladies' Home Journal* (June 1922), 51.

As these youthful, unencumbered bodies danced across the pages of women's and fashion magazines throughout the 1920s, the voluptuous Gilded Age ideal gradually receded from view. It would be incorrect, however, to suggest that fleshy curves were supplanted by hard edges altogether. In fact, the reality was quite the opposite. While slender bodies donning mere wisps of dresses rendered in weightless silk chiffon pervaded fashion editorials, fat bodies could be found populating advertisements for gimmicky weight-loss devices and miraculous fat-reducing compounds (Figure 4.3), as well as advertisements for products employing the curvaceous and racist "Mammy" stereotype, including Aunt Jemima Pancake Mix and Ole Mammy Creole Pralines, among others (Figure 4.4). The fat woman could also be found in stinging caricatures and sensationalist advice columns that warned against the social repercussions of overweight. In one 1920 *Vogue* article about automobile design, for instance, a woman of so-called "generous proportions" could be seen filling the cabin of a tiny cabriolet coupé (Figure 4.5). Whereas the slender body was one that hummed with the rhythms of the machine age, the image of a fat woman uncomfortably wedged into the cabin of a comically small automobile couldn't have been more out of scale with the streamlined aesthetics of modernity. Within contexts such as these, the fat woman functioned as an

Figure 4.3 La Mar Fat Reducing Soap advertisement (*c.* 1920). Bettman/Getty Images.

Figure 4.4 Aunt Jemima Pancake Mix advertisement (1915). Alamy.

Figure 4.5 Ann Fish, Illustration from "London Ladies and Landaulets," *Vogue* (January 1, 1920), 64. Image courtesy of Fashion Institute of Technology|SUNY, FIT Library Unit of Special Collections and College Archives.

anchor for the weightless bodies floating across fashion editorials—her body an ever-present reminder about the fragility and impermanence of youth and beauty.

This chapter explores the ways that fat bodies were portrayed within the American women's and fashion press during the 1920s through the structuring framework of the parable. In looking beyond advertisements and offensive caricatures, the "parables of overweight" discussed in this chapter reveal how other concerns, from aging to surveillance culture, were mapped onto the fat female body. It is within these spaces, and specifically through what Agnés Rocamora has defined as "fashion media discourses," that the fat female body was discursively constructed. Drawing upon Pierre Bourdieu's field theory and Michel Foucault's writings on discourse and power, Rocamora argues that fashion media discourse "sets out the parameters for an understanding of the way media texts work to create value and meanings within a given field … and a given culture."[9] Through this framework, she therefore seeks to delimit how discourse is created and disseminated within a particular field of cultural production (e.g., fashion), and to acknowledge the different institutions, sites, and mediums through which particular forms of knowledge are created and dispersed. The field of fashion, she argues, is "a space of knowledge with porous boundaries, a wide constituency of layered nodes and ideas, themes and concepts, that cut across disciplines and fields."[10] These "interwoven discourses" function to "invest fashion—its products, practices and agents—with a variety of values whose 'truth' is as much a part of the object of discourse as the material reality it refers to."[11] Rocamora's interest lies in the discursive construction of "la Parisienne" in the fashion media and beyond, but this framework can be applied to similar investigations into the discursive construction of the fat or "stout" woman, too. Indeed, by applying Rocamora's conceptualization of fashion media discourse throughout this chapter, I similarly seek to unravel the ways in which the women's and fashion press not only perpetuated but *produced* certain "truths"—namely, biased ideas and stereotypes—about fat embodiment, which, I argue, permeated beyond fashion's "porous boundaries."

Although idealized depictions of fat woman were largely absent within the rarefied pages of the American fashion press, fat women were occasionally the topic of discussion, criticism, and censure in advice columns, beauty features, and what can only be described as cautionary tales of sartorial misfortune that had dire social consequences. Different from the sympathetic stoutwear advertising tropes discussed in the previous chapter, these parables told stories of social embarrassment, adversity, and bad taste, while also perpetuating negative stereotypes about fat women as lazy, gluttonous, and unlovable. Fashion and beauty were central concerns of these stories; however, any advice offered was less instructive than didactic. Much like biblical parables or secular fables, these parables of overweight demanded interpretation and introspection from the reader. Rather than selling a product or providing the reader with specific fashion advice per se, they deployed embarrassment or shame to bring about a shift in perspective or a change in behavior in order to close the gap between deviant fatness and idealized femininity. Similar to female archetypes Minna Thornton and Caroline Evans explore in their book *Women & Fashion: A New Look* (1989), these parables shed light on the critical and constructive ways that women engage with fashion media and, conversely, the ways that the fashion media engages its female readership. Beyond just seeking out information about what is currently fashionable, women read magazines in order to escape, but also in order to "picture themselves, position themselves and [to understand] how they are themselves positioned" by the fashion industry.[12]

The parables discussed here—including "the parable of the deluded," "the parable of the matron," "the parable of the domestic," and the "parable of the style-blind"—gave texture and shape to modern weight bias and, in doing so, allowed readers to better understand their social standing as well as the place that they occupied not just in the fashion system but in American life more generally. Each of these parables therefore reveals the ways that the fashion media functioned as a site in which the expectations of modern femininity, as well as the contradictions therein, were discursively constructed, disseminated, and thereafter negotiated by the reader. While these parables were for readers perhaps unwelcome departures from the escapism and high glamor that fashion magazines afforded, the relatable, if pitiable, figures portrayed within them helped readers to identify potential shortcomings and areas of concern, while also reinforcing the notion that it was possible to transcend the excesses of the corpulent body through vigilance, persistence, good taste, and a bit of savvy consumerism.

The Parable of the Deluded

In the parable of the deluded, a woman is typically described or depicted standing in front of a large vanity or full-length mirror. More often than not, the woman departs in one way or another from the slender, youthful beauty ideal. In the mirror's reflection, she can be seen scrutinizing what the article identifies as potential flaws or, as one *Vogue* article put it, bearing witness to her crumbling "self-delusion."[13] The lesson espoused within the parable of the deluded is that mirrors, in tandem with other technologies, should be incorporated into a woman's daily beauty regimen to observe and measure fluctuations in her figure. If she does not engage in these practices of bodily self-surveillance, she may find herself out of step with fashion, or worse, socially or romantically ostracized.

Within the context of the parable of the deluded, the full-length mirror stands as a proxy for the societal gaze—an exceedingly mundane, if somewhat new, technology that, alongside the scale, introduced more precise ways of assessing the body's flaws. In the last decade of the nineteenth century, a number of technological innovations, including new processes for silvering glass and better manufacturing and transportation systems, enabled mirrors to become both larger and more widely available.[14] Although the mirror itself was not entirely novel, the intrusion of the mirror into couture salons, department stores, and even middle-class bedrooms *was* to the extent that it facilitated immediate and highly intimate practices of viewing the (often nude) body in its entirety. The image in the glass was one that few had had the privilege of seeing before this point. This was the real body—a seemingly truthful depiction of the body seen in its unvarnished entirety. For consumers unaccustomed to seeing their bodies in this manner, the effect was beguiling if somewhat confusing.[15] As Evans writes, as it became more ubiquitous, the mirror increasingly became a "place in which the script of the self [was] written."[16] This process, however, did not occur in a vacuum. Rather, these new practices of looking at the body and seeing all its flaws were reinforced by illustrations, moving images, and photographs—a dialectic that permitted women to see their bodies, as well as their flaws, with greater clarity and, one would assume, greater accuracy. It was within this context that the mirror became not just a site in which a woman could witness her self-delusion crumble but also an invaluable tool in the maintenance and preservation of her figure and thus an essential component of modern beauty regimens.

Beauty advice written by dieticians and experts underscored the importance of closely scrutinizing the nude body with the aid of full-length mirrors in pursuit of the "naked truth." For instance, a 1924 *Vogue* article instructed readers on how to use their mirrors to correct their posture and comportment:

> Upon stepping from your bath in the morning, step in front of your mirror. Stand in the position that comes most natural to you and look at your figure from the side. This requires courage. Unless you are one of the very few exceptionally fortunate women who have naturally perfect figures, what you see is apt to give you a distinct shock.
>
> Much more likely than not, your lines will not have the symmetrical arrangement that you had been led to believe most figures possess by the drawings you have seen here and there ....
>
> Do not weaken, above all do not despair. The worst is really over. You have seen the naked truth.[17]

Accompanied by an illustration depicting the silhouette of a woman standing before a full-length mirror (see Figure 4.1), the article underscores the notion that, in order to attain beauty, women had to engage in a daily practice of studying their bodies no matter how displeasing the reflection. A caption appearing to the right of the illustration further emphasizes this notion by putting forth this sentiment: "The naked truth imagined in the glass, may not, at first, appear beautiful, but a little time and attention can make it so." The mirror, according to *Vogue*, was thus a vital tool in the construction and maintenance of the fashionable body.

When invoked within these advice discourses, the mirror was often framed as more revealing than the gaze alone. One *Vogue* article even went so far as to describe the mirror as "a woman's truest friend; it tells the whole truth, even when it hurts."[18] If the mirror was a harbinger of truth, the gaze—corrupted by the influx of images of ideal bodies and beauty—had become unreliable. Another *Vogue* article explained how, in spite of being exposed to countless examples of ideal beauty on a daily basis,

> Few of us realize what we look like; that is the basic psychological fact that explains why so many of us are ill dressed. We have an ambition, a hope, a delusion about our personal appearance. We dress that ambition, hope, or delusion—and not ourselves.[19]

According to *Vogue*, the slender bodily ideal had become so powerful, so omnipresent, that women had grown accustomed to dressing for that ideal. This sentiment was echoed by illustrations accompanying the article depicting several women as it is revealed to them how others see them, demonstrating how one's self-perception—or self-*delusion*—is oftentimes at odds with reality (Figure 4.6).

In one, a woman recoils at the sight of four portrait photographs that amplify her drooping under-eyes and soft profile, while in another a woman gasps in horror as she looks upon her own ponderous physique reflected back at her in a full-length mirror—her modish tubular dress bulging where there should have been straight lines. Yet, where slender women saw mere imperfections, fat women saw not just their corporeal shortcomings but their moral failings, too. While bodies could "fail" in innumerable ways in their physical departures from the ideal, in parables of the deluded the fat woman's failings were especially egregious. Indeed, while the article argues that many women fail to grasp how time can ravage their appearances, particular ire is reserved for the woman who gazes upon her excessive curves in the mirror but fails to react. *Vogue* goes on to note how the reader is surely familiar with the "countless pathetic women" who have gained weight but have evaded the mirror's reflection. Rather than dressing to suit her figure, this woman, the article explains, dresses her "ambition, hope, or delusion" that she can embody the slender ideal.

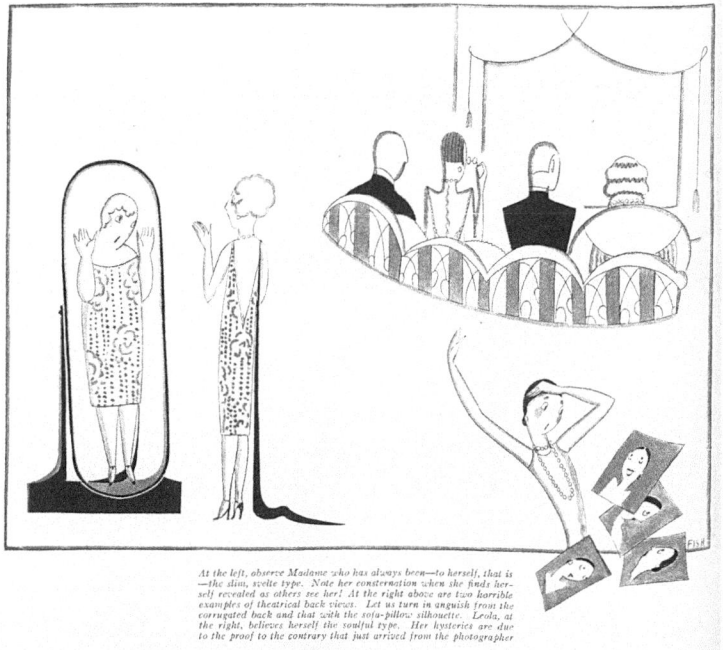

At the left, observe Madame who has always been—to herself, that is—the slim, svelte type. Note her consternation when she finds herself revealed as others see her! At the right above are two horrible examples of theatrical back views. Let us turn in anguish from the corrugated back and that with the sofa-pillow silhouette. Leola, at the right, believes herself the soulful type. Her hysterics are due to the proof to the contrary that just arrived from the photographer

Figure 4.6 Detail from "Delusions in Dress," *Vogue* (May 15, 1926), 69. Published with permission from *Vogue*, © Condé Nast.

Within this article, the mirror stands as a powerful symbol of the twentieth century's culture of self-surveillance, permitting what historian Sabine Melchior-Bonnet has described as a "doubled gaze" that inspired new ways not just of seeing but of being in the world. Through the image refracted back at the beholder from the glassy, silvered surface of the mirror, a woman could see herself as well as how *others* see her.[20] The mirror thus created a complex visual relay in which the beholder both came to understand her body more intimately while at the same time being alienated from it in experiencing the critical gaze of others. Georges Vigarello suggests that a product of this doubled gaze was a new and intensified attention to the body that did not exist before and which permitted the beholder to worry over even the most minute (and previously invisible) fluctuations in her physique.[21] The mirror thus permitted more intelligent, more explorative, and more incisive ways of monitoring the body's deviations from the norm.

Beyond the bedroom and dressing room, however, the mirror was a potent symbol within advertising, too.[22] In the first decades of the twentieth century, mirrors appeared within advertisements for various body-shaping garments, weight-loss products and cosmetics, as well as within countless fashion editorials, as powerful reminders of the societal gaze. Drawing upon Western artistic tropes, advertisers utilized mirrors to, for instance, show two angles of a product or garment at once, but also more powerfully as surrogates for the societal gaze.[23] For these advertising creatives, the image of a woman sitting with a mirror distilled the essence of womanhood; for consumers, these images functioned as a reminder of the ephemerality of beauty and the necessity of vanity in pursuit of preserving it. As such, these mirrors could reflect two divergent images of the body: the ideal body sufficiently transformed by whichever fashion or beauty product was being advertised or, conversely, the failed body. In either case, the potential of the body as a sort of corporeal work-in-progress was made manifest.

In one such advertisement, a young woman with bobbed hair sits with her back to the readers as she gazes in a vanity mirror (Figure 4.7). With the caption, "Must I Give Up—and Be Fat?" hovering over her head, her disconsolate expression reflected in the mirror divulges her shock and perhaps frustration over an apparent weight gain. The advertising copy further illuminates her plight:

Can I ever forget that moment, as I stared at myself in the mirror, and my mind grasped the miserable truth that I WAS ACTUALLY GETTING FAT? "Nothing makes a woman look so matronly, so middleaged [sic] and unattractive—nothing makes a man shun a woman so readily—nothing tends to relegate a woman so rapidly to the background—nothing … " My mind trailed off, I gazed vacantly, unhappily into space, as I recalled these words I had read somewhere, it seemed only yesterday. Then I was so beautifully, youthfully slim and the idea of my ever putting on weight had never even entered my mind.[24]

The mirror is here invoked as a tool reflecting the "doubled gaze" of the beholder and of society at large by engaging a dialectic of seeing and believing. The young woman

Figure 4.7 Corrective Eating Society advertisement, *The Red Book Magazine* (July 1922), 23. Courtesy the Internet Archive.

encounters her compromised reflection in the mirror, regarding it within the context of advice discourses—as well as in relation to the male gaze—that associate her perceived weight gain with social and moral failure. Put simply, the young woman realizes that she *looks* fat—a condition made apparent when she compares her own reflection to the world of images she encounters on a daily basis. With the female reader positioned directly behind the woman, however, her reflection exists as our collective reflection; her failure is our failure.

The duality of the mirror and its ability to engage in the viewer a slippery dialectic of seeing and becoming also points to its potential untrustworthiness. Illuminating this idea, a *The New York Times* piece published in 1926 reported on a case in which a French couturier was brought before a judge after being accused of using a trick mirror to deceive his fat customers:

> Before the mirror of a certain popular ladies' tailor patrons inclined to excessive embonpoint were stationed that they might see how slender Madame's deft art made them appear. What they saw in the glass they were charmed, and great were the profits that flowed into the couturière's till.
>
> The clients presently began to observe that arrayed in these costumes before the mirror at home they did not appear sylph-like as at the dressmaker's. Finally, the secret came out. Madame had been posing them before a convex mirror.[25]

With a dozens of indignant fat women serving as witnesses, the judge ruled on the side of the customers, imposing a fine of 2,000 francs on the couturier; however, the *The New York Times* reports that the judge ultimately "sympathized with the dressmaker who had successfully capitalized on [their] vanity." The problem was thus less the couturier's use of a convex mirror than the fact that the customers' home mirrors reflected an inconvenient truth. In the space of the couturier's dressing room, the women encountered a fantasy image—their bodies magically transformed through dress and brought into alignment with the slender ideal. Yet, upon returning home to their ordinary mirrors, they found that their own imperfect bodies awaited them in the glass, their self-delusion crumbled.

The Parable of the Matron

As it was discussed within early twentieth-century fashion media, stoutness was most often framed as a natural, if unfortunate, by-product of the aging process—even something taken for granted in discussions about dress for the older woman. Indeed, in his 1915 stoutwear survey, Albert Malsin delineated the most common type of stout figure in his three-part taxonomy—the "stout all over type"—as being typical of older, more "matronly" women.[26] In the fashion media more widely, the lion's share of references to stoutness appeared within the context of articles about fashion and age.[27] In the parable of the matron, however, age-related weight gain was not presented as a problem per se. According to some sources, a little extra weight at the hips was even deemed more desirable than a gaunt or emaciated appearance in older women, although this sentiment was not widespread. It was, however, framed as a condition that could be mediated through tactful dress practices. Yet, even as women could grow old gracefully—or even perhaps a little "broad" at the hips and bust as above—the same, however, could not be said for growing stout or, worse, *fat*. The central lesson of the parable of the matron was that age-related weight gain, if left unchecked, would result in a woman's fall from grace.

An article published in *The Ladies' Home Journal* in 1919 described just such a scenario in which a fictional character named "Mrs. Blank" has let her beauty, and therefore herself, go:

> The English women have always marveled at the willingness of our slender girls to grow almost universally into fat, short-winded women.
>
> "Of course, she's fat, but you have to expect it at her age," we always used to hear …. Now I hear: "Isn't it too bad that Mrs. Blank has let herself get so disgustingly fat? Why does she do it? She would be a beautiful woman if she'd take care of herself."[28]

As this recounting suggests, the shift in the 1920s was swift as the threshold for unacceptable fat had become both more minute and more concrete as aging women—once content to grow comfortably stout in later life—increasingly found themselves the targets of the self-preservationist discourses of consumer culture. Fatness, the article suggests, was no longer an "unfortunate degree of Providence" but rather a result of "too much food and too little exercise," or an overall lack of attention paid to preserving the body and, perhaps more importantly, to maintaining a youthfully slender figure. A woman grew fat because she did not "take care" of herself.

Certainly, by the 1920s, fatness was increasingly recognized as a health concern.[29] Within the women's and fashion press, however, preachments against fat had little rational basis beyond aesthetics. Even within medical discourses, references to fat women almost invariably focused on appearances.[30] The message was clear: there was no viable excuse for a woman to grow fat, not even in old age. As the matron increasingly became a relic of the nineteenth century, the youth-centric twenties brought with them a decisive shift in how aging and weight gain were perceived.[31] While "broadness" or "middle age spread" seemed to be regarded as age-related, if unwelcome, inevitabilities, fatness was more problematically likened to a woman's lack of self-control. As one 1926 *Vogue* article explained disparagingly, "The woman who lets go gets fat inevitably—and fat and forty might as well go and knit in the chimney corner,"[32] a clear reference to the perceived worthlessness of a woman past her so-called "prime," or past childbearing age. Swayed by the self-preservationist ethos of consumer culture, Americans increasingly fed into the notion that one could no longer age or gain weight gracefully; rather, extra weight on a woman had above all come to be regarded as an outward manifestation of her moral laxity. This point was underscored in an April 1924 *Harper's Bazaar* article titled "To Meet The Silhouette," which discussed new methods to weight loss and, in doing so, explained how training down to a normal weight now becomes so simple a matter that no longer will the stout woman be considered unfortunate. She merely will be looked upon as indolent.

Overweight may be dieted off, exercised off, or, by a new, easy, and utterly harmless method rolled off; but it cannot simply be laughed off as a joke, for the silhouette is now, more than ever before, a serious problem.[33]

Bodies that did not actively combat the visible signs of aging were therefore doomed not only to be failed bodies, rendered all but inert in a culture that so valued youth, but to also be conspicuous bodies. Perhaps somewhat ironically, the ubiquity of slender, youthful bodies within fashion, cinema, and visual culture only made the heavy, aging body all the more conspicuous, or, as was claimed in the above *Harper's Bazaar* article, "a serious problem."

Within the fashion media, however, fat women were assured that, in spite of the public scorn of fat and the media and culture industries' reinforcing of these values, they could be made to look decent, so long as they committed to monitoring themselves for and actively mediating the telltale signs of age- and pregnancy-related weight gain through dress. As one *Vogue* article titled "A Guide to Chic for the Stout Older Woman" so aptly put it, the clever older woman "has no illusions about herself and is well aware that her weak points are her sagging chin, overdeveloped bust and hips, and fleshy upper arms." Equipped with this knowledge, the article went on to explain how this woman now possessed the ability to "bring out [her] advantages and, above all, conceal the defects."[34] At the same time, however, the older fat woman was simultaneously warned of too conspicuously trying to arrest the visible signs of aging. In short, for women, the aging process was mired in contradictions.

These contradictions were addressed within beauty and advice columns that provided tips on how to dress as an older (and fatter) woman. In a 1928 *Vogue*, article, the magazine explained to its "matronly" readership that

As times change, our vocabularies change with them, and certain words, once popular, look strange to our eyes. The word "matron" is one of these—once such a favourite with those who sold their customers the richly fur-trimmed "matrons' coats," the important looking velvet "matrons' hats," and the dresses of exaggeratedly long line that were supposed to disguise the matronly figure, even though they succeeded only in proclaiming the extra pounds that the extra years had added to it.[35]

In the above quotation, *Vogue* points out that the days in which a woman could hope to age gracefully and with dignity were long gone. "To-day [*sic*] there are no matrons," the article also claims, evidenced by the fact that "older women are as slim as they were in their twenties, owing to a strenuous espousal of the gospel of diet and exercise." Here, *Vogue* first and foremost correlates a "matronly" appearance with body weight, a "slight increase in curve," for instance, being a telltale sign of one's advancing age. However, the article also touches upon the fact that looking matronly also encompassed a particular manner of dressing that harkened back to a bygone era, and specifically to the Gilded Age. Women who still clung to this opulent manner of dressing—as, for instance, by employing rigid corsetry to constrain the waist and round out the hips and bust to create a balanced hourglass silhouette—therefore showed their age. In a youth-obsessed culture, the matronly appearance had become associated with a certain former conservatism in dress that, as *Vogue* claims, succeed "only in proclaiming the extra pounds that the extra years had added" to the figure.[36]

The notion that a woman's manner of dressing could make her appear "matronly"—an appearance that met at the confluence of both extra curves and one's age—was further emphasized in an editorial entitled "A Guide to Chic for the Older Woman," in which *Vogue* assured the reader that it was not a woman's age per se that made her unfashionable but rather "the fact that her figure is different, and that the whole thought of the mode has changed since she first began considering clothes." Continuing, *Vogue* argued that by clinging to the fashions of her youth, the older fat woman will only "be—at best—[a] well-preserved and tightly corseted matron, dressed in good taste, but far from smart!"[37] This notion of being "well-preserved" is one that *Vogue* returned to time and again in articles and editorials commenting on dress and age. A 1926 article entitled "A Guide to Chic for the Woman of Forty or More" described the so-called "well-preserved look" in the following manner:

> The woman who starts out to convey the fatal well-preserved impression has her clothes fitted too tightly, uses too much make-up and never sits down without giving her audience the idea that she finds the operation complicated on account of her corsets.[38]

A far cry from being fashionable or, as above, "smart," the idea of being well-preserved conjured a manner of dressing perhaps more fit for the shelves of a reliquary than for bustling urban streets. Where modern garments like tubular shifts were designed to float weightlessly over the body, their matronly counterparts were both too covering and fit too tightly in all the wrong places. Where the straight-line style found charm in simplicity, matronly two-piece dresses were excessive in their ornamentation. And finally, where the youthful silhouettes allowed for freedom of body and movement, the matron—encumbered by her antiquated undergarments and heavy drapery—had only a limited range of movement, aging her not only in her dress styles but also in her posture and carriage.

In a fashion system that so profoundly hinges on its own constant regeneration, there occurs what Julia Twigg has aptly described as "a growing discordance between the processes of fashion renewal and the physical basis for them in the form of the aging body."[39] Fashion, consequently, leaves the older woman behind in order to capitalize on the fickle and ever-changing tastes of youth. As the parables of the matron illustrate, however, this inconvenient truth was no excuse for older women to succumb to the inevitabilities of aging, and specifically weight gain. Even though the trappings of the aging body did not coincide well with the aesthetics of a youth-centric culture, matrons were required to, as one *Vogue* article suggested, "spend even more time in fitting the figure to the frock than in fitting the frock to the figure"[40] in a somewhat hapless pursuit of a youthful appearance.

The Parable of the Domestic

If the fashion media is any indication, the young fat woman in the 1920s had a deeply ambivalent relationship with mass-produced stoutwear and the particular matrix of ideals it extolled. In the parable of the domestic, a younger fat woman finds herself navigating the paltry options available to her in the stoutwear department. Less than a form of escapism, the experience of shopping in these stories is an agonizing one that is rife with contradictions. On the one hand, she had been physically marginalized by the producers of mainstream, standard-size fashions who did not make garments in her size. On the other, however, she is too young to be resigned to wearing drab, covering stoutwear designed for the bodies of older women. These stories, however, are about much more than a lack of choice. In them, the young fat woman's sartorial exile is framed as a root cause of her romantic and sexual failures. Although the physical size of the young fat woman's body certainly bolstered her precarious relationship with fashion, the reasons for this discord lie in the expectations of fashionable femininity, but also of female sexuality.

As has been discussed, the feminine ideal of the 1920s was an inherently youthful one from which, as was suggested in a *Harper's Bazaar* article, "hips and waistlines are banished."[41] Although the modern silhouette was more androgynous and therefore less ostensibly feminine than those that had come before, the backward, conservative design of stoutwear reflected the fact that, increasingly, the aging process for a woman was experienced as her sexual demise. In terms of how this affected individual self-fashioning practices, whereas youthful modes of dressing underscored a woman's sexual allure through bodily liberation, the dress conventions of the matron signaled the fact that the wearer was old and therefore past her sexual prime. The sartorial disconnect for the young, fat woman in the 1920s therefore emerged from the contradiction that while she was in her reproductive prime, both her non-normative body and her manner of dressing suggested otherwise. In brief, she was a young woman dressed in an old woman's clothes.

Although the young fat woman was an ambiguous figure who did not fit neatly into any prescribed archetypes of contemporary femininity (e.g., "the flapper" or "the matron"), a 1924 *Vogue* article attempted to account for her in an article delineating a blunt, tongue-in-cheek taxonomy of the various female "figgers." Evocatively labeled as the "domestic type," the young fat woman was a figure to which "Nature has been inexplicably unkind ... depriving it of most of the attributes which femininity covets."[42] With the fashionably slender body standing as an implicit point of comparison throughout the article, the young fat woman is repeatedly disparaged for her abundance of mature curves. In underscoring the importance of the slender silhouette, this article places the domestic type at the top of a hierarchy resembling an upside-down pyramid, with the others diminishing "gradually in size almost exactly as the individuals involved diminish in bulk … [constituting] a mysterious unkindness on the part of nature."[43] Bodily curves are here associated with home and the domestic realm, or a form of femininity at odds with the expectations of modern womanhood.

Although the women depicted in the pages of *Vogue* during this period were, with extraordinarily few exceptions, white, the domestic type shares traits with the racist stereotype of the "Mammy," also prevalent in American society at this time. According to Patricia Hill Collins, the Mammy was created to "justify the economic exploitation of house slaves and sustained to explain Black women's long-standing restriction to domestic service" and was later used in the marketing of domestic goods and food products.[44] As Andrea Elizabeth Shaw further argues, within the white imaginary, her dark skin and maternally large body signaled "an inclination, if not need, to serve as a caretaker."[45] Physically and symbolically bound to the home and to domestic servitude, the Mammy was a defeminized, asexual figure—a figure through which "Black femininity [was] effaced" and, concomitantly, "a shadow against which white women's beauty [was] foregrounded" and the norms of liberated womanhood and sexuality were defined.[46] Not unlike the Mammy, the domestic was, as *Vogue* described her, a "soft solace in a world of sharp curves" who was more fit for the home than for bustling, urban streets.

By contrast, the stereotype of the liberated, modern woman was an embodied critique of domesticity and motherhood. Critics saw her body as a tacit rejection of "the set of norms, values, and social practices that had structured female identity in terms of a maternal, domestic role throughout the nineteenth century."[47] While this figure could not be boxed in by the traditional expectations of appropriate femininity, the domestic type, on the other hand, was the too-fleshy incarnation of these ideals. Continuing, the article describes (or perhaps debases) the domestic in more concrete terms:

Its chief characteristic is a sort of obviousness—it's all there, so to speak. You can see exactly where it begins and where it ends; it is a solid convexity not admitting of dispute. The word "stout" was invented to describe it with all its solidity and comparative shortness of breath. It was known to our grandmothers as a "matronly figure," and the married women of that time endured it, apparently, without resentment. Times have changed, but the matronly figure, young and old, is still with us, though somewhat under a cloud. Enlightened women have realized that it isn't an act of God, inevitable to the proper bringing up of children and the virtuous administration of a home, but something that holds for them an abrogation of youth—a defeat of their desire to attract.[48]

Vogue's final point, about how the domestic's appearance signals a "defeat of [her] desire to attract," parallels Banner's assertion that while the archetypal flapper—whose essence was distilled in filmic representations of modern femininity and through screen icons such as Clara Bow—was a living embodiment of the new freedoms women were enjoying after the war, she nevertheless reinstated the conventions of normative nineteenth-century femininity. Bent on attracting the male gaze, the modern woman was, more than anything, "intent on securing a husband, and that goal was the ultimate message."[49] Exacerbated by the social and political upheavals that occurred in Europe and the United States in the aftermath of the First World War, the new and dramatically different discourse of fashionable femininity was no longer defined by a woman's proficiency as a wife, homemaker, and caregiver, but rather was expressed by what she did outside of the home.

Permitting freedom of both breath and limb, 1920s fashions were well suited to the New Woman's active lifestyle and rejection of traditional female roles. In describing the essence of 1920s femininity in France via the figure of the *femme moderne* (also known as the flapper in the United States), Roberts has remarked upon the "starkness and sterility" of the new woman and her dress, which was designed to diminish any hint of a matronly curve and which transformed her into "a being without breasts, without a waist, without hips."[50] Likewise, Banner has argued that the low-slung waists and lack of bust lines in 1920s fashions actually functioned to draw attention *away* from women's bodies. The New Woman's sexuality was not expressed through womanly curves but through the dynamic movements of her body.[51] By comparison, the fat female body was an inert body burdened by the visible signs of lethargy and complacency: a body both "solid" and "short of breath."[52] However, with the ideal body being defined more by its corporeal lacks than any salient features—such as the nipped waist or the monobosom, which so defined ideal femininity only two decades prior—the fat woman was condemned for the overall "obviousness" of her body. Simply put, there was *too much* of her in none of the right places. Forced to don retrograde fashions, the young fat woman was made even more conspicuous by the datedness of her clothing.

In describing the dress of domestics, *Vogue* explains how they are, "curiously enough, the most serious decorators of the female form," and in them, one may observe "a courageous enthusiasm in adoring [the fat body's] well established protuberances with all manner of elaborate garniture."[53] Illustrated by the English cartoonist Ann Fish (Figure 4.8), the domestic is pictured gazing at her cartoonishly excessive appearance in a full-length mirror on one half of the double-page spread, and, on the other half, pointing at the Venus de Milo as if to underscore for the reader her deviations from the Venus' "enviable" figure—here elevated as the historical zenith of feminine beauty. Wearing a mismatched ensemble of a black-and-white checkerboard pattern skirt with a top featuring a stylized floral motif, her hair unfashionably piled in fussy ringlets, the garishness of the domestic's ensemble clashes with the exaggeratedly sylph-like "anemics" who surround her.

While the domestic's appearance signaled her acquiescence to be relegated to the home, her body was also, somewhat paradoxically, a symbol of her ineptitude as a partner and as an object of the male gaze. According to *Vogue*, any man, given the choice, would choose a slender woman over "a wife or lady-love tangibly fat." Why else "do husbands of plump wives linger by the drug-store windows where ladies of ephemeral slenderness and more ephemeral drapery are depicted advertising cures for the too fat?"[54] Here,

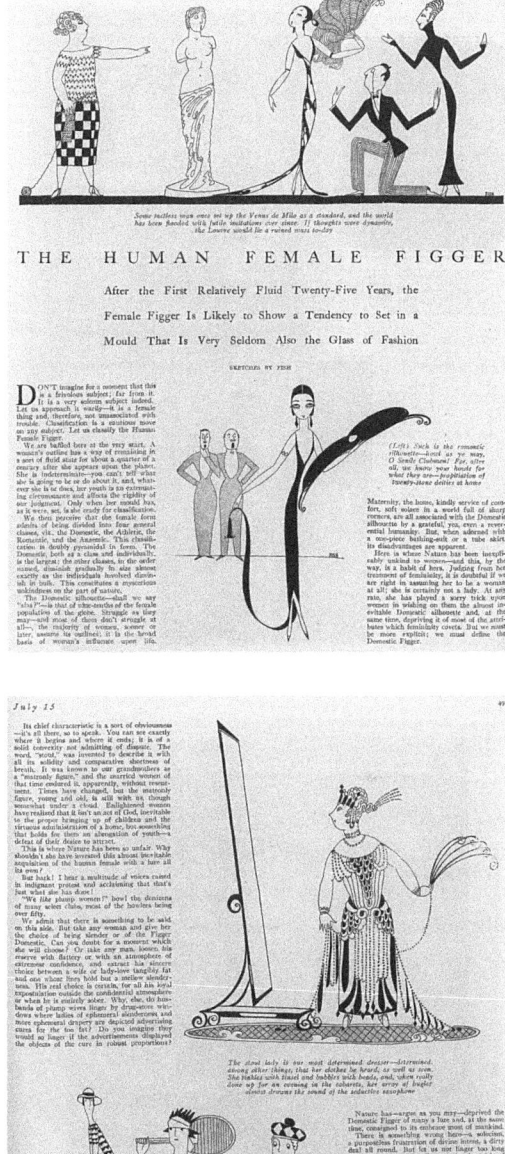

Figure 4.8 "The Human Female Figger," *Vogue* (July 15, 1924), 49. Published with permission from *Vogue*, © Condé Nast.

Vogue taps into growing consensus about the root causes of marital dissatisfaction during this period, and namely the expectation that marriage be grounded by sexual attraction.[55] This notion was alluded to in a 1929 *Harper's Bazaar* story titled "Make Yourself over for Spring," which discussed the marital repercussions of premature weight gain via the fictional figure of Perdita. In discussing how "the little demon FAT [*sic*]" had befallen Perdita, the narrator observed how "the comfortable state of matrimony is fast rounding [Perdita] out ... giving [her] an almost premature matronly appearance."[56] A popular diet book author of the period perhaps best articulated the basic precept of 1920s femininity when she wrote, "To get and hold a man, women need to preserve their youth and their physical attractiveness."[57] Yet, looking youthful and slender far surpassed simply reducing. From garments that fit too tightly, were too outmoded with their drab colors and dowdy cuts, or were simply too "obvious" in their ornamentation, the appearance of fatness was also sewn into the seams of stoutwear itself.

The Parable of the Style-Blind

> There is hope for the woman whose clothes are wrong, but whose mind is open, but there is no hope for the woman whose clothes are wrong and who is not only perfectly satisfied with them, but even proud of the points of difference! For every gown has its weakest spot, the place where mistreatment shows most clearly, and it is the woman wise in chic who recognizes these points and is ever wary of them.[58]

The above quotation comes from a feature that ran in the September 1927 issue of *Vogue* titled "A Guide to Chic for the Complacent" in which the author explains how a woman should not be content to just wear the latest fashions off-the-rack. Rather, the article suggests that the chicest woman will instead work with her seamstress to re-construct off-the-rack fashions to complement her unique bodily proportions. Recalling the parable of the deluded, this article invokes the mirror as a crucial device for obtaining knowledge about one's silhouette, recounting how a chic woman stood "before a triple mirror, [and] demonstrated to [a] style-blind woman ... exactly which lines must be respected." Looking through or past her flaws, the "style-blind" woman instead demanded "that a gown must follow some prejudiced idea that was in her mind." In doing so, the article explains, she achieves little more than an "unfashionable tightness above or below the hips" or the "disastrous effect of emphasizing the wrong line." Equipped with this knowledge, *Vogue* explains how the chic woman does not fit her body to the slender silhouette—and in the process showing a garment's so-called "weakest spot"—but rather concerns herself with the garment's fit in achieving the illusion of slenderness. "To achieve the right lines," the article goes on to explain, a woman has to know her body and also the "right lines, graceful in themselves, correct as pointers of the mode. There are so many ways of being wrong for every one way of being right!"[59]

Parables of the style-blind follow a familiar formula, similar to that outlined above: two women are pitted against each other, one chic, the other "style-blind." While the former has a clear-eyed understanding of her shortcomings and how to minimize or camouflage them with dress, the latter follows the dictates of fashion without regard to her so-called "weak spots." The lesson conveyed in the parable of the style-blind is that one must have an eye for both fashion and her bodily flaws. Good or "flattering" fit was the key to chicness; conversely, following fashion trends slavishly and without regard to fit was a recipe for disaster.

Much like the ideal body, the notion of "good fit" is a historically contingent concept that has evolved over time and in tandem with the rising and falling of hemlines, as well as with the fickle tastes for artificially nipped or natural waists. Indeed, looking fat in the early twentieth century was ultimately more so a matter of fit, or the relationship between the body and dress, than of physique alone. In the mid-1920s, a well-fitting, fashionable dress was one that had a certain degree of ease, and which fell in a straight perpendicular from the shoulders, skimming the flesh, but also concealing any signs of the body's natural curves. A decade prior, however, a well-fitting dress would have accentuated the fullness of the bust and hips. While stiff corsetry would have helped most women to approximate the beauty ideal of decades past, the streamlined look, by contrast, was difficult for all but the slenderest of women to achieve.[60] What was therefore regarded as "bad fit" was further exacerbated by the still somewhat crude state of mass manufacturing and standardized sizing at this time, coupled with the fact that consumers were increasingly expecting to be able to purchase garments off-the-rack that, as Schwartz writes, "would keep to a minimum all signs of deviation from the physical standard—no bulges, no unnecessary material, no obviously forced stitching, no awkward flapping or goring."[61] By the mid-1920s, *Vogue* was writing that it was "hardly possible to fit too closely to the hips, that is, where the fabric is drawn from the precise point of one hip-bone to the other."[62] For the fat woman, however, tightness in a garment merely made her so-called "points of decision" all the more obvious. "Good" or "flattering" garment fit was ultimately achieved when the body approximated the slender ideal as much as the recalcitrant flesh would permit. "Poor" or "bad fit," on the other hand, only emphasized the body's deviations from the slender norm and made the body appear larger, if only by comparison. That being said, good fit was not entirely out of reach for fat women.

One of the most basic, if mundane, instruments employed by women of all sizes to achieve a slender appearance (and therefore a good fit between body and garment) in the 1920s was the lightly boned corslette and, later in the decade, the elasticized "reducing" corset, both of which were foundations created to give the wearer a supple appearance and to allow maximum freedom of movement and which, in some instances, even promised permanent weight loss (Figure 4.9). In order for fat women to achieve the fashionably slender silhouette, however, they oftentimes had to rely upon more forceful or drastic means in order to reshape superfluous flesh. A July 1927 *Vogue* article paints a picture of the problems that older women with more "matronly" figures faced in attaining this foundation:

Figure 4.9 Bonton Mysteria Rubber Reducing Corset advertisement, *Vogue* (November 15, 1924), 19.

The average older woman fails to realize the value of suppleness, and, from this failure, all of her failures begin. All too often, she still wears a modified version of the old ironside corset! It makes her feel more slender, but it makes her look larger, and it puts her outside of the fashion picture ...

A great many older women make serious mistakes in the matter of fitting. They believe that tight fitting makes them look smaller, when, as a matter of fact, it merely reveals their inches. They are afraid of material, and they fail to see the advantage of leaving the world in doubt as to which is flesh and which is fabric.[63]

Here, *Vogue* establishes a crucial disconnect between the fashionable appearance of "suppleness," or an agile comportment, and an unfashionably tight, albeit slender, appearance. Many older women, the article points out, had resorted to stiff corsetry that achieved the all-important slenderizing effect, but which, puzzlingly, only made the body appear larger. What this article illuminates is the fact that mere slenderness alone was not synonymous with fashionability; rather, the ideal body expressed a sense of movement. The fashionably modern body was not an encumbered body, nor was it a cold, hard, and exceedingly slender body. Rather, it was an agile, animated body upon which garments floated effortlessly.

In numerous articles appearing within the pages of the women's and fashion press, fat women were advised to avoid tight or ill-fitting garments that made the body appear overly rigid or stiff. For instance, a 1928 article explained how when shopping for new clothes the "first thing to avoid is the over-fitted look—tightness under the arms, across the bust, or a too tight sleeve."[64] A 1927 article similarly advised that "never, under any circumstances, should [the fat older woman] allow her dressmaker to fit her sleeves too tightly, for nothing gives a more definitely 'matronly' appearance."[65] In this same article, however, concerns over tightness were also substituted for more redolent descriptions. Recounting the exertions of a fat older woman winkingly named "Lydia Bulkley" who struggled to fit her too-fat body into the season's unforgiving sleeves and skirts, *Vogue* colorfully animates the struggles of achieving good fit:

Sleeves, this season, are often short or very long and tight, neither of which are good for Lydia's unfortunately fleshy arm. The first reveals all, and the second gives an unpleasing, stuffed effect. Happily, however, sleeves can usually be changed without spoiling the design of the gown. Lydia finds that the straight, moderately wide model, with a fairly large armhole, beloved of Vionnet and Chéruit, is the best .... Lydia does not wear long skirts, but moderately short skirts with long lines obtained by panels, apron effects, and pleats. She avoids the sausage-like effect of a long, tight skirt over a full figure.[66]

Lingering on the too-tight sleeve and the body-skimming long skirt, this article suggestively describes the "unpleasing, stuffed effect" that the appearance of a large arm fitted to a narrow sleeve created, while remarking upon the "sausage-like effect" of a too-tight skirt on a too-large body. In an uncomfortable mental image that manifests for the reader the discomfort of the wearer herself, *Vogue* likens the poorly outfitted fat body to a "sausage"—the flesh forcibly stuffed into a fabric casing—evocatively demonstrating how ill-fitting garments limited the wearer's mobility and rendered the body all but inert.

Even as the body was increasingly regarded as plastic, fat flesh, however, seemed to remain stubbornly resistant to change. As in the above examples, even as the fat woman could use corseting to achieve a slender appearance, or even physically "stuff" her liquid flesh into modern garments—therein technically fitting the garment to the body but falling short of achieving a "good fit"—her body, literally too large for its coverings, belied her vain attempts to appear unencumbered. It was a body fit to the garment but which burst at the seams, so to speak. In other excerpts culled from the pages of *Vogue* that invoke the parable of the style-blind, the intractability of fat flesh is discussed in even more explicit terms.

In one 1929 article titled "The Older Woman and the New Mode," for instance, the three sartorial offenses fat woman should avoid in fitting her body to the new fashions were outlined. While the low waistline was identified for its tendency to widen the figure and ever-rising hemlines were castigated for revealing less-than-youthful legs, it was the third and final "effect [of] extreme tightness across the hips and back, giving what might be called a spanked look" that was the most distasteful.[67] In this text, the fat woman's physical struggle with her own excess is put into stark relief—the onomatopoeia of a "spank" viscerally evoking the tension of fat flesh pressing and pushing on fabric. In another instance from the aforementioned article, "A Guide to Chic for the Stout Older woman," *Vogue* explained how for the chic older woman,

> her waist-line no longer bothers her, for has not the clever Parisienne, who is the most successful dressmaker in the world, told her that to confine it is unnecessary for the present mode and would, moreover, press the superfluous flesh towards the bust and hips?[68]

Here again, the flesh itself is framed as a burden, with *Vogue* describing how, by confining flesh through constricting undergarments, the fat woman only displaces "superfluous flesh," pressing it upward and outward toward the already ample bust and hips. This so-called "pushed up" look, another article confirms, had fallen by the wayside, departing "with the hourglass waist of twenty years ago, but which one still sees on women of misguided judgement."[69] Perhaps even more devastatingly, an article that appeared in *Women's Wear* described the stout woman's feeble attempts to attain the slender silhouette through cumbersome corseting as creating an appearance "as nearly comparable as possible to an obese pillow tightly tied in the center."[70]

The discourses of tightness—or the tension between flesh and fabric—embedded within the advice that *Vogue* proffered to its stout and matronly readership throughout the 1920s recalls Hillel Schwartz's observation that the first decades of the twentieth century ushered in a shift in how the body was idealized. As he observes, the static body was replaced by the body-in-motion and, in consequence, "fatness became literally upsetting ... [an] unnecessary weight and an intolerable burden."[71] He attributes this important shift to how technologies, both big and small, from the camera to the airplane, changed "the experience of movement," creating a modern kinesthetic of "energy without volume."[72] Fashion itself, however, should not be underestimated as a key factor in precipitating this shift, rather than just a by-product of this new kinesthetic. In the years after the war and with the growing ubiquity of the portable camera, feminine gestures that had been limited to the head, neck, and hands throughout most of history had been replaced by spontaneous, expansive gestures, even to the point of affecting the design of women's clothing.[73] A 1923 *Vogue* article titled, "Figures That Do and Do Not Lie" addressed the new relationship between dress and the body:

> Comparatively few years ago, steel, whalebone, and buckram controlled any disposition of the female shape to swerve from that of the hour-glass. Corsets of this kind were not so absolutely restricting as the iron ones of the Middle Ages, but they were restricting enough to keep the occupants of them from undue activity. A discreet breath of interest might be drawn from the croquet lawn, but not the deep, dangerous inhalations following such rough and rapid movements as those on the tennis ground …. Now, every woman can breathe to the full depth of the lung power she has developed; the far stride of the mountaineer is within her scope; no sport indulged in by man is denied her.[74]

As this excerpt suggests, the new garments and undergarments did not only permit a greater range of motion; they also freed the breath so that women could draw "deep, dangerous inhalations." While the new styles showed off more of the body than ever, they equally, if more subtly, permitted greater freedom of breath. Recalling Valerie Steele's idea of the "internal" or "muscular" corset, which replaced whalebone and steel in the second decade of the twentieth century,[75] suppleness ultimately triumphed over mere slenderness alone, so much so that *Vogue* suggested that a fat woman must never be "too tightly corseted or brassièred. She must look and feel comfortable or she will not be to advantage. It is better to be a little broad than completely breathless."[76]

With supple simplicity reigning supreme, reaching its apogee in the mid-1920s, fat women were routinely admonished within the fashion media as notorious over-dressers. In his analysis of the slender silhouette, for instance, Leon Bakst claimed that "the majority of [stout women] find it very hard to abandon a type of costume which outlines all too plainly their robust silhouettes. Exaggerated efforts to confine an abundant figure are, to put it plainly, in very bad taste."[77] The idea that the fat woman lacked taste was a persistent one that appeared within the fashion media as early as 1912 when Anne Rittenhouse of *The New York Times* remarked, "It looks as though all the fat women in the world were running a race to see who could wear the greatest number of colors and attach themselves to the greatest number of pendants."[78] The question of how to dress well—one that *Vogue* argued should be "ever present" on the fat woman's mind—was made even more difficult by the "glittering temptations" in department store windows.[79] So prevalent was the stereotype of the style-blind fat woman that one fashion writer even commented that "with the suggestion of her … there comes into mind gay, brilliant flowers, downy creatures feathered and furred, that nestle and chatter and are gathered to one's arms as pets …. It is the dearest of missions, this of being the bright bird of home."[80] Beyond satire or sheer mean-spiritedness, however, the stereotype of the fat woman as a variously "determined" or "style-blind" dresser pointed, perhaps, to a more complex set of biases concerning the very competence of fat women as consumers.

***

As the parables of overweight discussed in this chapter demonstrate, the task of cultivating an appropriately slender, and therefore feminine, appearance was far from inconsequential and less than straightforward. While advertisements promoted the idea that slenderness should be at the forefront of the fat woman's mind when getting dressed, it was the discursive device of the parable that lent this idea weight, so to speak. A streamlined appearance was not just fashionable; it symbolized moral and bodily self-discipline in the face of unconstrained consumption. As discussed in the previous chapter, however, fat women were perceived to be voracious, reactive consumers who lacked basic self-awareness. Hers, to borrow the words of Joy and Venkatesh, was a body that was "loathed" because it did "not meet the aesthetic norms of commodity culture," nor those of "appropriate" consumption.[81] Excessive appearances—both in body and in dress—were therefore not merely unfashionable; taken together (a sort of sartorial "double-strike"), they were potent symbols of the fat woman's inability to navigate modern femininity.

The parables discussed throughout this chapter purported to be about fashion and beauty, and specifically how to consume and dress in a manner that was in keeping with the prevailing ideal; however, they were also about how fat had come to be regarded in American society during the interwar years, and specifically the confluence of anxieties that were mapped on to it. From fears of aging to concerns about the construction and presentation of modern femininity, body fat became a potent symbol not just of a body in decline but of the fallibility of the body in consumer culture more broadly. Fat, perhaps more so than other, more subtle, markers of bodily decline, was an obvious scapegoat for the excesses of modern life. Alongside weight-loss products and diet advice, fashion media discourses emphasized the aesthetic rewards of diligent body maintenance while also touting its spiritual and social returns—or a transformation of the inner life of the consumer. Within this context, a woman could strive to attain not just a transformed appearance but a transformed mode of existing in the world unburdened from the stigma, and quite literally the *weight*, of fat. As with everything pertaining to fat, however, the lessons proffered by these parables were rife with contradictions, especially with regard to the articulation and presentation of appropriate femininity. How women actually navigated, and in some cases subverted, these lessons was another matter altogether.

CHAPTER 5
THE FORGOTTEN WOMAN

It is true that nobody admires a fat woman—that is, if she *looks* fat. To avoid looking fat, the stout woman must constantly be on the alert for correct dress suggestions. She must use good judgment regarding every part of her costume, disregarding the fads and fancies that come into fashion's realm each season.[1]

The above advice is typical of that which a fat woman would have encountered in magazines, newspapers, and style guides in the first decades of the twentieth century. It comes from a book titled *Harmony in Dress* (1925) by the home economist Mary Brooks Picken. In this volume, Picken extended advice to women of all shapes and sizes; however, she dedicated no less than an entire chapter to the fat woman. While she remains optimistic, arguing that a fat woman can mitigate the negative stereotypes associated with overweight with little more than a bit of sartorial restraint and some good judgment, her directives nevertheless underscore what many fat women already knew: getting dressed was an act not to be taken lightly. Indeed, throughout her book, Picken frames fashion less as a medium of self-expression than one used for carefully managing appearances in order to fit a narrowly defined standard of idealized femininity. In this way, she was in keeping with other advice writers of the period who tended to stress that it was more important that clothing was becoming to the individual than at the height of fashion.[2] For the fat woman, however, the proverbial "do's" and "don'ts" of dressing proved to be particularly restrictive.

As Carmen Keist has observed, early twentieth-century style advice for fat women—both proscriptive and prescriptive—foregrounded slenderizing as the single most important thing to take into consideration when getting dressed, and spanned everything from how to choose corsets to how to identify the most becoming silhouettes, fabrics, and even accessories.[3] Also pervading these advice discourses was the tacit recognition that with the growing availability of ready-made dress women had more choice than ever before as well as more opportunities to make sartorial blunders. For fat women who, as discussed in previous chapters, were believed to be particularly voracious and emotional consumers, the stakes were even higher. This sentiment was perhaps best expressed by the home economist Helen Goodrich Buttrick, who saw "a real need for a definite kind of education … to overcome our natural vice, extravagance, amidst a sea of goods."[4] Different from the vast array of cheap products that promised fast remedies for fat, there was a steep learning curve to dressing to look slender. It encompassed not only the nineteenth-century precept of how to achieve "harmony" in dress through thoughtful applications of color and pattern,[5] but also advice on how to comport the body so as not to appear clumsy or lumbering and, in some instances, even patronizing bathing and grooming directives that cast doubt on fat women's knowledge of basic hygiene.[6] Because these texts were frequently penned by self-identifying (or reformed) fat women, they tended to strike a more compassionate tone than the parables discussed in the previous chapter; however, they still framed getting dressed as a perilous act—the goal of which was to achieve sartorial and aesthetic equilibrium in order to simply *blend in*.

Although style advice for the fat woman was far-reaching, most authorities tended to offer guidance on how to select garments that made the wearer appear both smaller and less conspicuous. For instance, fat women were advised to eschew many of the most popular styles of the era, which could have the undue effect of highlighting parts of the body that would be better off concealed.[7] They were also advised to avoid heavy fabrics, cumbersome silhouettes, noisy attention-grabbing fabrics, and bright colors that would cause them to stand out in an urban sea of black and muted gray.[8] In the most rigid advice texts, these mandates were rattled off simply as a list of "don'ts," as, for instance in a 1925 column written by *Brooklyn Daily Eagle* fashion correspondent Rita Stuyvesant:

> Don't wear gay designs in your frocks if you are short and stout.
> Don't wear a number of colors in the same costume if you are stout.
> Don't try and dress in a juvenile style if you are not that type.[9]

According to many style authorities, the last thing the fat woman wanted to do was draw attention to herself with overtly flamboyant or intrepid sartorial displays that might invite scrutiny from onlookers. In many ways, dressing to look slender was as much an exercise in self-restraint as it was a performance of deception, for these tactics worked only if others perceived you as slender. A discernable undercurrent of anxiety therefore ran through advice for the fat woman, for any minor infraction could have the unwanted effect of drawing attention to or accentuating her size; or, as one writer bluntly stated, "the illusion of slenderness can be made or marred by a single accessory."[10] Having evolved from the previous century's etiquette manuals, the literary genre of style advice was, for many women, a crucial lifeline that helped them to navigate the newfound freedoms of public life and sartorial expression.[11] For fat women, however, style advice was yet another channel for the perpetuation of weight bias—one that not only established appropriate ways of being and appearing in the world but also reified their status as fashion outsiders.

The phrase "getting dressed," according to Joanne Entwistle, "captures the idea of dress as an activity … that is as intimate as it is social," for when an individual gets dressed, they do so "within the bounds of a culture and its particular norms."[12] Because the bodies of fat women broke with cultural conventions of appropriate femininity, these norms of dress revolved around making their bodies decent, acceptable, and, perhaps more than anything, *slender* if only in appearance. Drawing upon a variety of sources that illuminate the nuances of getting dressed at the intersections of size, race, class, gender, and age—from autobiographies, to interviews, to portrait photographs—this chapter explores how fat women navigated the written and unwritten rules of dressing to look slender within the context of their daily self-fashioning practices. In a departure from previous chapters that focused primarily on fashion industry practices and fashion media discourses, the lived experiences of fat women are foregrounded here. Following Buckley and Clark, their stories are employed to cast light on how fat women practiced fashion, or how "they performed socially constructed identities via fashion."[13] Also considered, however, is how they used dress to *resist* these socially constructed identities, disrupt stereotypes, and resignify fat embodiment. As I define it throughout this chapter, self-fashioning may be understood as a process that occurs upon the surface of the body, and which renders the disorderly fat female body socially intelligible by helping it inch ever-closer to a prevailing beauty ideal, or, conversely as a strategy of resistance and subversion. Self-fashioning is thus framed as an everyday, self-reflexive practice undergone in response to and in dialogue with the norms of American culture, fashion media discourses, and, as is particular to this chapter, style advice discourses.

The title of this chapter acknowledges the extent to which fat women's stories, and specifically those stories that speak to the ordinary, everyday practices of self-fashioning, are too often forgotten to fashion history. With the exception of the home economist Jane Warren Wells, however, the women discussed here are not necessarily forgotten, even if the more mundane aspects of their dress practices are. Indeed, the vaudeville performer Sophie Tucker and the blues singer Gertrude "Ma" Rainey exist in the cultural imaginary as women who accepted, if not *embraced*, their size. While fashion was a key facet of their glamorous, proud, and at times defiant public images, as this chapter will reveal, dressing for even the most admired of fat women was a practice that was as challenging as it was mired in contradictions, and which—in spite of the promises made by stoutwear manufacturers and advertisers—went far beyond merely slipping on a stoutwear dress.

The Everywoman: Jane Warren Wells

In the introduction to her 1924 style guide, *Dress and Look Slender*, Jane Warren Wells describes the predicament she found herself in when, due to an unexpected weight gain, she crossed over the threshold from standard to stout sizes. Unable to wear her old clothes, she retreated to the stoutwear department but found that the goods on offer only had the effect of making her look, in her words, "heavier and older" in spite of advertisers' promises to the contrary. Influenced by the countless advertisements for weight-loss products that seemed to be overflowing from magazines and newspapers, she began to try various methods—from diet breads to rubber fat-melting corsets—but had little success reducing her weight. When she asked her doctor for a more permanent solution, he explained that he could give her something (likely amphetamine-laced diet pills) "that would take off the fat, but that it would age the tissues of the body ten to fifteen years." Keen to hold on to her youth a little while longer and resigned to the fact that her weight-loss journey was all but over, Wells left his office thinking,

If only he knew how much the heavy woman wants to appear thin enough to wear smart clothes, if could only know how she actually longs for the lovely things that fashion creates for the slender types, he would be more sympathetic.[14]

It was then that an idea came to her. "If I could not safely reduce," she wrote, "I could at least give the *appearance* of having reduced."[15] As Wells observed, fashion—from corsets to crinolines—had for centuries been used to alter the silhouette, yet little attention had been paid to how to use the armature of dress to effect the appearance of all over bodily slenderness. Part how-to-guide, part memoir, *Dress and Look Slender* is the culmination of Wells' research into the "science" of looking slender, and more specifically "The Principles of Optical Illusion," or what she describes as the knowledge of how to make "things appear to the eye to be different than they really are."[16] Different from the prescriptive or even reproachful tone of other advice texts, Wells' book is written from a place of empathy; her struggle is the readers' struggle. Of her qualifications to tender such advice, one reviewer remarked, "The author confesses that she belongs to the sisterhood herself and therefore writes from personal study and experience as well as from observation of others."[17]

In addition to discussing the challenges of finding slenderizing ready-made clothing in shops and department stores, Wells also reflected on the broader social consequences of overweight and why dressing to look slender was something that fat women should pursue for reasons that transcended mere aesthetics. Perhaps nowhere is her stance more clearly revealed, however, than in the first sentence of the book in which she bluntly observes, "If there is any one thing in the world that is not wanted it is too much fat on a woman."[18] In the conclusion to the volume, she further expounds on this idea, arguing that the virtues of dressing to look slender are especially urgent "in this day of competition and progressive freedom of women ... [for] perfect proportions are the aim of every woman who wants to make the best of herself."[19]

While these sentiments may, at first blush, seem overstated, Wells' worries were not entirely unfounded. As Stearns argues, there was a perceptible shift in the 1920s when weight bias assumed a decidedly misogynistic tone. Sustained by the erosion of gender distinctions and a broader societal backlash to the freedoms—social, sexual, and political—that women were enjoying after the First World War, the burden of weight morality came to bear "disproportionately on women precisely because of their growing independence, or seeming independence, from other standards."[20] This state of affairs was further compounded by the fact that in the early twentieth century the body had replaced the face as the focus of beauty culture, creating the conditions under which slenderness came to be more or less synonymous with (or was at least a requisite aspect of) outward physical beauty.[21] The fashion and cosmetics industries, buoyed by the explosion of the women's and fashion press, along with the growing popularity of beauty pageants more concretely established the "rules" of feminine beauty than in previous decades.[22] Ascendant, too, was the democratic belief that with hard work and enough capital investment, any woman could be beautiful.[23] As a result, dieting moved to the center of American women's lives as a somewhat unlikely cornerstone of contemporary beauty culture. Wells' beliefs about the importance of dressing to look slender thus reflect the extent to which women, fat or thin, had come to internalize weight bias and specifically the belief that overweight was as much a physical burden as it was a social impediment, as well as the insidious idea that within consumer culture the body is never "finished."[24]

While stoutwear was advertised as having the extraordinary ability to liberate fat women from the social, if not physical, burden of overweight (for stoutwear only effected the *appearance* of slenderness), Wells' firsthand accounts expose the ways that "slenderizing stoutwear" fell far short of its lofty promises. In addition to making fat women appear "older and fatter," as she claimed in the introduction to her book, mass-market stoutwear did not take into account the particular shortcomings (or, for that matter, strong points) of the individual consumer's physique. Rather, it seemed that stoutwear manufacturers were content to drape fat women in yards of gloomy fabric in order to simply hide their bodies. Of her own attempts to find slenderizing stoutwear, Wells mused that she "felt like an Eskimo on a summer's day on Fifth Avenue." In spite of all that was promised to fat women in stoutwear advertisements in the way of figure flattery and fashionability, she found that the goods on offer had "written all over them, 'built especially for a stout.'"[25] Rendered in shades of brown and gray and featuring "long surplice effects," Wells believed that stoutwear garments only drew attention to the wearer's "condition" to the degree that they departed from the fashionably streamlined silhouette.[26] Too often as well, stoutwear simply failed to achieve the promise of a perfect fit.[27] Although stoutwear pioneers like Albert Malsin tried in good faith to create sizing and grading systems that were more accommodating of different shapes, standardization by its very nature proved to be ill-equipped for accommodating the particularities of the fat woman's physique.

Wells thus proposed the science of dressing to look slender as a method for adapting off-the-rack garments to the individual needs of the consumer. Her approach was in many ways a practical response to what many stoutwear manufacturers had quietly come to acknowledge: that aftermarket alterations were an unwelcome but necessary by-product of the move toward greater standardization. While in the early twentieth century many manufacturers, beholden to their guarantees of perfect fits, had previously shouldered the cost of alterations, by the 1920s the cost burden had largely shifted to consumers.[28] Different from making custom garments from scratch—a practice that was growing increasingly cost prohibitive and outmoded as the market for ready-made dress continued to expand—dressing to look slender involved selecting and, if necessary, altering garments that served the dual purpose of highlighting the wearer's strong points while camouflaging parts of the body that impeded the illusion of slenderness. For Wells, this process involved choosing restrained but modish dresses, frequently rendered in slenderizing black or featuring subtle patterns, that accentuated her height and diminished her width (Figure 5.1). Occasionally, in order to transform a "dumpy fat woman's dress" into something more becoming, she changed a neckline, removed an ornament, or fixed the line of a sleeve—all of which Wells claimed were simple alterations well within the capabilities of the average home sewer.[29] Although she advised against

These two pictures illustrate improper and proper choice of fabrics for a stout figure. Above, the large-figured material adds size, the fur trim shortens, the round beads shorten the neck. All conspire to emphasize weight.

118

Here a small all-over pattern minimizes size, the plaits and tassels lengthen, the necklace adds a slenderizing touch. The appearance as a whole is graceful and youthful.

119

Figure 5.1 Illustration from *Dress and Look Slender* by Jane Warren Wells (Scranton: International Textbook Press, 1924), 118–9.

sacrificing beauty altogether just for the sake of looking slender, Wells believed that a fat woman's primary garment should fit well, but should more or less function as backdrop for more expressive shoes and accessories. In addition to drawing the eye away from "a great 'mother lap' or a shoulder of Gibraltar to weep on," Wells furthered that carefully chosen accessories could highlight a slender ankle or wrist, or even elevate a simple look into a more markedly fashionable one. And even though there were certain double-chin-accentuating hat shapes, such as "squatty mushroom types" and those with "roll brims," that were to be avoided, accessories were generally one area in which she permitted readers to indulge their more fashionable impulses.[30]

Ruffles, color, and exuberant patterns, on the other hand, were sartorial flourishes that Wells believed were the sole preserve of the thin and youthful. Acknowledging what she described as her and her readers' natural "appetite for color," Wells sympathized, stating,

Because we love red, orange or King's blue is no sign we must wear it on our backs for all to see. Buy a little piece of fabric with just the colors you revel in; put it in the dresser drawer, or let it ornament a chair back, look at it every day, and thus satisfy your longing for color. Then wear those very simple things you know will be becoming.[31]

Certainly, advice such as this was given with the best of intentions, and namely with the goal of helping fat women to find social acceptance in an increasingly fat-phobic culture. At the same time, however, such advice discourses merely reproduced the hierarchies and power structures of a fashion system that had for so long marginalized the fat woman. As a product of culture, advice discourses impose that culture's values onto individual bodies, constraining it to appear and behave in certain ways, while also reifying biases and prejudices.[32] *Dress and Look Slender* takes as its starting point the flawed notion that all fat women must want to lose weight, and will therefore sacrifice other pleasures—and namely that which is derived from fashionable consumption—for the sake of looking slender, while also perpetuating harmful stereotypes. In the above quotation, specifically, Wells evinces the stereotype of the fat woman as an emotional, if not gluttonous, consumer. Because of their inability to practice restraint in the way of fashion consumption, Wells urges her readership to largely forego fashion trends and fads in the service of cultivating an anonymous public persona. Unfortunately for the fat woman, color was something only to be enjoyed in the home and thus safe from the withering public gaze.

Throughout *Dress and Look Slender*, Wells acknowledged that the fashion and beauty industries bore some responsibility for the fat woman's marginalization; however, she assigned most of the blame to fat women themselves, explaining how "we deserve to be dowdy if we haven't enough pride, ingenuity and perseverance to conceal intelligently and comfortably a few extra pounds."[33] Her text thus reveals the great pressure fat women were under to conform to a narrowly defined standard of slender, youthful beauty in early twentieth-century America—this being in spite, or perhaps *because*, of the wealth of products that promised them the opportunity to have their proverbial cake and eat it too. Because consumer culture promised so many fast and affordable solutions for the problem of fat—from pills, to stoutwear, to the ever-growing style advice economy—there was no one for the fat woman to blame for her shortcomings and failures of willpower except herself. In spite of Wells' at times reproachful tone, however, she remained stalwart in her belief that dress was a more effective means of achieving the appearance of slenderness than any weight-reducing gimmick or quick fix, which could not only result in premature aging but actually endanger a woman's health and well-being. The practice of dressing to look slender was thus framed in Wells' book as a safer and empowering (if not emancipatory) act, albeit one that somewhat paradoxically was accomplished in the service of a culturally sanctioned body ideal. Herein, the extent to which self-fashioning is less of an individualistic practice than one performed in response to external social forces and pressures is made manifest, as is the extent to which style discourses (well-intentioned as they may be) reinforce beauty ideals, affirm gender norms, and normalize body maintenance practices among their readership.[34]

While presented as a straightforward style guide, in its entirety, *Dress and Looks Slender* opens a window onto what it was like for one ordinary woman to navigate the constraints and contradictions of early twentieth-century weight bias in the pursuit not just of a suitable appearance but of admiration and social acceptance as well. Although Wells' personal disclosures are central to the text—sometimes to great emotional effect—it is unlikely that the book was actually written by Jane Warren Wells, or that there was even a home economist who ever went by that name at all. Indeed, a number of sources suggest that Wells was actually a pseudonym used for a period in the early 1920s by Mary Brooks Picken.[35] Picken, who was quoted at the beginning of this chapter, was among the many home economists who in the early twentieth century penned the books, pamphlets, and advice columns that taught millions of American women how to navigate the new consumer culture and, specifically, how to dress and shop.[36] Although it is unknown precisely why Picken, a prolific and respected author, chose to write under the pseudonym Jane Warren Wells, one can reasonably assume that it was done in order to strike an emotional chord with her readership and to imbue her advice with the weight of lived experience. Like fashion journalism and photography more broadly, style advice is used by women to imagine different modes of dressed embodiment. As Rebecca Arnold, drawing upon the work of psychologist Paul Schilder, writes, this process of "appersonization" is not a passive one through which readers reflexively adopt behaviors and attitudes. Rather, it is an active process in which readers reflect upon and internalize the various aspects of the author's body and lived experience and use them in the construction of their own body image.[37] The fictional character of Jane Warren Wells is thus more than just the author of the text and translator of sophisticated design theories into layman's terms.[38] Not unlike a glossy, editorial photo of a fashion model, she is an idealized but deeply relatable figure against whom readers can formulate their own body images, as well as a window onto a different, perhaps more successful, way of being in the world.[39]

As compelling and useful as it may have been to readers, *Dress and Look Slender* nevertheless raises some important questions about how and to what extent one can take the author's admissions about the struggles of shopping and getting dressed and extend them to the experiences of fat women more generally. On the one hand, one could write off this book as a work of fiction, and Picken (a slender woman) as an unreliable narrator. On the other, it could be argued that *Dress and Look Slender* is an example of what Anne Buck calls "dress in action" to the extent that it reveals the nuances of dress and the experiences of self-fashioning within "the author's world,"[40] which in this instance is an America in which modern weight bias was rapidly calcifying. While the personal anecdotes in *Dress in Look Slender* may themselves be works of fiction, the overall tenor of the volume aligns with other interpretations of what it was like to shop and get dressed as a fat woman in early twentieth-century America, which is to say, neither simple nor straightforward. Spread out over two hundred pages, Picken's ruminations on the most seemingly insignificant details of dress and the dire social and romantic consequences of looking fat lend weight to the idea that the average fat woman lived in what *Women's Wear* described in 1915 as a natural state of "self-conscious distress."[41] Where the volume falls short, however, is in accounting for the breadth and diversity of fat women's experiences. While the fictional character of "Jane Warren Wells" may be a proxy for the "everywoman" belonging to the white middle class—and thus subject to white middle-class norms and values—other fat women were exempt from the rules altogether. For some women, it was far better to stand out than to blend in among the anonymous masses.

The Vaudevillian: Sophie Tucker

I don't want to lose weight.
The boys tell me I'm great, and my sweetheart loves me just the way I am.
I have no fear that he'll go chasing round with other mamas.
He may find one who will fill my shoes but not my pajamas.
I don't care what I weigh. I eat pie every day ...
I don't want to get thin.
You can laugh and you can grin, but I'm doing very well the way I am.[42]

Sophie Tucker wrote the above lyrics in 1929, two decades into her nearly sixty-year career as an actress, singer, and comedian. During her long and storied tenure on the American vaudeville circuit, Tucker was known for her risqué, brash, and defiant song lyrics that, among other things, celebrated her sizable physique. In 1929's *I Don't' Want To Get Thin*, for instance, Tucker tackled the issue of her weight with her characteristic good humor, suggesting that it was the reason for her sexual appeal, and that at one hundred sixty-three pounds she had even lured married men away from their "slender-waisted mamas." Partly because of ribald lyrics such as these, Tucker came to occupy a vaunted place in the cultural imaginary as a fat icon—a woman who flaunted her weight in the face of immense societal pressure to reduce, long before such public acts of self-acceptance by women were common or accepted.

Although voluptuous nineteenth-century stage actresses like Lillian Russell (who famously weighed two hundred pounds at the height of her popularity) and Fanny Davenport arguably paved the way for Tucker, the conditions under which she sought fame were markedly different. As Susan A. Glenn writes, during the first decades of the twentieth century the American stage became a space in which "proto-feminist" ideas about equality, gender relations, and sexuality were explored and in which female performers consciously developed modern expressions of liberated womanhood.[43] Even though Tucker's natural inclination to off-color humor was well suited to this environment, her body would prove to be somewhat less so. Just as women's and fashion magazines were sites in which the slender, youthful beauty ideal embodied by the liberated "New Woman" was cemented as the norm, so too was the American stage. Thus, as the voluptuous ideal exemplified by Russell and Davenport fell into eclipse in the early 1900s, Tucker found herself being compared to willowy beauties such as Sarah Bernhardt and Lillie Langtry, who just a decade prior were criticized for being too slender.[44] Tucker's rise to fame was therefore as unorthodox as it was hard fought. Although she projected an unflinchingly confident public persona—proclaiming to audiences in 1929, "I don't care what I weigh ... I eat pie every day"—Tucker's insecurities, especially in the way of fashion, ran deep.

Sophie Tucker's memoir, *Some of These Days* (1945), chronicles her career beginning in 1906 when she sang in restaurants in Hartford, Connecticut, through to her brief foray as a Hollywood film actress in the 1940s. Interspersed throughout her nostalgic reminiscences about her travels, celebrity friends, and of the dissolution of the vaudeville circuit are intimate insights into the role that fashion played in the creation of her legendary public persona. In spite of her fame and vast resources, however, Tucker's relationship with fashion was complicated by her lifelong struggle with her weight. During her early years in particular, Tucker found it difficult to reconcile what she describes in *Some of These Days* as her "big and strong" body with those of her less developed peers. With her big body, however, came a big voice and an equally big personality. By the time she was thirteen, she was singing for tips in her Russian-born Jewish immigrant parents' faltering restaurant during the week and performing in local singing competitions on weekends. While her undeniable talents won over audiences, some unruly patrons were nevertheless quick to take note of her well-developed 145 pound frame with shouts of "let the fat girl to do her stuff" and "give us the fat girl!" Even from an early age, however, Tucker was able to use her sharp wit to diffuse the sting of these verbal injuries, willing herself to believe that "maybe in show business size doesn't matter if you could sing and could make people laugh."[45]

Tucker's coping mechanisms would prove especially useful when she left home at the age of seventeen to pursue a career on Broadway. Success did not come quickly, however, and between her failed auditions, Tucker attended vaudeville shows where she took note of the "smartly dressed" performers with "beautiful figures" to whom she compared herself and her wardrobe of plain, well-worn dresses. As Marlis Schweitzer observes, during this period, stage girls had to choose fashionable costumes but also had to display them to good effect.[46] Streamlined fashions required streamlined bodies and therefore fat performers like Tucker could not expect to get by on their talents alone. Rather, they had to reproduce themselves as "desirable and saleable objects" by demonstrating their acquiescence to the emergent "cult of clothes" on the American stage.[47] Because there was little that Tucker could do to reduce her weight in such a short period of time, she had to settle for adopting a more modern hairstyle and purchasing an "on time" outfit of a shirtwaist and walking skirt for $10, which she paid for on a $1-weekly installment plan.[48]

Tucker's new, more polished look helped her land auditions; however, the growing preference for slender performers meant that there were simply fewer and fewer opportunities for someone of her size on the American stage. Deeply problematic and racist roles that permitted fat white women to masquerade as another race were the exception. Blackface, as M. Alison Kibler writes, "was one route to success and celebrity in vaudeville for women who were not conventionally attractive."[49] For Tucker, whose deep, belting voice was commonly mistaken for that of a Black woman, minstrelsy was a singular path to stardom, albeit one she claims to have initially rejected.[50] In *Some of These Days,* Tucker recalls attending an audition in Harlem, where a club runner remarked, "This one's so big and ugly the crowd will razz her. Better get some cork and black her up."[51] According to Andrea Elizabeth Shaw, this was a decision steeped in the recognition that "Black femininity was one of the final frontiers of socially acceptable womanhood—the domain of the woman dispossessed of her femininity" into which a fat white woman could be incorporated without issue.[52] Although Tucker claimed to have initially felt "sick and frightened" by the prospect of performing in blackface, as soon as she began earning top billings as a "World Renowned Coon Shouter," she easily cast aside any lingering reservations.[53] Of her rapid rise to fame, a reporter for the *San Francisco Examiner* remarked that she seemed to naturally possess all of the requisite skills, from an expressive face to a booming voice, to master the "fine art" of minstrelsy, but that it was the "spirit of fun" that she "exuded from every pore of her roly-poly [body]" that put her "over the top."[54] While she did not like having to hide under the "nasty mess" of burnt cork that stained her expensive stage clothes, Tucker seemed to have a knack for racist masquerade.

Blackface minstrel shows, which became popular in the United States in the 1840s and remained so through the 1920s, created an outlet for white performers to broach taboo subjects and traverse racialized boundaries.[55] Popular among white audiences across the industrialized North and the rural South alike, minstrelsy, as Susan Gubar argues, played an important role in the social fabric of the United States in the early twentieth century for the extent to which it affirmed the racial hierarchy.[56] Because minstrelsy framed African Americans as inherently inferior to white Americans, it was also a medium that allowed racial, religious, and ethnic Others, including Jewish performers like Tucker, to distance themselves from their ethnic and religious backgrounds and align themselves with American constructions of whiteness. On the American stage, the "racial mask" of blackface functioned to highlight the perceived positive traits associated with whiteness while affirming racist stereotypes associated with those being impersonated.[57] For female performers, blackface minstrelsy was typically rooted in one of two racist archetypes: that of the "Mammy" or the lascivious jezebel.[58] In both instances, the fat woman's robust physique, concealed under a layer of burnt cork or black paint, appealed to white audiences' fascination with fat Black female bodies—a fascination that was deeply rooted in racism, nativism, and the ascendance of the slender beauty ideal, and which was heightened by the knowledge that the performer was subversively broaching racialized boundaries.[59] In her own performances, Tucker played into the lascivious jezebel stereotype by signing bawdy songs while donning figure-hugging white and champagne-colored satin dresses that contrasted starkly with her painted skin. By embodying two forms of deviant femininity—Blackness and fatness—Tucker traversed into the realm of spectacle and engaged in metaphorical performance of miscegenation.[60] Further heightening the effect, at the end of each performance, she was known to seductively peel off her opera gloves to reveal the unpainted, alabaster skin underneath, an action that both titillated and affirmed her whiteness. The overall effect won over audiences who delighted in the sexualized, racial masquerade that bordered on burlesque. Tucker, however, grew to dislike performing in blackface night after night not because of any moral misgivings but because it was a persistent reminder of her inability to conform to narrowly prescribed standards of white beauty.[61]

After several successful years performing on the minstrel circuit, Tucker sought out new opportunities to perform as herself: a fat Jewish woman. In this process of reclaiming her identity, what she wore on stage played an even more crucial role.[62] Because she was no longer able to wear a racialized disguise, Tucker had to go to greater lengths to self-fashion an acceptable appearance—one that was distinctive but which also conveyed her willingness to conform to contemporary beauty standards (Figure 5.2). Of her early performances in which she took the stage in a simple wool suit and white cotton shirtwaist, Tucker remarked that she felt "stripped," albeit relieved to be rid of the sticky burnt cork residue of her blackface period. Her solution was to assemble a wardrobe of glamorous dresses in order to fashion a more conventional stage persona. In her memoir, she recalls

Figure 5.2 Portrait of Sophie Tucker (1918). Hulton Archive/Getty Images.

purchasing a tightly laced, black princess seam gown with a train of red chiffon ruffles that, while more conspicuously fashionable, proved ill-suited to performing and made her "feel like a baloney in mourning." Already feeling self-conscious in her new gown, Tucker, whose torso was tightly constricted by the gown's stiffly-boned bodice, struggled to draw a deep breath throughout her performance; however, her greatest humiliation came at the end of the show when she got caught in her train and tumbled "like a ton of bricks" as she was attempting to exit the stage.[63]

For Tucker, this performance was an abject failure; however, as far as her manager was concerned, it marked an important turning point in which she secured her reputation as both a talented singer and a comedian. Even as Tucker blushed with embarrassment, the audience roared at what from their vantage point looked less like an accident than a slapstick punchline to her act. Indeed, comedy, much like minstrelsy, was one other narrow avenue for fat female performers to achieve fame in early twentieth-century America.[64] Both mediums created an outlet for audiences to engage in a form of pleasurable voyeurism since fatness, much like Blackness, incited within them a mix of curiosity and revulsion.[65] There was thus no greater thrill than seeing the negative stereotypes associated with overweight humorously play out on the stage. What made Tucker's performance especially amusing to audience members, however, was the depth of her sartorial failure. In addition to breaking several of the cardinal rules of dressing to look slender—including squeezing into a too-tight gown that featured a bulky, brightly colored train—her clumsy bodily comportment betrayed her self-conscious attempts to refashion herself in the image of the liberated New Woman. In spite of Tucker's public humiliation, comedy would nevertheless prove to be a more palatable route to stardom than blackface.

With Tucker's rapid rise to fame came greater access to fashion—especially designer and bespoke garments—as well as a loosening expectations around what constituted an "appropriate" appearance. In *Some of These Days*, she describes commissioning expensive gowns from famous French and English couturiers like Madame Isobel, Madame Francis, and Lucien Lelong, from whom she commissioned a favorite black sheath dress.[66] Still, Tucker struggled throughout much of her career to fully liberate herself from the written and unwritten rules of dressing to look slender even as she outwardly reclaimed her fatness on stage and in her song lyrics. To celebrate her first headlining performance in Atlantic City, for instance, Tucker purchased an expensive, floor-length leopard skin coat and a sealskin muff similar to those worn by other, more slender, starlets. On her large frame, however, she felt that the bulky coat was "unbecoming" and "too showy," and therefore put her at risk of alienating potential friends and suitors.[67] Even so, Tucker recognized the power of dress, remarking in her memoir that her obsession with fashion had less to do with her vanity than with the simple fact that, "in show business, clothes matter."[68] Putting her reservations aside, Tucker made it a point to use fashion, both onstage and off, less to flatter her figure than to make headlines. Indeed, as she told *Women's Wear* in October 1922, it was better for fat women to simply accept their figures and dress accordingly. Continuing, she added, "there is nothing more pathetic, it seems to me, than a large mature woman trying vainly to look slim and girlish."[69]

Among her many sartorial transgressions, Tucker recalls wearing a "very, very daring … headline-making" tight sheath skirt with a knee-high slit while on tour in Ohio, and a $600 custom beaded gown made by Madame Francis that was paired with a billowing, royal-blue velvet wrap and imposing feather headdress.[70] Entertainment journalists routinely commented on her head-turning fashion choices, including vibrantly colored costumes "that would make you gasp" if you saw them on the street and her "wonderful, glittering, dazzling gowns of silver and gold."[71] However, Tucker's proudest moment came when in 1931, at the height of her popularity, she was photographed on a transatlantic cruise wearing a pair of bespoke blue tweed afternoon pajamas by Paul Poiret (Figure 5.3). Recounting this moment in her memoir, Tucker wrote,

> The minute I saw the reporters and photographers come aboard, I rushed to my stateroom and got into a Paul Poiret royal blue suit trimmed in gray caracul. What a laugh when I barged in in front of the camera boys, leading the two German police dogs I'd bought in Berlin, and the boys saw I was wearing *pants*! Yes, it was Sophie Tucker, not Marlene Dietrich, who introduced pants in the U.S.A. They got me into the headlines and newsreels and were good for laughs any place. Yes, I beat Marlene to pants, but I've got to admit she beat me in them as far as looks go.[72]

While the history of women wearing pants is much more mundane and spans a decades-long period of adoption and normalization from the 1850s to the 1930s, this incident, while embellished for dramatic effect, reveals the important role that dress played in fortifying Tucker's reputation as a provocateur. Even as she acknowledges in her memoir that the style was perhaps not the most flattering on her curvaceous frame, there is also a tacit recognition that there is truly no bad publicity. In the photo, a beaming Tucker strikes a haughty pose with her hand casually resting on her thigh and her right foot alighting a stair to show the billowing culottes to their best effect. In doing so, she breaks one of the cardinal rules of dressing to look slender, repeated across numerous style guides and advice columns, which directed fat women to comport themselves in such a manner so as to physically diminish their size.[73] Summarized by Wells in *Dress and Look Slender*, a large woman "with her feet spread apart … makes a very heavy and unattractive picture." Rather, fat women, she explained, should strive to "cultivate grace and ease of motion" and "endeavor to overcome heaviness in" their posture so as not to "appear to weigh a thousand pounds."[74] Such acts of taking up space, however, were an essential facet of Tucker's bawdy on- and offstage persona, ascendant in the 1930s, as "The Last of the Red Hot Mamas."[75] Although Tucker had hoped to make headlines for introducing American women to trousers with this carefully orchestrated publicity stunt, perhaps of greater significance was the way that she comported her body inside of the trousers. With her expansive pose, Tucker presented an alternative model of fat female embodiment—one that rejected rigid social prescriptions for how fat women should dress and carry themselves in public.

While Tucker was growing more and more famous and, ostensibly, more confident in the 1930s, offstage she was quietly fighting a number of personal

Figure 5.3 Sophie Tucker on the ship SS Isle de France in blue afternoon pajamas by Paul Poiret (September 26, 1931). Imagno/Hulton Archive/Getty Images.

battles. From failed romantic relationships to a faltering career, these issues risked undermining her self-possessed public image.[76] It was her weight, however, that proved to be one of her more enduring struggles. When vaudeville began to be eclipsed by Hollywood, Tucker attempted to translate her onstage talents to the big screen. After seeing some of her early screen tests, however, Tucker feared that she was not destined for Hollywood stardom. Of this painful realization, she wrote, "I looked as large as the Rocky Mountains ... I had neither the beauty nor glamor to offer the screen."[77] Although she does not discuss this in her memoir, at the age of forty, Tucker received a facelift during a stopover in Chicago. When confronted by a reporter after leaving a plastic surgeon's office with bandages on her face, she remarked with her characteristic frankness, "The operation? Just a little fat and loose skin taken off my face .... Only a small cut in front of each ear. Had to look a little younger for films."[78] Her decision to get a facelift was ultimately made in vain, for her Hollywood résumé amounted to little more than a string of supporting roles. Later in her career, and buoyed by the success of several residencies and one-woman shows, however, Tucker became more outspoken about the challenges faced by fat and older women to remain relevant in American society. In 1937, for instance, Tucker decided to formally drop her title of "The Last of the Red Hot Mamas" and to embrace the "stylish stout" moniker in order to draw attention to the plight of "the thousands of stout women who are never considered by the fashion designers of today."[79] At the age of sixty, she even lent her name and likeness to a line of mass-manufactured stoutwear blouses produced by the ready-to-wear brand Vicki Lynn. Speaking to *Women's Wear* about the somewhat controversial move to align herself with a simple clothing line that paled in comparison to the glamour of her onstage wardrobe, she stated that her decision was informed by the fact that she'd grown weary of seeing clothes modeled by "perfect 12s." "That's all very well," she told the trade publication, "but how would it look on someone like me?"[80]

Throughout much of her career, Tucker struggled to find belonging on the American stage due to her unruly body, which defied the norms of appropriate white femininity. From her racist blackface period to her star turn as a vaudeville performer, however, clothing proved to be a crucial tool that helped her navigate the beauty ideals demanded by the industry. Just as important, however, was the way Tucker strategically used dress to cultivate a stage persona befitting her self-proclaimed title as "The Last of the Red Hot Mamas," and in the creation of which she abandoned many of the rules of dressing to look slender. As her career progressed, Tucker, at least publicly, seemed to have grown more at ease with the prospect of dressing more for herself than for an externalized gaze. Yet, the ability to dress as she liked was a singular privilege conferred by her enormous celebrity. As can be gleaned from the fictional Jane Warren Wells' account, the average fat woman did not have the same sartorial freedoms enjoyed by a world-famous performer. Even as Tucker's experience provides a different perspective on what it was like to shop and get dressed as a fat woman in early twentieth-century America, it is something of a rarefied outlier that does not speak to the diversity of lived experiences of fat women, especially at the intersection of race, class, and ethnicity.

The Mother of the Blues: Gertrude "Ma" Rainey

In the opening scenes of the 2020 film *Ma Rainey's Black Bottom*—an adaptation of August Wilson's 1982 play of the same name—Gertrude "Ma" Rainey, played by a fat suit-wearing Viola Davis, sings the opening bars to "Deep Moaning Blues" under a canvas tent somewhere in the deep South. As the camera pans around the packed tent, boisterous audience members shout, dance, and fan themselves as a sweat-drenched Rainey writhes and moans to the thumping syncopation of her suit-clad instrumentalists. She wears a floor-length shift with kimono sleeves rendered in burgundy silk chiffon and embellished with a spray of onyx and champagne sequins. Everything about the scene exudes heat—from the sepia-toned cinematography, to the song's sexually-charged lyrics, to the beads of sweat dripping down Rainey's ample bosom. While there are no surviving film recordings of her performances, the scene is faithful to written accounts, which describe broken attendance records, sultry song stylings, and, perhaps most notably, Rainey's commanding stage presence. In addition to being physically large, Rainey was an expressive performer and ostentatious dresser. "Her gowns were most wonderful creations of the dressmaker's art," remarked one *Chicago Defender* reporter in 1924, while another exclaimed, "Oh boy! What a flash Ma does make in her gorgeous gowns."[81] Rainey's self-fashioning went far beyond her gorgeous gowns, however. As Donald Bogle writes, she was also known for "her gold bracelets, her gold fillings in her teeth, her string upon string of necklaces, and, most of all, there were her diamonds—in her hair, on her clothes, around her neck and [on her] arms."[82] Some described her as the "ugliest woman in showbusiness,"[83] yet there was no denying Rainey's powerful stage persona, nor the important role that fashion played in its construction.

Given the title of "The Mother of the Blues" by her record label, Paramount, Ma Rainey was the first female blues singer to achieve mainstream fame in the United States and an important pathbreaker for the many African American female jazz and blues singers who followed in her wake.[84] Born in 1886 in Columbus, Georgia, Gertrude Pridgett was one of five children born into a musical family with deep roots in the church. By the age of fourteen, she was singing in the choir of the First African Baptist Church and performing widely in tent shows where, as early as 1902, she had added blues to her repertoire.[85] In 1904 she was married to a fellow performer named William Rainey. Together, "Ma" and "Pa" Rainey toured the American vaudeville and minstrel circuits for several years until Ma's fame eclipsed that of her husband.[86] Propelled by the swelling popularity of the blues especially amongst white audiences, Rainey began to headline as a solo artist performing both blues classics and her own songs, which were soon to become classics in their own right. As her celebrity grew, so too did her productions, which at the height of her fame in the 1920s included chorus girls, contortionists, and even live chickens.[87] However, it was Rainey and her singular talents as a comedian, emcee, and "Assassinator of the Blues," as she was occasionally billed, that drew record-breaking crowds across America from the segregated Jim Crow South to the Rust Belt.

Ever the show woman, Rainey was known to take the stage in a Victrola-shaped box from which she would emerge as if by magic. Of these performances, Rainey's pianist, Thomas Dorsey, recalled,

> Ma would sing a few bars inside the Victrola. Then she would open the door and step out into the spotlight with her glittering gown that weighed twenty pounds and wearing a necklace of five, ten and twenty dollar gold-pieces. The house went wild …. Ma had the audience in the palm of her hand. Her diamonds flashed like sparks of fire falling from her fingers. The gold-piece necklace lay like a golden armor covering her chest. They called her the lady with the golden throat.[88]

Although her talents as a performer were legion—from her powerful vocals to the sheer magnetism of her personality—Rainey's fame was nevertheless something of an aberration, for there were many more technically skilled and beautiful female blues singers on the minstrel and vaudeville circuits, including Mamie Smith and her own protégé Bessie Smith.[89] Of her appearance, biographer Chris Albertson writes, "Looking closer to fifty than her real age of thirty-nine, Ma Rainey was no beauty by anyone's standards." Continuing, he adds that with "her thick, straightened hair going in every direction, large gold-capped teeth, a fan of ostrich plumes in her hand, and a long, triple necklace of shiny twenty-dollar gold coins hugging her neck … Rainey was a sight to behold"[90] (Figure 5.4). Such sentiments were even echoed by those closest to Rainey, including her trombone player, Clyde Bernhardt, who believed her to be ugly but conceded, "I'll tell you one thing about it, she had such a lovely disposition … and personality, you forget all about it. She commence to lookin' good to you."[91] By all accounts, Rainey was aware of the fact that she did not conform to contemporary beauty standards. Lieb and other historians agree that Rainey consciously employed her physicality to great comedic effect in her performances wherein she—a short, heavyset, mature woman—would poke fun at her weight during her comedy bits or playfully flirt with her younger, slimmer musicians in acts of good-humored self-deprecation.[92] These lighthearted moments, however, contrasted sharply with more uninhibited displays of her physicality such as that in the opening scene to *Ma Rainey's Black Bottom*. As a "big mama," or "a lover, a voluptuous and desirable woman … a sex symbol," Rainey did not hesitate to discuss sex or move her body in an overtly provocative manner—a fact which, if anything, made her an even more confounding figure.[93]

Even more so than their fat white counterparts, fat Black women had limited pathways to achieve mainstream stardom in early twentieth-century America. In particular, white audiences responded to roles in which Black performers played into racialized and weight-based stereotypes, and namely those that cast fat Black women as "sexual suspects—libidinous, carnal and generally disrespectful of the bodily controls that were supposed to … govern bourgeois white society."[94] These roles ranged from the sardonic minstrel performer to that of the sensual blues songstress. No matter the role, however, the fat Black woman's body was typically framed as the antithesis of appropriate white femininity and thus fetishized for its exotic excesses.

Figure 5.4 Portrait of Gertrude "Ma" Rainey (1923). Donaldson Collection/Getty Images.

As bell hooks argues, because it is not desirable in the conventional sense, the Black female body only gains attention in white America "when it is synonymous with accessibility, availability; when it is sexually deviant."[95] In her performances, Rainey knowingly fulfilled these stereotypes in lyrics that broached taboo subjects ranging from female desire to homosexuality, as well as in her bodily comportment and manner of dress.[96] Yet, whereas fat white performers could amplify these deviant traits on stage and, to a certain extent, retreat to modes of acceptable feminine embodiment off the stage—as, for instance, Sophie Tucker, who could "un-black" herself at the conclusion of her shows or publicly renounce her title as "The Last of the Red Hot Mamas"—there was no comparable escape for Black performers (fat, female, or otherwise) who bore the weight of white racism on a daily basis, while also having to navigate the expectations of respectable self-presentation within the context of a rapidly changing social and cultural landscape.

Ma Rainey was but one among the millions of African Americans who left the rural South during the 1910s and 1920s in search of better lives and livelihoods during the first Great Migration. In doing so, they traded the most malicious manifestations of racism and white supremacy in the South for cultural, political, and economic opportunities in cosmopolitan northern cities where urban Black populations more than doubled between 1920 and 1930.[97] Chicago in particular proved to be something of a magnet for singers and instrumentalists, making the city a jazz-and-blues hub rivalled only by New York City. Seeking to capitalize on the growing popularity of the blues, a number of Black- and white-owned record labels were founded in Chicago during this period, including Paramount Records with whom Rainey recorded over ninety-two tracks between 1923 and 1928.[98] It is in these bustling northern metropolises that African Americans like Ma Rainey created prosperous new lives, but also carved out spaces for themselves within the context of emergent cultural industries such as music, film, literature, and mass spectator sports. With its roots in slave spirituals and West African musical traditions, the blues in particular were an important medium for the exploration and expression of modern Black identity.[99] So too, however, was consumer culture.

According to Davarian L. Baldwin, the mass consumer marketplace was a crucial site of Black self-determination in the 1920s—one that enabled African Americans to seek out "race-based cooperative and capitalist strategies as possible solutions toward autonomy and self-control."[100] For all the freedoms the objects of consumer culture afforded African Americans in reimagining the parameters and possibilities of modern Black identity, however, self-presentation remained a contested subject. Older generations and some intellectual circles held tightly to the notion that African Americans should dress and behave in such a manner so as to communicate modesty, temperance, thrift, and subservience, or what Evelyn Brooks Higginbotham has called "the politics of respectability."[101] Eager to cast off these constraints, however, many southern transplants turned to the mass marketplace in pursuit of more exuberant and individualistic expressions of Black prosperity, intellectualism, and artistry. They were guided by the ideology of the "New Negro" movement, which encompassed a number of goals and strategies in the struggle for civil rights, as well as more diffuse ideas about racial uplift and Black identity that transcended politics and entered the wider realm of consumer culture.[102]

For African American women, beauty and fashion were two privileged sites in which they participated in this process. As Laila Haidarali has argued, beauty provided an important public terrain for women to reimagine race representations within a largely male-dominated movement.[103] By purchasing makeup and haircare products—such as those created by America's first self-made female millionaire, Madam C.J. Walker—Black women were engaging in very modern conceptions of self-fashioning, which only two decades prior would have been deemed inappropriate.[104] While hair-straightening products and skin-whitening solutions were ostensibly used in the service of diminishing the appearance of Blackness, Shane and Graham White argue that it was more so the case that Black women wanted the same freedoms to construct their self-identities as their white counterparts. Artificially made-up faces and bobbed, dyed hair were not, they argue, inept attempts to imitate white beauty standards. Rather, Black women undertook these beauty regimens in the service of distancing themselves from those practiced by their mothers and grandmothers, which foregrounded naturalness and were steeped in outmoded ideas about propriety and racial uplift.[105] No less important, however, was the simple desire, shared by many young Black women, to participate in the marketplace as fully fledged consumer-citizens.

Although frequently overlooked in the literature, fashion, too, was an important political realm for Black women within the context of the Great Migration and the Harlem Renaissance. "When Black women adopted the popular styles of the flapper in the 1920s," writes Einav Rabinovitch-Fox, "they made claims to be included as equals in mainstream culture, defying gender, race and class hierarchies of power."[106] All of the hallmarks of the "flapper" or "garçonne" style—including shorter hemlines, straight silhouettes, and uncorseted waists—conveyed the same messages on the bodies of Black women as they did on their white counterparts: that the wearer was stylish, modern, and, perhaps more than anything, free. Yet, freedom did not mean the same thing to Black women as it did within the context of white articulations of the liberated New Woman. For Black women, fashion was not just a medium of sexual and self-expression. It was also essential in combating racism, promoting integration, and claiming their equal place in American society and consumer culture.[107]

For blues songstresses at the vanguard of Black modernity, streamlined shifts and chemise gowns were essential styles that were torn from the pages of the white fashion press, but which were transformed on Black bodies. As Alphonso McClendon writes, these styles permitted maximum freedom of movement, but also freedom of expression. With their large, uninterrupted expanses of fabric, they were ripe for extravagant embellishment—from sequins, to feathers, to fur trimmings.[108] Historically, Black women had suffered from a lack of access to fashion due to financial constraints and because they were not perceived by white manufacturers and advertisers as a viable consumer group. Beyond constraining Black women's ability to dress how they liked, this historic lack of access to fashion contributed to the effacement of Black womanhood and provided a moral rationale for racism and discrimination.[109] With the freedom and anonymity afforded by northern metropolises, however, Black women seized the opportunity to direct more of their disposable income to fashion, employing it as both a political and expressive medium. The flamboyance of the blues singers' dresses should therefore be understood not just as a conspicuous display of their wealth and success but as part of a strategy to reject bodily regimes that had been historically imposed upon them by whites and by white consumer culture.[110] By the 1920s, the highly embellished shift had thus become a quintessential facet of the glamorous blues aesthetic and was worn by stars including Mamie Smith, Alberta Hunter, and Bessie Smith, among others. Although she was both older and larger than many of her fellow blues singers, this style was preferred by Ma Rainey, too.

In a 1924 portrait photograph depicting Rainey and her backing band, the Rabbit Foot Minstrels, for instance, she wears a floor-length shift, which she pairs with a beaded "headache band" and an ostrich plume fan (Figure 5.5). In a departure from the more streamlined, restrained versions promoted in the pages of magazines like *Vogue* and *Harper's Bazaar*—and perhaps best exemplified by Chanel's austere 1926 "Ford" gown rendered in humble wool jersey—Rainey's silk chiffon gown is heavily adorned with sequins and beads arranged in a geometric pattern that evokes both art deco

Figure 5.5 Portrait of Gertrude "Ma" Rainey and her band (1924). Redferns/Getty Images.

aesthetics and the "Egyptomania" craze that swept America after the discovery of King Tutankhamen's tomb in 1922. In addition to tapping into the ideology of the liberated New Woman and evolving ideas about Black modernity within the context of the New Negro movement, Rainey's gown reflects what McClendon interprets as blues singers' affinity for Egyptian motifs as a way to acknowledge the genre's African roots.[111]

While there are less than a dozen surviving photographs of Ma Rainey, a number of illustrated Paramount advertisements similarly depict her as a thoroughly modern, fashion-conscious woman. Different from her somewhat stilted studio portraits, however, in these advertisements Rainey is depicted wearing even more revealing and, one could argue, more modern dress styles. In one for her 1927 song, "Dead Drunk Blues," for example, she wears a sleeveless black chemise cinched at the waist with a simple white bow (Figure 5.6), while in another for her 1928 album, "Ma Rainey's Black Bottom," she wears a similar dress but rendered in white (Figure 5.7). Although simpler than the heavily adorned shift she wore in her 1924 portrait with her band, these gowns are more in keeping with the streamlined, "boyish" aesthetics that had so come to define women's fashion by the mid-1920s. Interestingly, however, the dresses are perhaps the least notable thing about these compositions. Rather, it is Rainey's bodily comportment that likely would have been the first thing to catch readers' eyes. Lifting her skirt to reveal a glimpse of her plump thighs, in one illustration she can be seen, according to the caption, "black-bottoming around those mean trombones and clarinets" as she would in her raucous live performances. In the other, a "dead drunk" Rainey dances on a table while hoisting a champagne coupe over her head as three tuxedo-clad men look on in amusement—a rowdy scene that the advertising copy reveals was plucked from real life. As the embodiment of the "Black flapper," Rainey rejoices in both her social and sartorial freedoms, while at the same time testing the limits of respectability politics. As scandalous as they may have been to some audiences, however, images such as these established female blues singers as the glamorous standard-bearers of the new, liberated ideal.[112] Different from other mainstream depictions of the Black flapper, however, Rainey was a highly unlikely fashion and beauty icon. Rather, with her dark skin, coarse hair, and large body, she stood in stark contrast to ideals promoted in Black beauty pageants and in the Black press. Just as the blues were, as Zandria Robinson writes, full of "paradox and contradiction,"[113] so too was Ma Rainey—a figure who resisted staid notions of idealized femininity not only through her self-fashioning practices and sexually charged song lyrics but through her deviant embodiment, too.

Historically, fatness has been more widely accepted within African Diasporic communities than in white mainstream culture. In African American communities specifically, larger bodies tend to be associated with power and abundance, rather than with disorder. As a number of scholars have observed, the greater tolerance for fat within the African Diaspora can be attributed to a number of factors, including the distinctive power and position of women as matriarchs, skepticism around mainstream diet culture, culinary traditions, and the historical legacies of loss and scarcity.[114] During the first Great Migration and with the rise of a distinctly Black consumer culture, however, a new beauty ideal emerged. Paralleling similar shifts within white beauty culture, by

Figure 5.6 Advertisement for Gertrude "Ma" Rainey's EP "Dead Drunk Blues," (1927). Pictorial Press Ltd./Alamy.

the 1920s, many popular Black female vaudeville performers, models, and beauty queens were thin, youthful, and light-skinned.[115] Even as African American fashion and beauty authorities—from fashion journalists to beauty pageant judges—claimed to be more inclusive of the "many types of Colored beauty" (as was claimed in a 1921 beauty pageant advertisement in the *Chicago Defender*), those with light skin and refined, anglicized features tended to be heralded as the most beautiful to the extent that they were the ones whose images were featured in advertisements and on cosmetics labels.[116] Although less of an emphasis was placed on weight within Black beauty culture—for excess weight was still permissible in African American life even if it wasn't elevated as an ideal per se—even a cursory examination of cosmetic and beauty pageant advertisements published in the Black press reveals that the ideal was almost universally slender, too. With their smart, bobbed haircuts and sleek dresses that skimmed over slender physiques, Rabinovitch-Fox argues that commercialized images of Black flappers "[moved] beyond traditional images of motherhood and devotion," and, in doing so, "conveyed messages of freedom, equality and modernity."[117] The new, more slender ideal that was promoted within

Figure 5.7 Advertisement for Gertrude "Ma" Rainey's EP "Ma Rainey's Black Bottom," (1928). Pictorial Press Ltd./Alamy.

Black beauty culture therefore functioned as a model of modern Black identity to the extent that it supplanted stereotypical and racist representations such as the subservient, maternal, and curvaceous "Mammy," which remained all too pervasive in mainstream advertising and popular culture.

Although there is evidence that Ma Rainey at least partially tried to conform to this ideal by, for instance, wearing heavy skin-lightening makeup that by some accounts gave her a ghoulish pallor underneath the bright stage lights,[118] by and large, she resided at the margins of both Black and white femininity. In the context of her performances, however, Rainey existed within a privileged space—one in which both fatness and Blackness were more permissible, if not celebrated. Andrea Elizabeth Shaw argues that not unlike fat white singers and actresses who performed in the aggrandized mode on America's minstrel and vaudeville stages in the early twentieth century, fat Black performers fulfilled the nation's collective, if racist, "yearning to free itself from imperatives of 'appropriate' cultural conduct," which in the case of female blues singers manifested in and through their hyper-sexualization.[119] As mentioned previously, Rainey's lyrics were highly suggestive and rife with sexual innuendo; however, this fact alone does not quite illuminate the reasons for her enormous popularity among both Black and white audiences. Rather, it was the powerful combination of her subversive lyrics, her glamorous self-fashioning, and her physicality that endeared her to audiences. Indeed, Rainey's rise to fame coincided with crucial shifts in popular and consumer culture that permitted her image to be strategically employed to promote her music, making it next-to-impossible to separate her image from her raw talents as a singer and songwriter.[120] If anything, her rule-breaking fashion choices were an essential facet of her commercial success. Key examples of this are previously discussed advertisements in which Rainey's skin-bearing chemise dresses function as sartorial shorthand by designating her a fully modern, liberated woman. This does not mean, however, her self-fashioning was perceived in the same way by white and Black audiences.

For white audiences, her fashion choices would have likely been interpreted within the limited, and racist, frameworks of minstrelsy wherein white performers like Sophie Tucker strategically employed dress purely for comedic effect, rather than in an attempt to look beautiful or composed. Within this context, Rainey's glamorous stage gowns would have been narrowly understood as a form of class and race masquerade—the fat Black woman trying, and failing, to imitate white beauty norms. Among Black audiences, however, Bogle argues, very much in spite of her weight and dark skin,

> Ma Rainey would have best represented the Black woman out to glorify herself, dressing up and stepping high, the "average" Black woman emerging onstage as the sophisticated, experienced woman of color determined to live high …. Her very look announced she was a queen, ready to flaunt her success in a world that had said no such thing was possible.[121]

The blues were an inherently subversive musical genre, and Rainey's deviant physicality and incongruous modes of self-fashioning—through which she patently rejected many of the rules passed down from white beauty culture that demanded austerity and restraint—cemented her status as both a provocateur and an icon. Indeed, as Maxine Leeds Craig writes, "African Americans have ceaselessly reinterpreted dominant culture. They have contested and revised the social meanings of Black racial identity through spectacles, protests and daily acts of self-presentation."[122] In her own self-fashioning, Rainey both adopted and reimagined the Black flapper ideal and, in doing so, became a beauty and fashion icon to audiences who perhaps looked more like her than the slender, light-skinned women who were heralded as beauty icons in the magazines. Rainey's body was thus a site of resistance wherein the possibilities of Black female embodiment were expanded beyond the narrow ideals that circulated within Black beauty culture, and upon which the aesthetics of respectability were cast aside in order to make way for more modern expressions of both Blackness and fatness.

***

This chapter opened with a definition of self-fashioning, provided by Joanne Entwistle, which framed it as a practice that is as intimate as it is social. As she observes, the everyday act of getting dressed is a highly personal one occurring on the surface of the body, but which is always performed within the context of culture and, specifically, in response to and in dialogue with the particular matrix of norms and customs that are imposed on individual bodies by that culture.[123] By its very nature, dress is always a limited and *limiting* medium of expression that materializes the social pressures that are brought to bear on bodies; however, these pressures are not universal, nor do they affect all bodies in the same way.

As has been demonstrated throughout this book, for instance, the fat female body was a particular target of early twentieth-century weight bias. From female-focused diet ads, to the emergent cult of slenderness, to the limitations of standardized clothes sizing, to be fat was to be relegated to the margins of both social and aesthetic acceptability. Well-meaning as they may have been, authors of style advice discourses—many of whom were fat themselves—further perpetuated weight bias and beauty norms by framing getting dressed as a perilous act singularly performed in the service of bringing the body more in line with culturally sanctioned ideals of appropriate femininity. At the end of the day, however, advice discourses were just that: *advice*. Although prescriptions for how to "dress to look slender" were pervasive within fashion media discourses, it was ultimately up to fat women to adopt, amend, or outright ignore these directives.

Investigations into how fat women navigated this fraught terrain have largely been absent in the fashion studies literature due in part to how challenging it is to locate personal testimonies that detail the exceedingly mundane, everyday practices of shopping and getting dressed. Here, however, I explored the sartorial biographies of three self-identifying fat women—Jane Warren Wells, Sophie Tucker, and Gertrude "Ma" Rainey—in order to shed light on how they performed socially constructed identities (and namely that of "the fat woman") in and through fashion. Specifically, I was interested in uncovering how they navigated the precepts of "dressing to look slender" in order to better understand how real women were affected by and implicated within the discursive regimes of power that rendered their bodies disruptive to the social order.

As the "everywoman," or an exemplar of the demographic targeted by most stoutwear, beauty, and diet companies, Jane Warren Wells was perhaps most susceptible to the expectations of appropriate dress as it was she who was most beholden to the expectations of white, middle-class femininity. Although Sophie Tucker and Gertrude "Ma" Rainey—as respectively fat, Jewish, and Black—perhaps resided farther outside the margins of normative feminine embodiment, their professions allowed them to circulate within privileged performative spaces wherein both fatness and exuberant sartorial displays were not only permissible but celebrated. As public figures, they were also given a platform to imagine new, more radical modes of feminine embodiment, thereby fortifying their status as fat feminist icons. Rather than the rule, however, Tucker's and Rainey's sartorial biographies are the exception since their ability to more or less dress how they liked was conferred by their enormous celebrity. Certainly, ordinary fat women would not have had the same freedoms of dress. Indeed, in everyday life, as Entwistle observes, "bodies ... that do not conform, bodies which flout the conventions of their culture ... are subversive of the most basic social codes and risk exclusion, scorn or ridicule."[124] Even so, the stories foregrounded here shed light on the important role of individual agency to the practice of self-fashioning, as well as the power of dress in the political project of resignifying fat embodiment.

CONCLUSION

"Stout" has outlived its usefulness as a designation of a type of dress….

There is a certain odium attached to the "stout" designation, that exists among merchandise managers, among buyers, among salesladies and among the consumer. All think back to a time when a "stylish stout" was anything but "stylish." …

Perhaps one of the best recommendations that could be made in this connection is to abandon the term "stout" entirely.[1]

In 1929—only fourteen years after it declared the imminent rise of the stoutwear sector—*Women's Wear* foretold stoutwear's demise. Paraphrasing M.F. Reuben, vice president of the New York-based Ru-Mark dress company, the trade journal remarked that the term "stout" had entirely "outlived its usefulness." While Reuben conceded elsewhere in the article that "of course, stout dresses have been developed more and more [and] the styling has improved greatly," customers had seemingly cooled to the novelty of being able to "get garments that would fit properly in the larger sizes [without caring] particularly whether the styling was conspicuously good or not."[2] More than that, however, he chalked up the slowing of the trade to the fact that stylish stouts were, in actuality, "anything but 'stylish.'"

Along with a collective of other stoutwear manufacturers, Reuben therefore sought to enact the "abolishment of a classification that [seemed] to have lost its usefulness, and to attempt to get a reasonable share of the regular size women's dress business."[3] A 1930 article also published in *Women's Wear* somewhat hyperbolically declared the industry's final death knell. Quoting William Hendricks, a veteran stoutwear manufacturer, the trade journal "reached the conclusion that there are no stout women."[4] According to Hendricks, this was due to the growing popularity of "Hollywood diets," new fads in exercise among American women, and, perhaps most importantly, the new, increasingly body-conscious fashions that "condemned curves" once and for all.[5]

While good for headlines, these sensational claims would prove, however, to be overstated. First and foremost, fat women did not simply "cease to exist" in 1930. Second, a number of stoutwear manufacturers continued to produce stoutwear well into the 1930s and beyond, albeit under different names. Not least of these was Lane Bryant, which pivoted to manufacture and sell so-called "junior plenty" and "chubby" garments to teens and young women during midcentury, and, beginning in the 1980s, "plus-sizes."[6] What the above articles did get right, however, was the fact that the fashion landscape in the United States had undergone a dramatic evolution between the 1920s and 1930s, as too had the culture of beauty, weight loss, and dieting. No longer could women expect to hide their excess flesh within the roomy folds of the more revealing but generously cut tubular dresses that were popular in the 1920s. With the effects of the Great Depression disrupting every facet of American life, clothes in the 1930s were themselves reflections leaner times, both literally and figuratively. As Caroline Rennolds Milbank has observed, "For the first part of the 1930s figures were almost emaciated [and therefore] clothes were narrow, long, and spare," or "simple to the extreme."[7]

Within this context, and specifically with regard to fashion, fatness had gone from being a burden that could be variously hidden or reshaped with dress to being utterly intolerable as the rift between fat and thin grew wider. As the science of "obesity" was becoming progressively sophisticated and as more drugs and cures emerged to combat overweight, fat people found themselves under even greater scrutiny.[8] More so than in previous decades, fat was a signifier of one's failings as a citizen, or what Georges Vigarello describes as a manifestation of one's "dereliction of duty ... at a time when working on oneself and adaptability [became] obligatory criteria of value."[9] Although she did not disappear—for every era has its fat woman even though conceptions of "normal" and "overweight" are constantly in flux—the stout woman found herself in eclipse, relegated once again to the margins of fashionability.

As a result of these changing circumstances, the stoutwear business—at least as it had been known—would slowly cease to exist. Under the leadership of M.F. Reuben, most of the remaining stoutwear manufactures reorganized their businesses to focus on the standard-size trade, while *Women's Wear* concurrently discontinued its "Styles for Larger Women" insert, which throughout the 1920s reported weekly upon goings on within the stoutwear sector. With no industry leaders championing the trade, the large-size dress sector quietly fell into decline. This would be to the detriment of the fat woman who in this new era was no longer an object or subject of fashion, let alone a "project" for enterprising industrialists. Options in the way of truly fashionable large-size garments were already relatively limited in the 1920s, but by the 1930s, manufacturers had all but abandoned their claims of melding fit with fashionability.

It wouldn't be until the 1980s that a new crop of designers, both in Europe and the United States, would turn their attention to the newly discovered and underserved "plus-size" market.[10] If there's one thing that can be gleaned with hindsight, it is that the fashion industry's interest in the fat woman ebbs and flows both with the market and with prevailing opinions about fat in American society—and thus the extent to which the fat woman is regarded as a viable "business opportunity." Indeed, as in the early twentieth century, the renewed interest the fat woman and her sartorial needs in the 1980s was, at least in part, the result of an increase in production capacity. Rather than the expansion of American industry and manufacturing, however, it was the possibilities of globalization and offshoring that had manufacturers in search of new markets. After a relatively quiet period between the 1990s and early 2000s—a period that notably coincided with the "heroin chic" aesthetic—the industry would again seek to bring the fat woman into fashion's proverbial folds in the 2010s. This was partly due to social media, and specifically the demands being made by fat activists and "fatshionistas," but also due to a strengthening economy and to the speeding up of the global fashion system.[11]

Fashion's Slenderness Imperative

After a decade of steady growth, in 2021, *Women's Wear Daily* reported that sales of plus-size clothing accounted for 19 percent, or $21.6 billion, of all women's apparel sales in the United States. More than that, the trade publication noted that it was one of the few sectors of the global fashion industry experiencing year-over-year growth.[12] The plus-size sector's remarkable turnaround over the last decade has, in no small measure, been propelled by the rise of fast fashion (and therefore a reduction in the cost of producing garments), but also by the growing number of American women who, according to industry standards, classify as plus-size. Although there persists a popular misperception that plus-size women comprise the minority—one that is, at least in part, fueled by lack of representation in fashion media and within retail spaces—a 2017 study published by Deborah Christel and Susan Dunn found that over sixty-seven percent of American women are, at least by industry standards, plus-size and that on average they wear a size sixteen, placing them solidly past the threshold between standard- and plus-sizes.[13]

Yet, in spite of the plus-size sector's impressive performance in recent years, there remains a clear discrepancy in the data. If two-thirds of American women are plus-size, shouldn't their patronage comprise greater than a nineteen percent share of the women's apparel market? One thing is for certain, plus-size fashion's relatively underwhelming performance (at least compared to the actual percentage of fat women) is not due to a lack of demand. As a number of researchers have found, the reason that fat women aren't buying plus-size clothes has more to do with a simple lack of choice. In addition to feeling underserved, fat women have cited retail discrimination, poor fits, and underwhelming aesthetics as reasons why they haven't been consuming plus-sizes with greater zeal.[14] Rather than providing opportunities for self-expression and identity formation, Calla Evans observes that the options afforded to fat women, especially at the larger end of the size spectrum, only serve to "remarginalize an already marginalized group" while fortifying the boundaries of "appropriate" or "desirable" fatness.[15]

Although it was a relatively short-lived phase in the longer history of plus-size fashion, and in spite of the massive convulsions that have reshaped fashion manufacturing over the preceding 100 years—from offshoring, to fast fashion, to automation—the legacies of stoutwear continue to dictate fashion practices and inform debates about what, we've come to learn, is a not-so-niche sector. The recent conversations being had about how to label large-size garments (and namely whether or not these labels have outlived their usefulness) and the controversies swirling around the segregation of large sizes in separate departments have clear origins in the early twentieth century. Questions about representation, especially at the intersections of race and ethnicity, in plus-size marketing and advertising materials can similarly be traced back over a century and specifically to the racist and xenophobic beliefs that shaped early twentieth-century beauty ideals and, particularly, notions of what constituted an "appropriately" American body. Perhaps more than anything, however, it is the design discourses of stoutwear that continue to shape and, I argue, constrain industry practice.

While throughout this book I have not made an argument for unbroken cultural and discursive continuities between stoutwear and contemporary plus-size fashion, I have set out to trace the first stirrings of the very particular complex of ideas, practices and biases that gave rise to stoutwear, and which continue to reverberate in the present. The goal of this search for "reverberations" and "conditions of emergence" was steeped in my desire to better understand why plus-size fashion remains such a contested terrain and to demonstrate that the fashion industry's elevation of the slender ideal has had broader implications for the ways about which fatness, especially on the bodies of women, is thought in American culture. While it has been claimed elsewhere that fashion was but a "small part" of the broader constellation of factors that gave rise to modern weight bias in the early twentieth century, this book has established that fashion—more than just reflecting cultural attitudes, biases, and beliefs—was actually one of its central engines.

Although the idea for a specialized large-size garment sector separate from mainstream ready-to-wear had seemingly altruistic origins, in their attempts to solve the problem of poor fit, stoutwear manufacturers imposed new, albeit slightly enlarged, standards that allowed the contours of deviant fatness to be seen and measured with greater clarity. Stoutwear sizing systems drew upon old ways of cutting and grading garments, which were themselves based on a romantic conception of an "ideal" or "normal" body and tapped into the rationalizing impulses of scientific management in the vein of trying to reduce waste and improve efficiency. Yet, with its unpredictable curves that stood in stark contrast to the streamlined aesthetics of modernity, the fat body revealed itself as a pressure point within this system. Thus, rather than designing for the individual fat body and all of its perceived flaws, stoutwear manufacturers designed with a *stout ideal* in mind.

It is not an overstatement to suggest that the stoutwear industry was built on the bedrocks of weight bias. Whether by physical means, such as reshaping the body with slenderizing and fat-melting undergarments, through the application of optical illusions to make the body merely appear smaller, or by simply rendering the fat woman's garments plainer in style and ornamentation than those designed for her slender counterpart, these methods revealed a deeply entrenched bias or *slenderness imperative* within stoutwear design discourse that not only impacted the construction of garments for larger women but affected design aesthetics, too.

Stoutwear design discourses furthered the notion that there was a correct way to inhabit a fat body. As it appeared within and was discussed across the fashion media in the early twentieth century, the idealized fat body was streamlined and contained. It was a big body at least when compared to the sylph-like bodies that appeared elsewhere in the fashion media, but it was one that was exceptionally clean, quiet, and had no flesh out of place. More than anything though, it was a body that evinced the time, resources, and energy that went into its care and maintenance—namely in the pursuit of achieving a slender appearance. While Paolo Volonté has argued that the thin ideal both perpetuated within fashion media discourses and materialized through the design of garments has left little room for the fat body in fashion, the place that fat bodies occupy within the fashion system is perhaps rather more ambivalent.[16] As has been demonstrated throughout this book, it is not so much that fat fashion was "nonexistent," as Volonté provocatively suggests, but rather that the basic principles undergirding the design and manufacture of large-size dress emanated from a different set of assumptions, concerns, and beliefs. Rather than being guided by trends or the creative the whims of designers, slenderizing continues to be one of the central organizing pillars around which design and self-fashioning decisions are made. In practice, this manifests not just in the notion, so prevalent in Western society, that one is improperly dressed if their clothing enhances rather than hides fleshy bulges; the ideology of slenderness is also sewn into the very fabric of garments.

This impulse can clearly be glimpsed in the conceptualization and execution of Lane Bryant's T3 denim, which launched in early 2019. Short for "Tighter Tummy Technology," T3 jeans featured panels of tightly woven mesh fabric sewn into the pockets and around the waistline to "keep the tummy under wraps" while "sculpting and smoothing every curve." As explained in the design patent, the jeans were meant to eliminate the "need" to wear reshaping undergarments like Spanx by making a "smooth transition to the wearer's body above the waistline" and eliminating "unsightly bulging" both above and below the waistband (Figure C.1). Continuing, the patent authors explain how

> Women who are abdominous or broad in their gluteus maximus area or just have a plus-size figure often wish to appear slimmer without relying upon uncomfortable foundation garments or bodysuit shapewear. They also want to wear fashionable pants garments made of stretch fabrics such as jeans made out of denim blended with elastic fibers without displaying unsightly bulging …
>
> There is thus a need for garments that are fashionable and capable of substantially slimming the wearer's appearance.[17]

While naturalizing the idea that most, if not all, fat people desire to appear slimmer, the patent also foregrounds slenderizing technology as an essential facet of large-size clothing design. Framed here as a "need," the patent authors argue that there is a noted gap in the market for garments that "substantially" alter the wearer's physique. The patent concludes by noting how the technology, which successfully eliminates the "undesirable muffin top" and "helps slim the wearer's appearance," is both a novel and "particularly important contribution [to fashion]." The patent authors' desire to intervene in the body by smoothing out "unsightly" bulges is, of course, not without precedent. Throughout this book, and especially in Chapter 2, I explored how stoutwear manufacturers endeavored to alter the fat woman's physique through "scientifically" designed garments in order to effect a slender and stylish appearance. Although the T3 patent authors claim theirs is a new and novel invention—so much so that it merits patent protection—this book has demonstrated that the fashion industry's stigmatization of fat has deep roots.

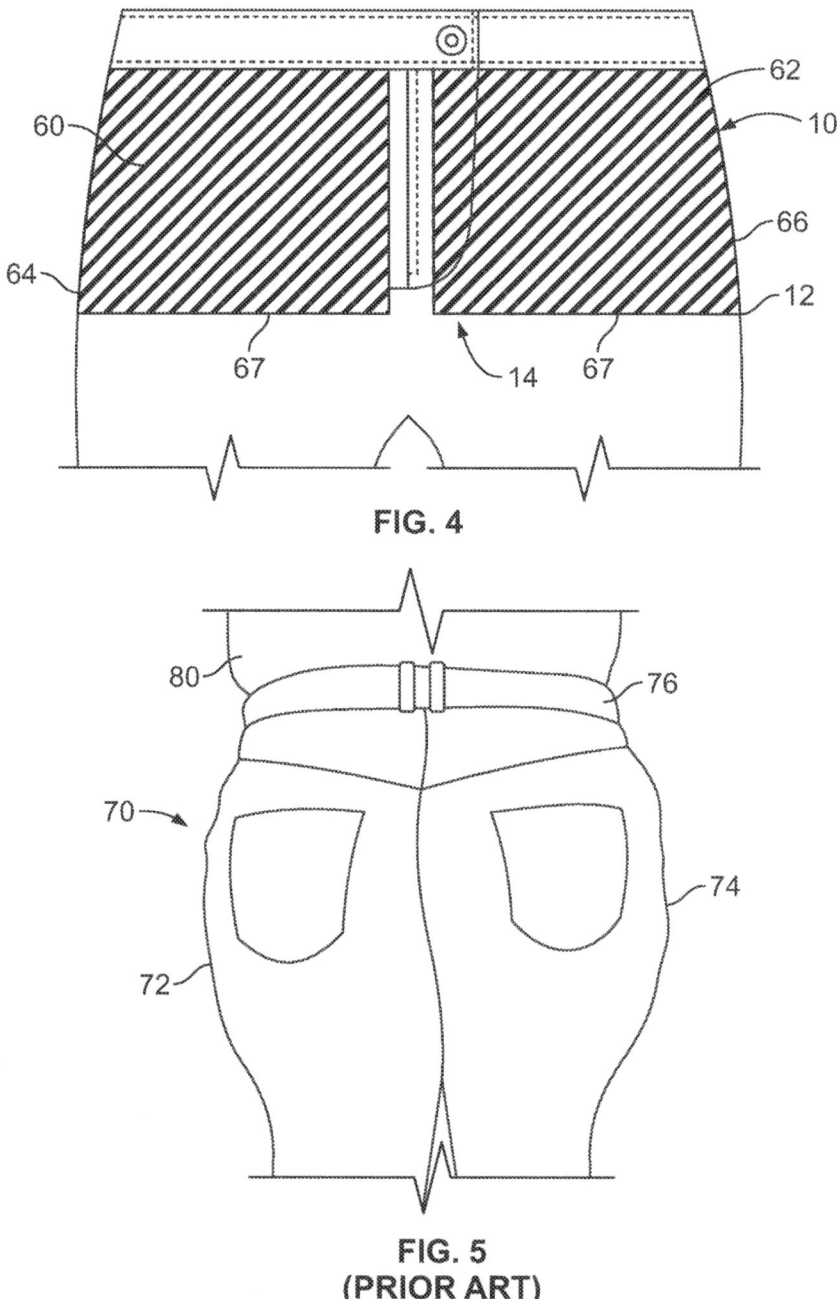

FIG. 4

FIG. 5
(PRIOR ART)

Figure C.1 Richard Zellinski, Illustration from US Patent No. 201301145516A1 for Slimming Garments (2011).

The impulse—so evident within both historical and contemporary large-size garment design discourses—to correct the perceived flaws of the fat physique recalls Mary Douglas' contention that bodily margins are "thought to be specially invested with power and danger."[18] Bodies that are leaky, malformed, or otherwise non-normative (e.g., the pregnant body, the sick body, or the fat body) are powerful symbols of disorder and uncleanliness in Western thought. Fat, as Richard Klein has written, is a particularly potent form of pollution—a kind of "cancerous growth … inessential to the body or its image."[19] Within this context, the natural response to such bodily disorder has been to impart order.

Separating body shapes into "standard" and "non-standard" categories as through the conventions of sizing is one means of doing so. Dress aesthetics buttress these categories by making the fleshy, "pre-cultural" body fit for the social world. Indeed, clothing effectively completes the body within societies that demand that bodies be properly dressed. Yet, as has been established, dress is more than the flimsy barrier between the self and society. As a materialization of cultural values, dress makes bodies legible. This is true for the slender beauty ideal as much as it is for its abject Other: the fat body. Fashion's slenderness imperative may therefore be understood as a disciplinary mechanism to the extent that it simultaneously naturalizes slenderness as the preferred mode of human embodiment—as well as the foundation for contemporary fashion design practice—while also stigmatizing fat. As this slenderness imperative is materialized in garments, it can bring fat bodies more in line with the thin ideal either through physical means (as is the case with the T3 denim or, in an earlier era, reducing corsets) or by merely hiding or camouflaging the points at which the fat body deviates from the norm.

Whereas stoutwear manufacturers were forthright in their ambitions to alter, and therefore improve, fat women's physiques—as, for instance, through their use of lofty language borrowed from the fields of architecture and Gestalt psychology—today the slenderness imperative manifests in more subtle and, one could argue, more insidious ways. With the rise of the Body Positivity Movement over the last two decades—a grassroots movement that was largely born within feminist blogging communities in the late twentieth century, but which has since been co-opted by fashion and beauty conglomerates from Dove soap to Lane Bryant—retailers are increasingly reluctant to explicitly market their wares as "beautifying" or "slenderizing."[20] These terms have therefore been replaced with the neoliberal discourses of "self-care."[21] While a nascent rhetoric of self-care can clearly be glimpsed in the self-fashioning advice discourses discussed in Chapters 4 and 5, in the twenty-first century, women are no longer urged to pursue an illusory, normativizing, and singular feminine ideal through their dress practices; rather, they are told to cultivate the best possible iterations of themselves and to define beauty on their own terms.

In the marketing of plus-size fashion, but also within popular plus-size fashion and style guides since the 1990s, this notion has manifested in and through the construct of "figure flattery," or the idea that clothing should complement, rather than compete with, a woman's curves. This is different from how self-care and self-love discourses are used within fat acceptance communities where they retain some of their political potency.

In particular, the precept of "radical self-love," or the idea that women should not only embrace but also flaunt their fleshy tummies and expose their cellulite by wearing tight, colorful, and revealing garments, has been embraced by "fatshion" communities, which have also reclaimed "fat" as a neutral descriptor.[22] While mainstream figure flattery discourses are similarly couched in the empowering notion that every body is a "good body" and that a woman can look good in the skin she's in, so to speak, they nevertheless uphold the hegemony of white, Western beauty ideals—or at least the vague notion that all women should aspire to *feel* beautiful—and perpetuates the idea that the body is an object of compulsory self-surveillance and routinized body maintenance. More than that, however, figure flattery discourses further the notion that there are both acceptable and unacceptable ways to not merely dress as a fat woman, but to inhabit a fat body. Although the standards for what constitutes the fat feminine ideal have perhaps expanded over the last century, commercial plus-size fashion, not unlike stoutwear, continues to promote a controlled, sanitized, and limited vision of fat female embodiment.

Although important inroads have been made in the plus-size sector in recent years, namely in terms of its unprecedented growth (especially with mainstream brands expanding their size ranges) and market valuation, this boom period (like all the others) will prove to be short-lived unless designers and manufacturers significantly reevaluate their design and manufacturing practices. Indeed, the spectacular rise and fall of Old Navy's "Bodequality" initiative in 2021—a widely publicized effort made by the brand to offer all styles in all sizes for the same price both in store and online—may be a bellwether for an industry that is already showing signs of strain, and which also seems to be moving past the trendy optics of inclusivity. While analysts are still trying to parse out where, exactly, Old Navy went wrong, initial reports suggest that poor fits and faulty size distribution ratios are largely to blame.[23] These findings indicate that Old Navy did not know who precisely their consumers were, nor did the company have a firm grasp on the fat woman's particular fit needs. Like many brands, they were operating within narrow constraints of accepted knowledge, which, as this book has demonstrated, has its origins in early twentieth-century fashion design practice. Because these frameworks are steeped in conceptions of the normal or ideal body, any efforts to reform or revolutionize plus-size design are doomed to fail. What is therefore required is a wholesale revisioning of conventional design wisdom. Rather than taking the standard or slender body as a starting point, what happens when fat people—as both producers and wearers of fashion—are centered?

What follows is not a conventional way to end an academic monograph to the extent that it does not offer a summary of the main points of this book, nor does it identify pathways for future research. For some readers this might be frustrating or confusing, especially given the extent to which I lay bare my social political and agendas in these final pages; however, as a self-identifying fat and fashion activist, as well as an educator who is tasked with training the designers of tomorrow, I feel compelled to offer if not a solution the problems identified in the preceding pages, then a call to action. Following Ben Barry and Deborah Christel's call for fashion studies scholars to use their platforms to "create a more just fashion industry and world" and to imagine "radically inclusive fashion systems,"[24] with the following provocation I encourage readers to use their learnings from this book to advocate for significant, systemic change within an industry that has for too long Othered and marginalized fat consumers in the vein of upholding fashion's slenderness imperative.

A Provocation: Toward an Epistemology of "Fat Clothes"

As calls for greater inclusivity in the fashion industry have become more urgent in recent years, some designers have come to recognize the aesthetic and creative limitations of fashion's slenderness imperative. Becca McCharen-Tran, founder of the gender fluid, queer, and size-inclusive design studio, CHROMAT, is one designer who has quickly made a name for herself with her innovative swim- and sportswear. Trained as an architect, McCharen-Tran is interested in exploring the intersections of architecture, fashion, and technology. Her studio produces garments that "augment and enhance the body's performance" and which are radically inclusive in their embrace of "different versions of beautiful."[25] McCharen-Tran became the darling of New York Fashion Week after her Spring 2015 collection, *Formula 15*, in which plus-size model Denise Bidot opened the show in an avant-garde, architectural black cage ensemble that loosely recalled eighteenth- and nineteenth-century panniers and crinolines (Figure C.2). Different from how these historic garments would have been worn, however, Bidot did not wear cumbersome petticoats and overskirts on top of the cage structure to create the illusion of a transformed silhouette. Her tanned thighs clearly visible through the graphic windows created by black spandex and plastic boning, McCharen-Tran's design called attention to the body underneath the garments, while also opening up possibilities to radically rethink the ways that garments could enhance, rather than diminish, the fat physique. A wearable work of art as much as a statement on the artifice and artificiality of dress, the garment was more concept-driven than it was functional in its critique of orthodox foundation garments designed to compress and reshape the body. This moment was truly a first in the world of plus-size fashion, which historically has favored ready-to-wear functionality over the fantasy of the high fashion runway.

While CHROMAT exists on one end of the design spectrum—that which includes conceptual, experimental, and couture design—Universal Standard is another example of a company that is radically rethinking the practice of designing for the fat woman but through the medium of ordinary, everyday dress. Founded in 2015 by Polina Veksler and Alexandra Waldman, Universal Standard set out to create a retail experience in which a woman who is a size forty could shop in the same way as a size double-zero. Through their innovative pattern grading system, FitLiberty, the technical designers at Universal Standard were able to make garments across their expanded size spectrum that fit all bodies the same, and which, as they write, enable women to shop "without anxiety, fear or regret."[26] While many plus-size retailers still rely upon antiquated and limited sizing conventions that have their origins in the early twentieth century and which established categories of normal and deviant bodies, Universal Standard is seeking to eliminate these categories altogether.

Figure C.2 Denise Bidot walking in CHROMAT fashion show, 2015, *Formula 15*. Getty.

Although the brand has been a favorite among fat consumers for the last half decade, in 2019, the brand began spotlighting size forty women in their advertisements, thereby giving so-called "infinifat" consumers—many of whom were unaccustomed to seeing themselves represented in media—the full glossy editorial fashion treatment.[27] Whereas many plus-size and "curve" retailers favor "mid-size" (US size 12–14) models or, conversely, larger models in slenderizing dress, Universal Standard does not camouflage or diminish the fleshy curves of the fat body through digital retouching or other means. Instead, they foreground fit—that is, their ability to eliminate hallmarks of poor fit, such as gaping and bagging common in much mainstream plus-size apparel—over figure flattery. Further, by including size forty models in their marketing materials, Universal Standard was fulfilling one of the central tenets of fat activism: to create neutral representations of fat embodiment within a media landscape that, historically, has relegated fat bodies to its margins.

Both CHROMAT and Universal Standard operate under the rubric of what I have come to designate as "fat clothes"—or garments that celebrate and flaunt, rather than stigmatize and hide, the fleshy bulges and bumps that stoutwear and plus-size fashion have for so long attempted to control, contain, and camouflage. They also constitute what has come to be known as "inclusive design," a term that has become something of a buzzword as much as a call to action in the fashion industry in recent years. Broadly referring to adaptive, non-gendered, and plus-size fashion, the ethos of size inclusivity aims to level the sartorial playing field by upending fashion's long-standing white, Western, slender-bodied ideal. While size-inclusive design too often frames fat people as the passive recipients of design—or as the unwitting objects of corporate diversity and inclusivity commitments—when done correctly, fat clothes help us to reimagine the relationship between dress and the fat body. An epistemology of fat clothes not only challenges long-standing assumptions about what large-size garments should "do"; it also opens up opportunities to "know" the fat body differently, and thus to redraw the contours of weight bias. Just as fat activists' reclamation of the term "fat" seeks to destigmatize fat embodiment, fat clothes alternately enhance or demonstrate an ambivalence toward the perceived "flaws" of the fat body, rather than fixing them. I argue that fat clothes might enable new paradigms of fat beauty and embodiment through the ways in which they unsettle widely held truths about fat and weight, and pluralize the ways that fat bodies are mediated through dress. Fat clothes, however, are not formulaic or prescriptive. Rather, they are loosely guided by the following seven design principles:

1. Fat clothes flaunt, rather than hide, lumps, bumps, bellies, and cellulite.

2. Fat clothes enable freedom of movement and breath, rather than compressing and constricting parts of the body deemed "too big."

3. Fat clothes reject the tenets of slenderizing and figure flattery, thereby embracing oversized and unconventional silhouettes.

4. Fat clothes are not *fast* clothes. They are created through sustainable, equitable, and enduring modes of production and with regard to the specific fit requirements of the consumer.

5. Fat clothes belong on fashion runways and in museums, rather than in the dark corners of department stores, specialized departments, and clearance racks.

6. Fat clothes are anti-assimilationist to the extent that they embrace the idea that fat consumers are not a monolith and that they should have the same freedoms to fashion unique expressions of identity as slender people.

7. Fat clothes are designed *by fat people* rather than by teams of designers who have not themselves experienced the sting of fat stigma.

More than anything, however, fat clothes present an opportunity to decenter (or "fatten") fashion's slenderness imperative. On the one hand, fat clothes enable fat people to find clothes that *fit their bodies*, rather than requiring them to *fit their bodies to their clothes*. On the other hand, fat clothes encourage multiple modes of embodiment. With an abundance of choice—from fat swimwear to fat couture—fat people are permitted to choose and perform multiple identities, rather than just that of the "fat person." Likewise, by not being hemmed in by the mandates of figure flattery and slenderizing, designers might come to perceive of the fat body not as a design problem but rather as a site of opportunity, experimentation, and play.

Of course, this is only an initial proposal—one with significant shortcomings and limitations. For instance, it is solely focused on design for women's bodies and therefore neglects menswear and nonbinary design. It also only briefly touches upon issues surrounding environmental sustainability. I therefore discourage readers from blindly adopting the tenets presented here and to instead regard them as a provocation. Indeed, different from the old rules of stout and plus-size design, these rules are meant to be broken.

NOTES

Introduction

1. "'Fat Women Hopeless,' Says Poiret—Is He Right?" *The South Bend Tribune* (January 14, 1923): 36.

2. Historian Peter Stearns observes that, in the history of fat stigma in the United States, the 1920s heralded a particularly misogynist phase. This, he argues, was partly a backlash to women's increasing political and social freedoms. See Peter Stearns, *Fat History: Bodies and Beauty in the Modern West* (New York: New York University Press, 1997), 71–7.

3. The publication changed its name to *Women's Wear Daily* on January 3, 1927. See "How Many Fat Women in Your Town?" *Women's Wear* (June 11, 1915): 3.

4. Although it's unclear how manufacturers arrived at this figure, it was repeated often in the trade press. See "Winning the Trade of Stout Women," *Women's Wear* (September 10, 1915): 5, 8.

5. See "Even the 'Freaks' Want to Look 'Nifty," *Women's Wear* (March 26, 1920): 51; "Gigantic Dress Is Never Sold, but Stimulates Sale of Stoutwear," *Women's Wear* (March 6, 1926): 5; Ready for the Big Ones: A New Angle on the Fat Woman's Wants," *Women's Wear* (July 2, 1915): 3.

6. E. McKenna, "Makers of 'Stouts' Band Together for Better Retailing," *Printers' Ink* (September 16, 1920): 154.

7. Carmen Keist, "'The New Costumes of Odd Sizes': Plus Sized Women's Fashions, 1910–1924" (Ph.D. diss., Iowa State University, 2012), 64.

8. "On Her Dressing Table," *Vogue* (July 1, 1918): 78.

9. Not only was stoutwear described as a growth sector, it was also heralded as a time- and labor-saving innovation. See "Garment Built to Figure of Customer Obviates Faulty Alterations," *Women's Wear* (Thursday, October 11, 1923): 30, 32; "Increase in the Stout-Wear Trade," *The New York Times* (February 11, 1923): 13; "Plan to Put Stout Dep'ts in Stores All over Country," *Women's Wear* (May 15, 1918): 27, 30; "Providing Dresses for Stout Women," *The New York Times* (August 10, 1924): 69; "Who's to Blame for Alterations? Ninety Per cent of Garments Must Be Altered," *Women's Wear* (August 29, 1917): 25.

10. Albert Malsin, "How Science Is Helping 'Stout' People to Look Less 'Stout," *Richmond Times-Dispatch* (April 9, 1916): 53.

11. Amy Erdman Farrell, *Fat Shame: Stigma and the Fat Body in American Culture* (New York: New York University Press, 2011), 3.

12. The Gilded Age is one such era that is frequently cited in the literature as a period during which more voluptuous silhouettes were permissible. It is worth pointing out, however, that even during this period, fatness at the waist was discouraged. For a discussion of Gilded Age beauty ideals, see Lois W. Banner, *American Beauty: A Social History ... Through Two Centuries of the America Idea, Ideal, and Image of the Beautiful Woman* (Los Angeles: Figueroa Press, 2005), 155–85.

13. "Diet Decimates Stouts, Dress Producer Says," *Women's Wear* (May 5, 1930): 5.

14. Because women's clothing was so highly tailored to the body, women's ready-made dress lagged somewhat behind that for men. Cloaks and crinolines were available to purchase ready-made as early as the 1860s. By the last quarter of the nineteenth century, mass-manufactured corsets and suits were available to purchase in a wide array of sizes. Simple shirtwaists and skirts could be purchased en masse by about 1890. See Claudia B. Kidwell and Margaret C. Christman, *Suiting Everyone: The Democratization of Clothing in America* (Washington, DC: The Smithsonian Institution Press, 1974), 101–11.

15. See, for instance, Michel Foucault, *Power/Knowledge: Selected Interviews and Other Writings 1972-1977* (New York: Pantheon, 1980), 85; Michel Foucault, *Discipline and Punish: The Birth of the Prison* (New York: Pantheon, 1977). Caroline Evans observes that Foucault's genealogy is not so different from the process of fashion design itself to the extent that it "reveals the complex historical relays between past and present." See Caroline Evans, *Fashion at the Edge: Spectacle, Modernity, Deathliness* (New Haven: Yale University Press, 2003), 11–12.

16. David Garland, "What Is a 'History of the Present'? On Foucault's Genealogies and Their Critical Preconditions," *Punishment & Society* 16, no. 4 (2014): 372.

17. Ibid.

18. Caroline Evans, *Fashion at the Edge*, 9; Ulrich Lehmann, *Tigersprung: Fashion in Modernity* (Cambridge: MIT Press, 2000); Elizabeth Wilson, *Adorned in Dreams: Fashion and Modernity* (New Brunswick: Rutgers University Press, 2003).

19. Caroline Evans, *The Mechanical Smile: Modernism and the First Fashion Shows in France and America, 1900-1929* (New Haven: Yale University Press, 2013), 207–11.

20. Lane Bryant is America's oldest and most well-known purveyor of large-size women's fashions. The history of Lane Bryant is discussed in Chapter 2.

21. Carmen Keist, "'Stout Women Can Now Be Stylish': Stout Women's Fashions, 1910–1919," *Dress: The Journal of the Costume Society of America* 43, no. 2 (2017): 100.

22. Ibid.

23. Kidwell and Christman, *Suiting Everyone*, 15.

24. William Leach has described this as the "democratization of desire." See William Leach, *Land of Desire: Merchants, Power, and the Rise of a New American Culture* (New York: Vintage Books, 1993), 3.

25. Although data is scattered, historians and epidemiologists agree that Americans did grow both taller and heavier in the twentieth century, but this process was a gradual one. Through the 1920s in particular, increase in Americans' average weight was negligible. For a summary of this research, see Peter Stearns, *Fat History: Bodies and Beauty in the Modern West* (New York: New York University Press, 2002), 129–34.

26. Hillel Schwartz, *Never Satisfied: A Cultural History of Diets, Fantasies and Fat* (New York: The Free Press, 1986), 159.

27. This exaggerated bust-to-waist ratio (e.g., with a larger bust and smaller waist) evidences the late nineteenth and early twentieth-century preference for the hourglass silhouette. It is also worth noting here that at the turn of the century, sizes were based either on a woman's bust or on waist measurement. Standard sizes ranged from a thirty-two to forty-four bust measurement, and twenty-three- to thirty-inch waist measurement. While these were typical size ranges, many manufactures devised their own set of measurements. See Kidwell and Christman, *Suiting Everyone*, 105–9.

28. "Vogue's Eye View of the Mode," *Vogue* (January 15, 1923): 41.

29. As Caroline Evans observes, a defining feature of dresses designed by French Couturiers like Lucile, Callot, and Drecoll, and which trickled down to American mass-manufactured versions, was a sheerness unseen in the previous decade, and which placed an emphasis on the body underneath the gown. See Evans, *The Mechanical Smile*, 9.

30. Schwartz, *Never Satisfied*, 5.

31. Weight loss and asceticism as forms of compensation for moral and ethical overindulgence are common within Christian societies. See Christopher E. Forth, *Fat: A Cultural History of the Stuff of Life* (London: Reaktion Books, 2019), 82–106; R. Marie Griffith, *Born Again Bodies: Flesh and Spirit in American Christianity* (Berkeley: University of California Press, 2004). These virtues would also manifest in twentieth-century consumer society. See Schwartz, *Never Satisfied*, 23–8; Stearns, *Fat History*, 64–8; Bryan Turner, "The Discourse of Diet," *Theory, Culture & Society* 1, no. 1 (1982): 23–32.

32. Although there were a number of popular fad diets in the mid-nineteenth century, these were mostly steeped in religious dogma. Secular fasting wouldn't become common until the early twentieth century. See Katharina Vester, "Regime Change: Gender, Class and the Invention of Dieting in Post-Bellum America," *Journal of Social History* 44, no. 1 (2010): 39–70; Joan Jacobs Brumberg, *Fasting Girls: The History of Anorexia Nervosa* (New York: Vintage Books, 2000), 228–54.

33. Nicholas Rasmussen, "America's First Amphetamine Epidemic 1929–1971: A Quantitative and Qualitative Retrospective with Implications for the Present," *American Journal of Public Health* 98, no. 6 (June 2008): 974–85. See also Schwartz, *Never Satisfied*, 178–80.

34. See, for example, Susan Bordo, *Unbearable Weight: Feminism, Western Culture and the Body* (Berkeley: University of California Press, 1993); Amanda Czerniawski, *Fashioning Fat: Inside Plus-Size Modeling* (New York: New York University Press, 2012); Karen de Perthius, "The Synthetic Ideal: The Fashion Model and Photographic Manipulation," *Fashion Theory* 9, no. 4 (2005): 407–24; Evans, *The Mechanical Smile*, 211–5; Anne Hollander, *Seeing Through Clothes* (New York: The Viking Press, 1978), 312–4, 336–7; Marianne Thesander, *The Feminine Ideal* (New York: Reaktion Books, 1997), 55–67, 107–29.

35. See Elena Levy-Navarro (ed.), *Historicizing Fat in Anglo-American Culture* (Columbus: The Ohio State University Press, 2010); Farrell, *Fat Shame*; Forth, *Fat: A Cultural History of the Stuff of Life*; Schwartz, *Never Satisfied*; Kerry Seagrave, *Obesity in America, 1850–1939: A History of Social Attitudes and Treatment* (Jefferson, North Carolina and London: McFarland & Company, Inc., 2008); Stearns, *Fat History*; Georges Vigarello, *The Metamorphoses of Fat: A History of Obesity* (New York: Columbia University Press, 2013); Sabrina Strings, *Fearing the Black Body: The Racial Origins of Fat Phobia* (New York: New York University Press, 2019).

36. Schwartz, *Never Satisfied*, 19.

37. Ibid.

38. Roy Porter, "History of the Body" in *New Perspectives on Historical Writing*, ed. Peter Burke (Cambridge: Polity, 1991), 206–7.

39. Michel Foucault, "Nietzsche, Genealogy, History" in *The Foucault Reader*, ed. Paul Rainbow (New York: Pantheon, 1984).

40. Garland, "What Is a 'History of the Present'," 373.

41. Porter, "History of the Body," 210.

42. Ibid., 211.

Notes

43. Joanne Entwistle, *The Fashioned Body: Fashion, Dress and Modern Social Theory* (Cambridge: Polity Press, 2000), 6.

44. Ibid., 7–8.

45. See Wilson, *Adorned in Dreams*, 3, 8; Elizabeth Wilson, "Fashion and the Postmodern Body" in *Chic Thrills: A Fashion Reader*, eds. Juliet Ash and Elizabeth Wilson (London: Pandora, 1992), 3–16.

46. Here, Entwistle draws upon Foucault's theory of panopticism, which draws upon Jeremy Bentham's designs for a "perfect prison." Featuring a central tower with a reflective, glass observation room around which cells are positioned in a circle in such a way so that no prisoner can see the guard, the "Panopticon" ensures "an automatic functioning of power." Foucault holds that modern society is not unlike Bentham's Panopticon to the extent that discipline is enacted on human bodies through more "mindful" rather than physical means. See Entwistle, *The Fashioned Body*, 11, 16–20.

47. Because Foucault does not account for embodiment, or the way that power is experienced at the level of the individual body, in discussing the relationship between dress codes and the act of getting dressed, Entwistle further draws upon Maurice Merleau-Ponty's phenomenology and Pierre Bourdieu's theory of practice in fleshing out the relationship between these two processes. See Entwistle, *The Fashioned Body*, 6, 12–16, 23–35.

48. Paolo Volonté, *Fat Fashion: The Thin Ideal and the Segregation of Plus-Size Bodies* (London: Bloomsbury, 2022), 79–94, 121–2.

49. Entwistle, *The Fashioned Body*, 37.

50. Paolo Volonté, drawing on Ashley Mears' scholarship, evocatively describes the relationship between the slender ideal and fashion design as the "internal law" of fashion. See Volonté, *Fat Fashion*, 109–10.

51. Rebecca Arnold, *Fashion, Desire and Anxiety: Image and Morality in the 20th Century* (New Brunswick: Rutgers University Press, 2001), 89–95.

52. For further discussion about the body as a "project" in consumer culture, see Mike Featherstone, "The Body in Consumer Culture," *Theory, Culture & Society* 1, no. 1 (1982): 18–33; Chris Shilling, *The Body and Social Theory* (London: Sage, 1993); Bryan Turner, *The Body and Society: Explorations in Social Theory* (Oxford: Basil Blackwell, 1985).

53. Valerie Steele, "The F Word," *Lingua Franca* (April 1991): 17–20.

54. Richard Klein, "Fat Beauty" in *Bodies out of Bounds: Fatness and Transgression*, eds. Jana Evans Braziel and Kathleen LeBesco (Berkeley: University of California Press, 2001), 27.

55. This is derived from an *Oxford English Dictionary* definition. See Heike Jenß, "Introduction" in *Fashion Studies: Research Methods, Sites and Practices*, ed. Heike Jenß (London: Bloomsbury, 2016), 21.

56. Sophie Woodward, "'Humble' Blue Jeans: Material Culture Approaches to Understanding the Ordinary, Global and the Personal" in *Fashion Studies: Research Methods, Sites and Practices*, ed. Heike Jenß (London: Bloomsbury, 2016), 45.

57. Rebecca Puhl, Tatiana Andreyeva, and Kelly D. Brownell, "Perceptions of Weight Discrimination: Prevalence and Comparison to Race and Gender Discrimination in America," *International Journal of Obesity* 32, no. 1 (2008): 992–1000.

58. Volonté, *Fat Fashion*, 12–13.

59. Strings, *Fearing the Black Body*, 6–7.

60. Katharina Vester, "Regime Change: Gender, Class, and the Invention of Dieting in America," *Journal of Social History* 44, no. 1 (2010): 54.

61. Collier Marshall, "Selling 'Stouts,'" *Printer's Ink Monthly* (August 1920), 34.

62. Strings' investigation focused mainly on dieting advice proffered by the American women's and fashion magazines *Godey's Lady's Book* and *Harper's Bazaar*. See Strings, *Fearing the Black Body*, 122–46.

63. Ibid., 76–9, 81–4.

64. Farrell, *Fat Shame*, 83.

65. Erving Goffman, *Stigma: Notes on the Management of a Spoiled Identity* (New York: Simon & Schuster, 1963), 11.

66. In posing this question, Evans was referencing and rephrasing a comment made by the film scholar Eirik Frisvold Hanssen, who during the seminar asked the question, "What is a film history without film?"

67. See Kevin Almond, "Fashionably Voluptuous: Repackaging the Fuller-Sized Figure," *Fashion Theory* 17, no. 2 (2013): 197–222; Keist, "The New Costumes of Odd Sizes."

68. In her recent scholarship, Kenna Elizabeth Mulroney Libes has found that large-size garments may actually be collected with greater frequency than previously thought. Instead, she believes that it is the common, and interrelated, practices of misinterpreting and mislabeling garments that, in their time, would have been worn by fat people as standard size. See Kenna Elizabeth Mulroney Libes, "Fat by the Wayside: Size Exclusion in Exhibitions and Collections of Dress" (MA thesis, S.U.N.Y. Fashion Institute of Technology, 2022), 30–6.

69. The exception is the Fashion Study Collection at Columbia College Chicago, where since 2018, I, as the collection's director, have set out to fill this gap by collecting examples of historic stout and plus-size fashion spanning the twentieth and twenty-first centuries. As of September 2022, this collection is numbered at thirty garments and growing.

70. Carolyn Steedman, *Dust: The Archive and Cultural History* (New Brunswick: Rutgers University Press, 2001), 2–3.

71. Lauren Downing Peters, "A History of Fashion without Fashion: Recovering the Stout Body in the Digital Archive," *Journal of Critical Studies in Fashion and Beauty* 10, no. 1 (2019): 97.

72. For a general discussion of the concepts of survival and selection bias, see Cheryl Buckley and Hazel Clark, *Fashion and Everyday Life: London and New York* (London: Bloomsbury, 2017), 18; Ingrid Mida and Alexandra Kim, *The Dress Detective: A Practical Guide to Object-Based Research in Fashion* (London: Bloomsbury, 2015), 120–1, 160–1; Alexandra Palmer, "Untouchable: Creating Desire and Knowledge in Museum and Textile Exhibitions," *Fashion Theory* 12, no. 1 (2008): 31–63; Lou Taylor, "Doing the Laundry? A Reassessment of Object-Based Dress History," *Fashion Theory* 2, no. 4 (1998): 337–58.

73. For further discussion of the privileging of object-based approaches in fashion studies and dress history, see Valerie Steele, "A Museum of Fashion Is More than a Clothes-Bag," *Fashion Theory* 2, no. 4 (1998): 327–35.

74. Charlotte Nicklas and Annabella Pollen, "Introduction: Dress History Now: Terms, Themes and Tools" in *Dress History: New Directions in Theory and Practice*, eds. Charlotte Nicklas and Annabella Pollen (London: Bloomsbury, 2015), 2.

75. Evans, *Fashion at the Edge*, 11–12.

76. Carmen Keist's dress historical research into the history of plus-size fashion is the notable exception.

77. Christopher Breward, *The Culture of Fashion* (Manchester: Manchester University Press, 1995), 304.

78. Evans, *Fashion at the Edge*, 12.

79. Marco Pecorari defines fashion ephemera as the transient, disposable objects "not intended to survive beyond their original purpose," but which lend clues to the nature and practices of fashion, and are not typically collected or saved in formal fashion archives. Fashion ephemera encompasses everything from fashion plates to personal snapshots. See Marco Pecorari, *Fashion Remains: Rethinking Ephemera in the Archive* (London: Bloomsbury, 2021), 3–8.

80. In devising this approach, Breward draws upon the cultural historian Charles Bernheimer. See Christopher Breward, *The Hidden Consumer: Masculinities, Fashion and City Life 1860–1914* (Manchester: Manchester University Press, 1999), 17–19.

81. Buckley and Clark, *Fashion and Everyday Life*, 14–22.

82. Marilyn Wann, "Foreword" in *The Fat Studies Reader*, eds. Esther Rothblum and Sondra Solovay (New York: New York University Press, 2009), xiii.

83. Kathleen LeBesco, *Revolting Bodies: The Struggle to Redefine Fat Identity* (Amherst: University of Massachusetts Press, 2004), 105.

84. Don Kulick and Anne Meneley, "Introduction" in *Fat: The Anthropology of an Obsession*, eds. Don Kulick and Anne Meneley (New York: Penguin, 2005), 2.

85. Almond, "Fashionably Voluptuous."

86. Wann, "Foreword," xii.

87. Woodward describes "sartorial biographies" as the life histories of research subjects as told through their wardrobes. See Sophie Woodward, *Why Women Wear What They Wear* (London: Berg: 2007), 31–50.

Chapter 1

1. "How Many Fat Women in Your Town?" *Women's Wear* (June 11, 1915): 3.

2. Ibid.

3. Stuart Ewen, *Captains of Consciousness: Advertising and the Social Roots of the Consumer Culture* (New York: Basic Books, 2001), 33.

4. Ibid., 25–6.

5. "Stout Wear: Promotion of Trademarks Is Held Responsible for Stoutwear Success," *Women's Wear* (August 3, 1922): 29.

6. See, for instance, Almond, "Fashionably Voluptuous."

7. Ana Carden-Coyne and Christopher E. Forth, "Introduction: The Belly and Beyond: Body, Self, and Culture in Ancient and Modern Times" in *Cultures of the Abdomen: Diet, Digestion, and Fat in the Modern World*, ed. Ana Carden-Coyne and Christopher E. Forth (New York: Palgrave MacMillan, 2005), 1–2.

8. Vigarello suggests that the last moment during which fat was idealized was in the Middle Ages during which time "massive bodies [were] praised … as denoting power and ascendancy." See Vigarello, *The Metamorphoses of Fat*, ix–x.

9. Aurore Bayle-Loudet, "The Corset, Essential Protagonist of Modern Femininity" in *The Body: Fashion and Physique*, ed. Denis Bruna (New Haven: Yale University Press, 2015), 164.

10. Banner, *American Beauty*, 186; Seagrave, *Obesity in America*, 1.

11. Carmen Keist, "How Stout Women Were Left Out of High Fashion: An Early Twentieth Century Perspective," *Fashion, Style and Popular Culture* 5, no. 1 (2018): 29.

12. Forth, *Fat*, 236–7; Samantha Murray, *The "Fat" Female Body* (New York: Palgrave MacMillan, 2008), 15–21; Seagrave, *Obesity in America*, 18–30; Schwartz, *Never Satisfied*, 115–45; Strings, *Fearing the Black Body*, 6–7, 126–7; Stearns, *Fat History*, 6–11; Vigarello, *The Metamorphoses of Fat*, 156–62.

13. Bantingism was invented by a London undertaker named William Banting. The diet was predicated on the consumption of lean meats, eggs, and green vegetables. Banting publicized his diet via a popular pamphlet that sold more than 58,000 copies in the UK and abroad. Founded by the temperance leader Horace Fletcher in 1895, Fletcherism was deemed a natural route to weight loss, wherein food was to be chewed into a liquid so that it could be more easily digested. This, according to Fletcher, would help the individual avoid "auto-intoxication," or the root cause of overweight. See Tim Armstrong, "Disciplining the Corpus: Henry James and Fletcherism" in *American Bodies: Cultural Histories of the Physique*, ed. Tim Armstrong (New York: New York University Press, 1996), 101–2.

14. "In the Effort to be Angular the Fat Woman Terrifies Her Thin Sister," *The New York Times* (August 11, 1907): 34.

15. Banner, *American Beauty*, 225.

16. Martha H. Patterson, *Beyond the Gibson Girl: Reimagining the American New Woman, 1895–1915* (Urbana and Chicago: University of Illinois Press, 2005), 4.

17. See Strings, *Fearing the Black Body*, 163; Cookie Woolner, "American Excess: Cultural Representations of Lillian Russell in Turn-of-the-Century America" in *Historicizing Fat*, ed. Elena Levy-Navarro (Columbus: The Ohio State University Press, 2010), 132.

18. Schwartz, *Never Satisfied*, 162.

19. Joyce L. Huff, "A Horror of Corpulence: Interrogating Bantingism and Mid-Nineteenth Century Fat Phobia" in *Bodies out of Bounds: Fatness and Transgression*, ed. Jana Evans Braziel and Kathleen Lebesco (Berkeley: University of California Press, 2001), 46.

20. "Fat Women Busy Reducing, Thin Ones Adding Weight," *The New York Times* (Sunday, July 26, 1925): 148.

21. Mark Seltzer, *Bodies and Machines* (New York and London: Routledge, 1992), 100.

22. Brumberg, *Fasting Girls*, 231.

23. Schwartz, *Never Satisfied*, 156.

24. Ibid.

25. Actuarial Society of America and the Association of Life Insurance Medical Directors, *Medico-Actuarial Mortality Investigation: Volume II*, 9.

26. Amanda Czerniawski, "From Average to Ideal: The Evolution of the Height and Weight Table in the United States, 1836–1943," *Social Science History* 31, no. 2 (2007): 276.

27. Schwartz, *Never Satisfied*, 157.

28. See "Cater by Method to Stout Persons," *The New York Times* (August 11, 1918): 28; "Looking Backward and Forward in the Development of Stylish Stout Wear," *Dry Goods Economist* (November 19, 1921): 459; Paul Nystrom, *Economics of Fashion* (New York: The Ronald Press Company, 1928), 466; "Say Leading Form Makers Have Right Sizes That All Others Should Adopt," *Women's Wear* (March 5, 1925): 20; "Scientific Specialization in Stouts," 8; "Stoutwear's Possibilities as Viewed by Leading Garment Buyers," *The American Cloak and Suit Review* (November 1922): 91.

29. "Lack of Attention to Stouts Deplored," *Women's Wear* (August 23, 1919): 2, 31.

30. "Finds More Women Needing Stouts," *Women's Wear* (April 15, 1922): 12.

31. "Stout Women Can Now Be Stylish," *The New York Times* (January 14, 1917): 33.

32. As Stearns has written, the history of American weight gain is an anomaly. During the twentieth century, as dieting and fitness have become increasingly compulsory, American weight has gradually gone up. The pace of weight gain intensified especially after 1920 in the American population as a whole. See Stearns, *Fat History*, 129–34.

33. "Ready for the Big Ones: A New Angle on the Fat Woman's Wants," *Women's Wear* (July 2, 1915): 3, 11.

34. Claudia Kidwell, *Cutting a Fashionable Fit: Dressmakers' Drafting Systems in the United States* (Washington, DC: Smithsonian Institution Press, 1979), 98.

35. Kidwell and Christman, *Suiting Everyone*, 105–6.

36. Ibid., 109.

37. "Altered Garments Cost a Huge Sum," *The New York Times* (September 2, 1917): 20.

38. Ibid.

39. "Who's to Blame for Alterations? Ninety Per Cent of Garments Must Be Altered," *Women's Wear* (August 29, 1917): 25.

40. Kidwell and Christman, *Suiting Everyone*, 107–8.

41. "Stout Women Can Now Be Stylish," *The New York Times* (January 14, 1917): 33.

42. "Business Notes: A Revolution in Fitting Stylish Stout Women," *Women's Wear* (November 17, 1915): 9.

43. "Poor Patterns and Scant Cut Stoutwear Problem," *Women's Wear* (March 23, 1922): 27.

44. "Looking Backward and Forward in the Development of Stylish Stout Wear," *Dry Goods Economist* (November 19, 1921): 191.

45. This insight emerges from an observation made by Schwartz, who writes, "The picture of a patient on a scale, nurse or doctor hovering by the balance beam, became *the* popular icon of [a medical] exam." See Schwartz, *Never Satisfied*, 156.

46. Here, Jeacle draws upon Foucault's conceptualization of "technologies of the body." For further discussion of this concept, see Chapter 2. See Ingrid Jeacle, "Accounting and the Construction of the Standard Body," *Accounting Organizations and Society* 28, no. 1 (2003): 357.

47. "Waist Line Increasing: New Standards Needed," *Women's Wear* (December 13, 1916): 1, 10.

48. Wendy Gamber, "'Reduced to Science': Gender, Technology and Power in the American Dressmaking Trade, 1860–1910," *Technology and Culture* 36, no. 3 (1995): 469.

49. Ruth O'Brien, *An Annotated List of Literature References on Garment Sizes and Body Measurements* (Washington, DC: United States Department of Agriculture, 1930), 3.

50. Kidwell and Christman, *Suiting Everyone*, 105.

51. Jongsuck Chun-Yoon and Cynthia R. Jasper, "Development of Size Labelling Systems for Women's Garments," *Journal of Consumer Studies and Home Economics* 18, no. 1 (1994): 72.

52. Jeacle, "Accounting," 361.

53. Kidwell and Christman, *Suiting Everyone*, 108.

54. Although these measurements are typically considered inclusive of standard sizes, Kidwell and Christman concede that manufacturers during this period generally arrived "at their own set of measurements by a process of trial and error" in spite of rampant claims about scientific accuracy. See *Suiting Everyone*, 105. For further discussion, see also Jane E. Workman, "Body Measurement Specifications for Fit Models as Factor in Clothing Size Variation," *Clothing and Textile Research Journal* 10, no. 1 (1991): 31–2.

55. O'Brien, *An Annotated List*, 2–3.

56. Winifred Aldrich, "History of Sizing Systems and Ready-to-Wear Garments" in *Sizing in Clothing: Developing Effective Sizing Systems for Ready-to-Wear Clothing*, ed. Susan P. Ashdown (Cambridge: Woodhead, 2007), 30–1.

57. Woolner, "American Excess," 132.

58. Nancy A. Schofield, "Pattern Grading" in *Sizing in Clothing: Developing Effective Sizing Systems for Ready-to-Wear Clothing*, ed. Susan P. Ashdown (Cambridge: Woodhead Publishing, 2007), 158.

59. Kidwell and Christman, *Suiting Everyone*, 108.

60. "Who's to Blame for Alterations?" *Women's Wear* (August 29, 1917): 25.

61. "Specially Designed Stouts Release Store from Limitations of Its Alteration Room," *Dry Goods Economist* (March 11, 1922): 117.

62. Keist and Marcketti, "The New Costumes of Odd Sizes," 262. See also Keist, "The New Costumes of Odd Sizes," 64–7. Another outgrowth of the move toward greater specialization in the American fashion industry was the development of half-sizes for short, fat women in the 1920s. See Lynn Malley and Carmen Keist, "The Origins of the New Half Sizes in the 1920s," *Dress*, online first (August 30, 2022). Accessed September 5, 2022.

63. "Science at Last Turns Its Attention to 'Stout' People," *Richmond Times-Dispatch* (April 2, 1916): 53–4.

64. "A Chance to Make Money," *The New York Times* (April 27, 1922): 27.

65. Evans, *Mechanical Smile*, 74.

66. Nancy L. Green, *Ready to Wear, Ready to Work: A Century of Industry and Immigrants in Paris and New York* (Durham: Duke University Press, 1997), 4–5.

67. Evans, *Mechanical Smile*, 74.

68. Green, *Ready to Wear*, 115.

69. O'Brien, *An Annotated List*, 1.

70. Tim Armstrong, *Modernism, Technology and the Body* (Cambridge: Cambridge University Press, 1998), 3, 65.

71. "Developing a Stouts Department," *Women's Wear* (January 3, 1917): 31.

72. "Cater by Method to Stout Persons," *The New York Times* (August 11, 1918): 28.

73. "Science at Last Turns Its Attention to Stout People," *Richmond Times-Dispatch* (Sunday, April 2, 1916): 54.

74. Klein, "Fat Beauty," 27.

75. Jessie Shepherd, "For Women of the Rubens Type," *Harper's Bazaar* (August 31, 1895): 707.

76. Schwartz, *Never Satisfied*, 79–80.

77. Hillel Schwartz, "Torque: The New Kinesthetic of the Twentieth Century" in *Incorporations (Zone 6)*, ed. Jonathan Crary and Sanford Kwinter (New York: Zone Books, 1992), 77. For a similar discussion, see also Jessica Burstein, *Cold Modernism: Literature, Fashion, Art* (University Park: Pennsylvania State University Press, 2012), 13.

78. "Quality as Important as Size in Handling Stouts Trade," *Women's Wear* (January 9, 1917): 48.

79. "Ready for the Big Ones," *Women's Wear* (July 2, 1915): 3.

80. Douglas, *Purity and Danger*, 5.

81. "How Many Fat Women in Your Town," *Women's Wear* (June 11, 1915): 3.

82. "Even the Freaks Want to Look 'Nifty,'" *Women's Wear* (March 26, 1920): 51.

83. Ibid.

84. Douglas, *Purity and Danger*, 115.

85. Ibid., 5.

86. Ibid., 50.

87. Peter Corrigan, *The Sociology of Consumption* (London: Sage, 1997), 64.

88. Ibid.

Chapter 2

1. A *Women's Wear Daily* puts her address at 111th street. See Samuel Feinberg, "From Where I Sit," *Women's Wear Daily* (March 19, 1968): 12.

2. Tom Mahoney, *50 Years of Lane Bryant* (New York: Lane Bryant, 1950), 5–7.

3. "Funeral Today for Founder of Lane Bryant," *Women's Wear Daily* (September 28, 1951): 31.

4. Born Lena Himmelstein, she took the last name Bryant when she married her first husband, David Bryant, in 1899. When she opened a bank account for her business in Jewish Harlem, a bank associate misspelled her name as "Lane." It is from this period henceforth that she went by Lane Bryant, but is occasionally referred to by her full name, Lena Himmelstein Malsin Bryant.

5. Mahoney, *50 Years of Lane Bryant*, 13.

6. "Selling 'Stouts': Studied Service to One Kind of Buyers Wins Success at Lane Bryant," *Printers' Ink Monthly* 1, no. 7–12 (June 1920): 36.

7. Albert Malsin, "Garment," US Patent no. 1119296, Filed May 2, 1911, Patented December 1, 1914 (accessed July 13, 2022), http://www.google.com.na/patents/US1119296.

8. Malsin was not the only one trying to claim space in the bourgeoning stoutwear trade. Between 1910 and 1928, at least forty-nine patents were granted for stoutwear garments and foundations. See Keist, "The New Costumes of Odd Sizes," 97.

9. Feinberg, Samuel, "From Where I Sit: Lane Bryant—And How It Grew," *Women's Wear Daily* (March 19, 1968): 12.

10. Mahoney, *50 Years of Lane Bryant*, 17.

11. The exact number of women Malsin measured is unclear. In another article, Malsin claims that he measured 250,000 women (see "Who's to Blame for Alterations"), while Tom Mahoney's Lane Bryant pamphlet claimed that Malsin measured 4,500 customers and examined the insurance policies of another 200,000 women. See Mahoney, *50 Years of Lane Bryant*, 19.

12. "Selling 'Stouts': Studied Service to One Kind of Buyers Wins Success at Lane Bryant," *Printers' Ink Monthly* (June 1920): 34.

13. "Scientific Specialization in Stouts," *Women's Wear* (July 9, 1914): 4.

14. Ibid.

15. Albert Malsin, "How Science Is Helping 'Stout' People to Look Less 'Stout.'" *Richmond Times-Dispatch* (April 9, 1916): 53.

16. Kidwell and Christman, *Suiting Everyone*, 15.

17. Grace Lees-Maffei, "Introduction—Writing Design: Words, Myths, Practices," *Working Papers on Design* 4, no. 1 (2010): 3.

18. Forth, *Fat*, 236.

19. "Making Designers: The Development of Five Years in Odd Sizes," *Women's Wear* (July 27, 1915): 1, 5.

20. Ibid., 5.

21. McNeil notes that the image of the couturier in a white artist's smock is a common one within the visual vernaculars of modernism. Beginning with Christian Dior, the white lab coat or smock became a mainstay or something of a uniform of couturiers. See Peter McNeil, "Fashion Designers" in *Berg Encyclopedia of World Dress and Fashion: West Europe*, ed. Lise Skov (Oxford: Berg, 2010), 131.

22. Baum & Wolff, Inc. advertisement, *The Dry Goods Economist* (January 26, 1918): 84.

23. Gamber, "'Reduced to Science,'" 458.

24. See Christopher Breward, *Fashion* (Oxford: Oxford University Press, 2003), 32; Jennifer Craik, *Face of Fashion: Cultural Studies in Fashion* (London: Routledge, 1994), 56–8; Ilya Parkins, *Poiret, Dior and Schiaparelli: Fashion, Femininity and Modernity* (London: Berg, 2012), 77, 123; Nancy Troy, *Couture Culture* (Boston: MIT Press, 2003), 6, 47. For further discussion of the posturing of the designer as artistic genius, see also Yuniya Kawamura, *Fashion-ology: An Introduction to Fashion Studies* (Oxford: Berg, 2005), 65; Gilles Lipovetsky, *Empire of Fashion: Dressing Modern Democracy* (Princeton: Princeton University Press, 1994), 64–6.

25. Victor Margolin, "Introduction" in *Design Discourse: History, Theory, Criticism*, ed. Victor Margolin (Chicago: University of Chicago Press, 1989), 10–11.

26. This argument is somewhat different from Troy's assertion that even as couturiers set themselves apart as singular artistic geniuses, they nevertheless engaged in practices of self-promotion while negotiating "the supposedly corrupting influence of commerce and commodity culture." Indeed, stoutwear manufacturers, unlike couturiers, were more forthright about their connections to the mass market. For further discussion, see Troy, *Couture Culture*, 6–8.

27. "Science at Last Turns Its Attention to 'Stout' People," *Richmond Times-Dispatch* (April 2, 1916): 54.

28. Ibid.

29. Gamber, "'Reduced to Science,'" 467.

30. "Science at Last Turns Its Attention to 'Stout' People," *Richmond Times-Dispatch* (April 2, 1916): 55.

31. "To Make Stout Folk Look Thin," *Oregon Daily Journal* (August 13, 1916): 48.

32. "How Science Is Helping 'Stout' People to Look Less 'Stout,'" *Richmond Times-Dispatch* (April 9, 1916): 53.

33. Ibid.

34. Patricia Mears, *American Beauty: Aesthetics and Innovation in Fashion* (New Haven: Yale University Press, 2009), 3.

35. Bradley Quinn, *The Fashion of Architecture* (Oxford: Berg, 2003), 133.

36. Mary McLeod, "Undressing Architecture: Fashion, Gender and Modernity" in *Architecture: In Fashion*, ed. Deborah Fausch (Princeton: Princeton Architectural Press, 1996), 39.

37. McLeod, "Undressing Architecture," 58.

Notes

38. Llewelyn Negrin, "Ornament and the Feminine," *Feminist Theory* 7, no. 2 (2006): 225; Parkins, *Poiret, Dior and Schiaparelli*, 25–45, 63.

39. McLeod, "Undressing Architecture," 55.

40. "Style Severity Lessened in this Season's Stout Suits—Easy Lines Prevail," *Women's Wear* (July 25, 1922): 5.

41. "Extensive Choice for Stout Woman: Fabric, Color and Line Closely Resemble Those for Slender Sizes," *Women's Wear* (April 15, 1922): 14; "Stoutwear Designers' Conceptions of Gowns for the Fall," *Women's Wear* (August 3, 1922): 23.

42. "Details from Openings in Paris Offer Inspiration to the Stoutwear Designers," *Women's Wear* (September 7, 1922): 17.

43. Parkins, *Poiret, Dior and Schiaparelli*, 1–2.

44. Breward, *The Culture of Fashion*, 186–7; Wilson, *Adorned in Dreams*, 39–42.

45. Evans, *Mechanical Smile*, 6.

46. Lipovetsky, *Empire of Fashion*, 66.

47. Christopher Breward and Caroline Evans, "Introduction" in *Fashion and Modernity,* ed. Christopher Breward and Caroline Evans, (London: Berg, 2005), 1–7; Evans, *The Mechanical Smile*, 7; Richard Martin, *Cubism and Fashion* (New York: Metropolitan Museum of Art, 1999); Radu Stern, *Against Fashion: Clothing as Art, 1850–1930* (Cambridge, MA: The MIT Press, 2005), 63; Valerie Steele, *Paris Fashion: A Cultural History* (Oxford & New York: Oxford University Press, 1988), 227–30; Troy, *Couture Culture*, 3; Wilson, *Adorned in Dreams*, 60–3.

48. Wilson, *Adorned in Dreams*, 62.

49. Ibid., 62–3.

50. Evans, *Mechanical Smile*, 6.

51. Armstrong, *Modernism, Technology and the Body*, 6.

52. Hollander, *Seeing Through Clothes*, 314.

53. "Smart Aids to Slenderness," *Vogue* (May 1, 1921): 116.

54. "The Problem of the Straight Silhouette: Fitting the Flat Back to the Full Figure," *Vogue* (November 1923): 44–5.

55. "Vogue's Eye View of the Mode," *Vogue* (January 15, 1923): 41.

56. Mark Wigley, *White Walls, Designer Dresses: The Fashioning of Modern Architecture* (Cambridge: MIT Press, 2001), xviii.

57. Here, Vigarello quotes a 1900 article in the French magazine *Le Caprice*, which, while early, nevertheless anticipated the continued narrowing of the silhouette in the decades to come. See Vigarello, *Metamorphoses of Fat*, 147.

58. "Popular Price Stoutwear of Improved Type Finds a Market," *Women's Wear* (September 7, 1922): 20.

59. "Accent Large Sizes to Stimulate Trade in Department for Women," *Women's Wear* (April 22, 1925): 22.

60. Nystrom's volume was mostly focused on fashion as a social process and therefore stands as an attempt to reveal the underlying logic of fashion change. John Styles places Nystrom's book within a canon of early twentieth-century fashion literature that rejected the trajectories of dress history, and which instead examined economic, sociological, and psychological theories of fashion. See John Styles, "Dress History: Reflections on a Contested Terrain," *Fashion Theory* 2, no. 4 (1998): 383–90.

61. Nystrom, *Economics of Fashion*, 117.

62. Ibid., 117–18.

63. The notion of "mass illusions" with regard to stoutwear design was also discussed in Carl N. Werntz, "Selling the Customer Smartness through Basic Art Principles," *Women's Wear* (August 23, 1924): 10.

64. Nystrom, *Economics of Fashion*, 117–18.

65. Ibid., 119.

66. Ibid.

67. "Style Features Are Incorporated in Stoutwear," *Women's Wear* (July 5, 1922): 28.

68. Keist, *The New Costumes of Odd Sizes*, 80–82.

69. "The Selling Points of Your Merchandise: Aids in Applying Principles of Better Selling to Apparel Now in Vogue," *Women's Wear* (January 30, 1926): 11.

70. "Stoutwear Designers' Conceptions of Gowns for Fall," *Women's Wear* (August 3, 1922): 23.

71. Ibid.

72. The Müller-Lyer illusion dates to 1889 and is named after the psychologist who discovered it. For further discussion about the history of the illusion and the debates surrounding it, see Marjory Bates, "A Study of the Müller-Lyer Illusion, with Special Reference to Paradoxical Movement and the Effect of Attitude," *The American Journal of Psychology* 34, no. 1 (January 1923): 46–72.

73. Carl N. Werntz, "Selling the Customer Smartness through Basic Art Principles: No. 5. Adapting a Model to Different Figures," *Women's Wear* (July 19, 1924): 14.

74. Ibid., 19.

75. Ibid.

76. Wilson, *Adorned in Dreams*, 62–3.

77. Richard L. Gregory, *Eye and Brain: The Psychology of Seeing*, 5th ed. (Princeton: Princeton University Press, 1997), 2–3.

78. Ibid., 3–4.

79. Ibid.

80. Although it is difficult to trace how and to what extent early modernists were actively engaging with Gestalt psychology, van Campen has identified clear currents between the two movements, arguing that "early abstract art and experimental Gestalt psychology share a common history. The discussed theories of perception were not entirely new. Although revolutionary within their disciplines of the visual arts and experimental psychology, the experiments with visual principles were in fact rooted in the *Kunstwissenschaft* (science of art) in the late nineteenth century." See Crétien van Campen, "Early Abstract Art and Experimental Gestalt Psychology," *Leonoardo* 30, no. 2 (1997): 135.

81. Stern, *Against Fashion*, 65.

82. Much like Delaunay, the Russian constructivist designer Nadezhda Lamanova was also interested in the relationship between the body and dress. Upholding the belief that even the most minor details were essential to the whole, Lamanova espoused the idea that, when working on a garment, "one has to keep in mind the integrity of the general project" in order to create harmony between the discrete parts of the garment and the "geometric planes" of the body. See Nadezhda Lamanova, "Concerning Contemporary Dress" ("O svremenem kostiume") in Stern, *Against Fashion*, 174–7.

83. Evans explains how Delaunay's partner, Robert Delaunay, applied the theories of Simultanism in his modernist painting *La Ville de Paris*, which like a three-way mirror permitted a simultaneous view of the body. Although Sonia Delaunay was not known for her figurative art, the same principles apply to her abstractions. See Evans, *Mechanical Smile*, 46–7.

84. Christina Kiaer, "The Russian Constructivist Flapper Dress," *Critical Inquiry* 28, no. 1 (2001): 185–243.

85. Martin, *Cubism and Fashion*, 11.

86. Ibid., 16.

87. Steele, *Paris Fashion*, 232.

88. Martin, *Cubism and Fashion*, 16.

89. Evans, *Mechanical Smile*, 23–4.

90. For instance, Michel Eugène Chevreul's groundbreaking work on the logic of color harmony was in no uncertain terms a precondition for the Impressionist movement, while Ogden N. Rood's *Modern Chromatics* (1879) formed the theoretical basis for the Neo-Impressionist work of Georges Seurat and Paul Signac. See Faber Birren, "Color Perception in Art: Beyond the Eye to the Brain," *Leonardo* 9, no. 2 (1976): 106.

91. Jonathan Crary, *Techniques of the Observer: On Vision and Modernity in the Nineteenth Century* (Cambridge: MIT Press, 1992), 9.

92. Lamanova, "Concerning Contemporary Dress," 175.

93. Leon Bakst, "A Famous Artist Analyses the Slim Silhouette," *Vogue* (December 1, 1923): 61.

94. "Color and Costume Theme of Bakst Lecture in Toronto," *Women's Wear* (March 8, 1923): 2.

95. "Leon Bakst Discusses Effect of Line and Color on Silhouette," *Women's Wear* (January 31, 1923): 5.

96. B. J. Perkins, "Sees Lelong as Disciple of Modern School," *Women's Wear* (August 3, 1925): 2.

97. "Lucien Lelong Declares 'Kinetic Design' Acceleration of Modern Era," *Women's Wear* (August 13, 1925): 2. See also Lucien Lelong Advertisement, *Women's Wear* (August 11, 1925): 9.

98. "Lucien Lelong Declares 'Kinetic Design' Acceleration of Modern Era," *Women's Wear* (August 13, 1925): 2.

99. "Lelong Terms His Models Suitable to Mature Styling," *Women's Wear* (October 20, 1925): 32.

100. "Lelong Ends Study of Business Here," *Women's Wear* (December 5, 1925): 16, 22.

101. "Lelong Considers Logic in Design for Present Modes," *Women's Wear* (August 16, 1926): 6.

102. Lucien Lelong double-page advertisement, *Vogue* (France) (August 1, 1925): xxvi–xxvii, quoted in Evans, *Mechanical Smile*, 132 no. 101.

103. Ibid., 133.

Chapter 3

1. "Take Up Stoutwear Wholeheartedly—Or Not at All," *The American Cloak and Suit Review* (July–December 1922): 122.

2. T.J. Jackson Lears, "From Salvation to Self-Realization: Advertising and the Therapeutic Roots of the Consumer Culture, 1880–1930" in *The Culture of Consumption: Critical Essays in American History, 1880–1980*, ed. Richard Wrightman Fox and T.J. Jackson Lears, 1–38 (New York: Pantheon, 1983).

3. William Leach, "Transformations in a Culture of Consumption: Women and Department Stores, 1890–1925," *The Journal of American History* 71, no. 2 (September 1984): 319–20.

4. Celia Lury, *Consumer Culture* (New Brunswick: Rutgers University Press, 2011), 9.

5. Ewen, *Captains of Consciousness*, 33.

6. Roland Marchand, *Advertising the American Dream: Making Way for Modernity, 1920–1940* (Berkeley: University of California Press, 1986), 1–2.

7. Walter Dill Scott, *The Psychology of Advertising* (Boston: Small, Maynard & Company, 1921), 2.

8. Ewen, *Captains of Consciousness*, 33.

9. Scott, *Psychology of Advertising*, 42–3.

10. Ibid.

11. Stuart Ewen and Elizabeth Ewen, *Channels of Desire: Mass Images and the Shaping of American Consciousness* (Minneapolis and London: University of Minnesota Press, 1992), 32–3. Ewen and Ewen's use of the term "civilizing" draws upon Norbert Elias' discussions of the "civilizing of the West," or the historical processes through which certain norms and customs are adopted within society as "civilized."

12. Lury, *Consumer Culture*, 108–36.

13. Marchand, *Advertising the American Dream*, 63–6.

14. The exception would have been in Black-owned newspapers. For further discussion, see Marchand, *Advertising the American Dream*, 64.

15. This recognition was preceded by earlier demographic trends, such as the fact that, as early as the 1840s and 1850s, shopping had become a woman's job, "reflecting the gender differentiation of roles that resulted from the separation of workplace and home that was supported by the rise of wage and salaried male labor." See Leach, "Transformations in a Culture of Consumption," 332–3; T.J. Jackson Lears, *Fables of Abundance: A Cultural History of Advertising in America* (New York: Basic Books, 1994), 183–92.

16. Leach, "Transformations in a Culture of Consumption," 333; Lury, *Consumer Culture*, 122–3; Kathy L. Peiss, "American Women and the Making of Modern Consumer Culture," *The Journal for MultiMedia History* 1, no. 1. (1998): n.p.

17. Marchand, *Advertising the American Dream*, 66–9.

18. Featherstone, "The Body in Consumer Culture," 18.

19. Ibid.

20. "Quality as Important as Size in Handling Stouts Trade," *Women's Wear* (January 9, 1917): 47.

21. Stearns, *Fat History*, 84.

22. Jane Arthurs, "Revolting Women: The Body in Comic Performance" in *Women's Bodies: Discipline and Transgression* (London: Cassell, 1999), 140.

23. "'Wonderland': A Coney Show: Fat Lady, Skeleton and All Moving to New York Theatre," *The New York Times* (January 20, 1913): 11.

24. Mikita Brottman and David Brottman, "Return of the Freakshow: Carnival (De)Formations in Contemporary Culture," *Studies in Popular Culture* 18, no. 2 (1996): 90.

25. "Ready for the Big Ones: A New Angle on the Fat Woman's Wants," *Women's Wear* (July 2, 1915): 3.

26. Stearns, *Fat History*, 84.

Notes

27. Annamma Joy and Alladi Venkatesh, "Postmodernism, Feminism and the Body: The Visible and the Invisible in Consumer Research," *International Journal of Research in Marketing* 11, no. 4 (1994): 337.

28. "Stouts' Trade Valuable," *Dry Goods Economist* (December 30, 1916): 51.

29. "Take Up Stoutwear Wholeheartedly—Or Not at All," *The American Cloak and Suit Review* (July-December 1922): 122.

30. "Stout Garments," *Women's Wear* (September 2, 1919): 33.

31. Vigarello, *Metamorphoses of Fat*, xii.

32. Schwartz, *Never Satisfied*, 89.

33. Keist has also noted the proliferation of the terms "large figure, full figure, large women, silhouette beyond their attainment, comfortably housed woman of flesh, woman of robust proportions, plump, Juno type of figure, well developed figure, fleshy woman, inclined to rounding curves, stately figure, mature figure, matronly figure … heavy, extra size, generous proportions, unfortunate proportions, portly people, not-so-slender, big woman, chubby figure, woman of dignity, and stout miss." See Kiest, "The New Costumes of Odd Sizes," 6. Most of these terms, however, were used less widely for commercial or advertising purposes.

34. "Manufacturers in Increasing Numbers, Concentrate on Small Women's Sizes," *Women's Wear* (July 29, 1924): 30.

35. "Large Stores Organize Reducing Sections in Corset Departments," *Women's Wear* (July 24, 1924): 20.

36. Edith Sampson, "Some Small Advertisements for Large Sizes," *Women's Wear* (July 17, 1920): 43.

37. "Quality as Important as Size in Handling Stouts Trade," *Women's Wear* (January 9, 1917): 47.

38. "Between the Lines with the Ad Men," *Women's Wear* (May 3, 1922): 37.

39. Stearns, *Fat History*, 23.

40. "Outline of Salesforce Talk at Jordan Marsh: The Knack of Selling the 'Stout' Person—The Importance of This Class of Trade," *Women's Wear* (October 20, 1916): 4.

41. "In the Ad World: Filene's Glad Tidings for the Stout Woman," *Women's Wear* (April 2, 1917): 23.

42. Edith Sampson, "Some Small Advertisements for Large Sizes," *Women's Wear* (July 17, 1920): 43.

43. This was the title of a recurring advertising commentary section in *Women's Wear* in the 1920s.

44. Lane Bryant Advertisement, *Brooklyn Daily Eagle* (June 26, 1927): 10.

45. Ibid.

46. By this point, Lena Bryant, the woman, and Lane Bryant, the company's sympathetic figurehead (and product of a clerical error), had fused into one individual. There was little mention of "Lena Bryant" in the professional media.

47. "Poem Citing Style Woes of Stout Woman Answered in Ad That Sells Store's Slenderizing Service," *Women's Wear* (July 2, 1927): 5.

48. Lears notes that in the early twentieth century, women's magazines regularly assailed the "fashionable woman" as "frivolous" even as she was held up in the fashion press. See Lears, *Fables of Abundance*, 184.

49. Lane Bryant Advertisement, *The Brooklyn Daily Eagle* (June 26, 1927): 10.

50. Marchand, *Advertising the American Dream*, 13.

51. Ibid., 14.

52. Ewen, *Captains of Consciousness*, 45.

53. Lane Bryant Advertisement, *The Ladies' Home Journal* (September 1923): 151.

54. Keist, "How Stout Women Were Left Out of High Fashion," 35; Keist, "Stout Women Can Now Be Stylish," 106.

55. See, for example, "Special Service for Stouts Brings Store Permanent Business," *Dry Goods Merchants Trade Journal* (March 1920): 56–9.

56. Lears, *Fables of Abundance*, 162, 165.

57. Susannah Walker, *Style and Status: Selling Beauty to African American Women* (Lexington: University of Kentucky Press, 2007), 8.

58. Lears, *Fables of Abundance*, 187.

59. Cheryl Buckley and Hillary Fawcett, *Fashioning the Feminine: Representation and Women's Fashion from the Fin de Siècle to the Present* (London: I.B. Tauris, 2002), 74.

60. Cally Blackman notes that photography first appeared in fashion magazines around 1900; however, the stylistic influence of Paul Poiret, who commissioned illustrations by artists like Paul Iribe and Georges Lepape to publicize his collections, would have ramifications across the fashion media landscape. The *Gazette du Bon Ton*, with its lavish, full-color, stylized fashion plates, would also prove highly influential, with illustrators working for both European and American publications throughout the 1920s and 1930s. See Cally Blackman, *100 Years of Fashion Illustration* (London: Laurence King, 2007), 9–10.

61. Breward, *Fashion*, 115.

Chapter 4

1. Forth, *Fat*, 241.

2. See, for instance, "Stouts' Trade Valuable," *Dry Goods Economist* (December 30, 1916): 51; "The Problem of the Straight Silhouette: Fitting the Flat Back to the Full Figure," *Vogue* (November 1923): 44–5.

3. Schwartz, "Torque," 77.

4. Rebecca Arnold, *The American Look: Fashion, Sportswear and the Image of Women in 1930s and 1940s New York* (London: I.B. Tauris, 2009), 52–60.

5. "The Importance of Being Beautiful," *Vogue* (June 1, 1924): 52–3.

6. Ibid., 53.

7. Helen Bullitt Lowry, "Getting Thin to Music," *Harper's Bazaar* (October 1923): 168, 170.

8. Kathy Peiss, *Hope in a Jar: The Making of America's Beauty Culture* (Pittsburgh: University of Pennsylvania Press, 1998), 11–12.

9. Agnès Rocamora, *Fashioning the City: Paris, Fashion and the Media* (London: I.B. Tauris, 2009), 54–62.

10. Ibid., 57.

11. Ibid., 56.

12. Caroline Evans and Minna Thornton, *Women and Fashion: A New Look* (London: Quartet Books, 1989), 81–3.

13. "Delusions in Dress," *Vogue* (May 15, 1926): 70.

14. While glass mirrors similar in clarity and appearance to the mirrors of today were in use as early as the sixteenth century, small vanity mirrors only began to enter bourgeois households at the end of the eighteenth century. It was not until the end of the nineteenth century, however, that the free-standing, full-length mirror, which allowed one to view the entirety of her body from head to toe, came into wide use. The Pittsburgh Plate Glass Company further modernized manufacturing techniques so that by the late 1920s, sheet glass could be produced en masse and affordably. See Sabine Melchior-Bonnet, *The Mirror: A History*, trans. Katharine H. Jewett (New York: Routledge, 2001), x.

15. Evans, *The Mechanical Smile*, 155–7.

16. Caroline Evans, "Masks, Mirrors and Mannequins: Elsa Schiaparelli and the Decentered Subject," *Fashion Theory* 3, no. 1 (1999): 18.

17. "The Importance of Being Beautiful," *Vogue* (June 1, 1924): 98.

18. "The Importance of Vanity," *Vogue* (November 15, 1924): 57.

19. "Delusions in Dress," *Vogue* (May 15, 1926): 70.

20. Melchior-Bonnet, *The Mirror*, 156.

21. Vigarello, *Metamorphoses of Fat*, 146.

22. Ibid.

23. Marchand, *Advertising the American Dream*, 175.

24. Ibid.

25. "Convex Mirror for Stylish Stouts," *The New York Times* (November 21, 1926): 20.

26. For further discussion of Malsin's survey, see Chapter 2.

27. Keist, "The New Costumes of Odd Sizes," 85.

28. "Suppose You *Are* 40-Odd!" *The Ladies' Home Journal* (November 1919): 33.

29. Brumberg, *Fasting Girls*, 238–40; Schwartz, *Never Satisfied*, 174–83; Stearns, *Fat History*, 38.

30. Stearns, *Fat History*, 82.

31. "Odds Against Chic in Middle Age," *Vogue* (November 10, 1928): 77.

32. "A Guide to Chic for the Woman of Forty or More," *Vogue* (September 15, 1926): 94.

33. "To Meet the Silhouette," *Harper's Bazaar* (April 1924): 168.

34. "A Guide to Chic for the Stout Older Woman," *Vogue* (April 15, 1924): 78.

35. "Chic in the Years of Discretion," *Vogue* (November 10, 1928): 77.

36. Ibid.

37. "A Guide to Chic for the Older Woman," *Vogue* (July 1, 1927): 52.

38. "A Guide to Chic for the Woman of Forty or More," *Vogue* (September 15, 1926): 94.

39. Julia Twigg, *Fashion and Age: Dress, the Body and Later Life* (London: Bloomsbury 2013), 14.

40. "Chic in the Years of Discretion," *Vogue* (November 10, 1928): 180.

41. "Graceful Lines for Large Figures," *Harper's Bazaar* (October 1914): 52.

42. "The Human Female Figger," *Vogue* (July 15, 1924): 48.

43. Underneath the domestic, in order of diminishing body mass, are the athletic, the romantic, and the anemic. Within this hierarchy, the romantic, or who with her youthfulness and slenderness, is "the universal ideal of femininity." Ibid., 76.

44. Patricia Hill Collins, *Black Feminist Thought: Knowledge, Consciousness and the Politics of Empowerment* (New York: Routledge, 1991), 71.

45. Andrea Elizabeth Shaw, *The Embodiment of Disobedience* (Lanham: Lexington Books, 2006), 20.

46. Ibid., 20, 23.

47. Mary Louise Roberts, *Civilization Without Sexes: Reconstructing Gender in Postwar France: 1917–1927* (Chicago and London: University of Chicago Press), 72–3.

48. "The Human Female Figger," *Vogue* (July 15, 1924): 48.

49. Banner, *American Beauty*, 412.

50. Roberts, *Civilization Without Sexes*, 68.

51. Banner, *American Beauty*, 406.

52. "The Human Female Figger," 48.

53. Ibid.

54. Ibid., 49.

55. Stephanie Coontz, "The Origins of Modern Divorce," *Family Process* 46, no. 1 (2006): 11; Stearns, *Fat History*, 83.

56. Rebecca Stickney, "Make Yourself over for Spring," *Harper's Bazaar* (April 1929), 130.

57. This quote comes from fitness guru Anette Kellerman's massively popular diet book *Physical Beauty: How to Keep It* (New York: George H. Doran Company, 1918). In this book, Kellerman foregrounded the importance of staying slender and youthful in order to for a woman to retain her husband's admiration.

58. "A Guide to Chic for the Complacent," *Vogue* (September 1, 1927), 76–7, 102.

59. Ibid.

60. It's worth underscoring that only a decade prior, a slender woman would have been out of sync with the fashionable, hourglass silhouette and would have had to rely upon bust ruffles and bum pads to achieve the desired silhouette.

61. Schwartz, *Never Satisfied*, 160.

62. "A Guide to Chic for the Complacent," *Vogue* (September 1, 1927): 76.

63. "A Guide to Chic for the Older Woman," *Vogue* (July 1, 1927): 52.

64. "Shopping for the Older Woman," *Vogue* (December 15, 1927): 75.

65. "A Guide to Chic for the Stout Older Woman," *Vogue* (April 15, 1924): 52.

66. Ibid., 100.

67. "The Older Woman and the New Mode," *Vogue* (November 23, 1929): 88.

68. "A Guide to Chic for the Stout Older Woman," *Vogue* (April 15, 1924): 78.

69. "Smart Aids to Slenderness," *Vogue* (May 1, 1921): 118.

70. "Business Notes: New York—A Revolution in Fitting Stylish Stout Women, Says Mr. Ellis of Steinberg, Ellis & Schofield—The 'Pillow Tied in the Middle' Shape Is Passé," *Women's Wear* (November 17, 1915): 9.

71. Schwartz, *Never Satisfied*, 80.

72. Ibid., 81.

73. Hollander, *Seeing Through Clothes*, 338.

74. "Figures That Do and Do Not Lie," *Vogue* (November 15, 1923): 63.

75. Valerie Steele, *The Corset: A Cultural History* (New Haven: Yale University Press, 2003), 143.

76. "Odds Against Chic in Middle Age," *Vogue* (February 15, 1924): 72.

77. "A Famous Artist Analyses the Slim Silhouette," *Vogue* (December 1, 1923): 60.

78. Anne Rittenhouse, "Desirable Clothes for Stout and Elderly Women," *The New York Times* (August 11, 1912): 78.

79. "For the Woman with Grown Daughters," *Vogue* (July 1, 1923): 64.

80. Florence Hull Winterburn, *Principles of Correct Dress* (New York: Harper & Brothers Publishers, 1914), 108.

81. Joy and Venkatesh, "Postmodernism, Feminism and the Body," 337.

Chapter 5

1. Mary Brooks Picken, *Harmony in Dress* (Scranton: Woman's Institute of Domestic Arts and Sciences, 1925), 40.

2. Valerie Steele, "Artificial Beauty, or the Morality of Dress and Adornment" in *The Fashion History Reader*, ed. Giorgio Riello and Peter McNeil (London: Routledge, 2010), 276.

3. Keist, "The New Costumes of Odd Sizes," 86.

4. Helen Goodrich Buttrick, *Principles of Clothing Selection* (New York: The MacMillan Company, 1927), 6–7.

5. Charlotte Nicklas, "One Essential Thing Is Colour: Harmony, Science and Colour Theory in Mid-Nineteenth Century Fashion Advice," *Journal of Design History* 27, no. 3 (2014): 219.

6. Schwartz observes that "fat women were … to be especially clean, dry, odorless. As if, almost, they would leave no trail." There was no shortage of advertisements for deodorants, anti-perspirants, colognes, and lozenges that were targeted specifically to fat women. See Schwartz, *Never Satisfied*, 161–2. The fat woman's table manners were also a particular subject of concern. See, for instance, "Some Toothsome Dishes: Don'ts for Stout Women," *The New York Times* (May 29, 1910): 63.

7. Kiest, "The New Costumes of Odd Sizes," 86–7.

8. See Marie Cary, *Style and the Woman* (New York: The Textile Publishing Company, 1924), 7; Mary Brooks Picken, *Harmony in Dress* (Scranton: Women's Institute of Domestic Arts and Sciences, 1925), 42; Jane Warren Wells, *Dress and Look Slender* (Scranton: International Textbook Company, 1924), 130.

9. Rita Stuyvesant, "Even as You and I: Vertical Stripes Add Height," *The Brooklyn Daily Eagle* (February 6, 1925): 16.

10. Anne Rittenhouse, *The Well-Dressed Woman* (New York and London: Harper & Brothers, 1924), 95.

11. Featherstone, "The Body in Consumer Culture"; 27; Edwin L. Battistella, "The Yardstick of Manners," *Culture and Society* 46, no. 1 (2009): 363–7. For further discussion of how etiquette manuals related to the women's and fashion media in the late nineteenth and early twentieth centuries, see Craik, *The Face of Fashion*, 49–50.

12. Entwistle, *The Fashioned Body*, 11.

13. Buckley and Clark, *Fashion and Everyday Life*, 17.

14. Wells, *Dress and Look Slender*, 1–3.

15. Ibid., 4.

16. Ibid., 16.

17. "Books Received," *The Indianapolis Star* (December 21, 1924): 53.

18. Wells, *Dress and Look Slender*, 1.

19. Ibid., 179.

20. Stearns, *Fat History*, 71–2. For similar arguments, see also Douglas, *Purity and Danger*; Featherstone, "The Body in Consumer Culture"; Turner, *The Body in Society*.

21. Brumberg, *Fasting Girls*, 229; Peiss, *Hope in a Jar*, 7.

22. Banner, *American Beauty*, 291–8; Stearns, *Fat History*, 105; Vigarello, *Metamorphoses of Fat*, 170.

23. Featherstone, "The Body in Consumer Culture," 22.

24. Brumberg, *Fasting Girls*, 236; Entwistle, *The Fashioned Body*, 19.

25. Wells, *Dress and Look Slender*, 6.

26. Ibid., 15–16.

27. Ibid., 78.

28. This was an issue that was discussed at great length in the professional media in the early twentieth century, but which has gone largely overlooked in the histories of American fashion, sizing, and ready-to-wear. See, for instance, "Discuss Charges by Stores for Alterations," *Women's Wear* (May 14, 1926): 8, 39; "Discussing High Costs of Alterations," *Women's Wear* (August 19, 1919): 3; "Paull Outlines Aid Promised Retail Trade," *Women's Wear* (July 23, 1923): 1, 43; "Who's to Blame for Alterations?" *Women's Wear* (August 29, 1917): 25.

29. Wells, *Dress and Look Slender*, 16.

30. Ibid., 9, 172–3.

31. Ibid., 12.

32. Entwistle, *The Fashioned Body*, 14–15.

33. Wells, *Dress and Look Slender*, 10.

34. Entwistle, *The Fashioned Body*, 20–3. For further discussion on self-fashioning as a dialogic, rather than expressive, practice, see Wilson, *Adorned in Dreams*, 137; Buckley and Clark, *Fashion and Everyday Life*, 27–51.

35. Frank Crane, "Dress and Look Slender," *Wisconsin State Journal* (November 4, 1925): 3; Madelyn Shaw, "American Fashion: The Tirocchi Sisters in Context" in *From Paris to Providence: Fashion Art and the Tirocchi Dressmakers' Shop, 1915–1947* (Providence: The Rhode Island School of Design, 1999), n.p.

36. Linda Przybyszweski, *The Lost Art of Dress: The Women Who Once Made America Stylish* (New York: Basic Books, 2014), 8.

37. Arnold, *The American Look*, 44. Here, Arnold is referencing Paul Schilder's book *The Image and Appearance of the Human Body: Studies in Constructive Energies of the Psyche* (New York: International Universities Press, 1970).

38. Often drawing upon sophisticated theories drawn from disciplines as disparate as psychology and physiology, a distinguishing quality of style advice literature—and partly what made it so popular with American women—was the manner its authors translated complex ideas into layman's terms, frequently through personal anecdotes. See Przybyszewski, *The Lost Art of Dress*, 16, 24.

39. For further discussion about how fashion images "work" in the construction of body image, see Arnold, *The American Look*, 39–45.

40. Anne Buck, "Clothes in Fact and Fiction, 1825–1865," *Costume* 17, no. 1 (1983): 89–104.

41. "How Many Fat Women in Your Town?" *Women's Wear* (June 11, 1915): 3. Stearns similarly describes the shame and guilt that fat women must have felt when faced with the early twentieth century's onslaught of weight-reducing products. See Stearns, *Fat History*, 71–85.

42. Sophie Tucker and Ager Yellen, "I Don't Want to Get Thin," *I Don't Want to Get Thin* (London: His Master's Voice, 1929).

43. Susan A. Glenn, *Female Spectacle: The Theatrical Roots of Modern Feminism* (Cambridge: Harvard University Press, 2000), 5–7.

44. Banner, *American Beauty*, 218–9.

45. Sophie Tucker, *Some of These Days: The Autobiography of Sophie Tucker* (self-pub., 1945), 11.

46. Marlis Schweitzer, *When Broadway Was the Runway: Theater, Fashion and American Culture* (Philadelphia: University of Pennsylvania Press, 2009), 107.

47. Schweitzer, *When Broadway Was the Runway*, 106.

48. Tucker, *Some of These Days*, 26–8.

49. M. Alison Kibler, *Rank Ladies: Gender and Cultural Hierarchy in American Vaudeville* (Chapel Hill: University of North Carolina Press, 1999), 129.

50. Kathleen B. Casey, "'The Jewish Girl with a Colored Voice': Sophie Tucker and the Sounds of Race and Gender in Modern America," *The Journal of American Culture* 38, no. 1 (2015): 16; Lori Harrison-Kahan, *The White Negress: Literature, Minstrelsy, and the Black-Jewish Imaginary* (New Brunswick: Rutgers University Press, 2011), 16–17, 28.

51. Tucker, *Some of These Days*, 33–4.

52. Shaw, *The Embodiment of Disobedience*, 104.

53. "Coon" is a racist, derogatory term used to label African Americans. "Coon shouting" specifically referred to performances in which entertainers, donning blackface, would sing ragtime tunes in an overly theatrical manner that drew upon common racist stereotypes. For Tucker's description of her blackface period, see Tucker, *Some of These Days*, 35.

54. Al C. Joy, "Coon Shouting as a Fine Art Form," *San Francisco Examiner* (September 25, 1910): 75.

55. Robert C. Toll, *Blacking Up: The Minstrel Show in Nineteenth-Century America* (New York: Oxford University Press, 1974), 30–4.

56. Susan Gubar, *Racechanges: White Skin, Black Face in American Culture* (Oxford: Oxford University Press, 2000), 55–6.

57. Maria De Simone, "Sophie Tucker, Racial Hybridity and Interracial Relations in American Vaudeville," *Theater Research International* 44, no. 2 (2019): 156; Eric Lott, *Love and Theft: Blackface Minstrelsy and the American Working Class* (New York: Oxford University Press, 2013).

58. Harrison-Kahan, *The White Negress*, 18–20.

59. Sander L. Gilman, "Black Bodies, White Bodies: Toward an Iconography of Female Sexuality in Late Nineteenth Century Art, Medicine and Literature," *Critical Inquiry* 12, no. 1 (1985): 204–42; Glenn, *Female Spectacle*, 51; Shaw, *The Embodiment of Disobedience*, 101–4; Strings, *Fearing the Black Body*, 90–8.

60. Shaw, *The Embodiment of Disobedience*, 104.

61. Schweitzer, *When Broadway Was the Runway*, 110.

62. Ibid., 111.

63. Tucker, *Some of These Days*, 63–5.

64. Glenn, *Female Spectacle*, 45–6, 56.

65. Brottman and Brottman, "Return of the Freakshow," 90; Jennifer-Scott Mobley, *Female Bodies on the American Stage: Enter Fat Actress* (New York: Palgrave MacMillan, 2014), 128–30.

66. Tucker, *Some of These Days*, 116, 204.

67. Ibid., 105.

68. Tucker, *Some of These Days*, 106.

69. "Sense of Proportion Vital in Costuming Stout Woman, Declares Actress," *Women's Wear* (October 5, 1922): 14.

70. Tucker, *Some of These Days*, 106, 116.

71. Al C. Joy, "Coon Shouting as a Fine Art Form," *San Francisco Examiner* (September 25, 1910): 75; "Jazz Improves New Music Show," *The Evening Sun* (September 30, 1919): 14.

72. Tucker, *Some of These Days*, 204.

73. See, for instance, Florence Hull Winterburn, *The Secrets of Distinctive Dress* (Scranton: International Textbook Press 1918), iii; "Some Toothsome Dishes: Don'ts for Stout Women," *The New York Times* (May 29, 1910): 63; "The Importance of Being Beautiful," *Vogue* (June 1, 1924): 98.

74. Wells, *Dress and Look Slender*, 39–40.

75. Grace Overbeke, "Subversively Sexy: The Jewish 'Red Hot Mamas' Sophie Tucker, Belle Barth and Pearl Williams," *Studies in American Humor* 3, no. 25 (2012): 40–2.

76. Ibid., 45.

77. Tucker, *Some of These Days*, 206–7.

78. "Sophie Tucker Has Fat Taken Off Face; Reveals Her Third Marriage," *Salt Lake Telegraph* (January 3, 1929): 1.

79. "'Red Hot Mama' Cools Off, Now 'Stylish Stout,'" *Cuming County Democrat* (February 25, 1937): 2.

80. "Use of Sophie Tucker Endorsement in Large Size Blouse Promotion Works Well," *Women's Wear* (November 26, 1946): 48.

81. "Ma Rainey Packs 'Em in at Monogram," *The Chicago Defender* (February 21, 1925): 6; Bob Hayes, "Ma Rainey's Review," *The Chicago Defender* (February 13, 1926): 6.

82. Donald Bogle, *Brown Sugar: Eighty Years of America's Black Female Superstars* (New York: Da Capo Press, 1980), 18.

83. Bogle, *Brown Sugar*, 21.

84. Angela Y. Davis, *Blues Legacies and Black Feminism: Gertrude "Ma" Rainey, Bessie Smith, and Billie Holiday* (New York: Vintage Books, 1998), 35.

85. Sandra Lieb, *Mother of the Blues: A Study of Ma Rainey* (Boston: The University of Massachusetts Press, 1981), 2–4.

86. Driven in part by the popularity of white minstrel shows, versions featuring Black performers emerged by 1855 and were common by the 1870s. See Toll, *Blacking Up*, 30–40.

87. Daphne Duval Harrison, *Black Pearls: Blues Queens of the 1920s* (New Brunswick: Rutgers University Press, 1988), 37; Lieb, *Mother of the Blues*, 7, 12.

88. Hans R. Rookmaaker, Liner notes, *Ma Rainey, Mother of the Blues*. Riverside RM 8807, quoted in Lieb, *Mother of the Blues*, 30.

89. Bogle, *Brown Sugar*, 21.

90. Chris Albertson, *Bessie* (New Haven: Yale University Press, 2005), 115.

91. Lieb, *Mother of the Blues*, 8.

92. Ibid., 131. See also Albertson, *Bessie*, 115; Bogle, *Brown Sugar*, 18.

93. Lieb, *Mother of the Blues*, 10.

94. Glenn, *Female Spectacle*, 51.

95. bell hooks, *Black Looks: Race and Representation* (Boston: South End Press, 1992), 65–6.

96. Mobley, *Female Bodies on the American Stage*, 101; Shaw, *The Embodiment of Disobedience*, 8.

97. James R. Grossman, *Land of Hope: Chicago, Black Southerners, and the Great Migration* (Chicago: University of Chicago Press, 1989), 4.

98. Lieb, *Mother of the Blues*, 22, 92.

99. Monica L. Miller, *Slaves to Fashion: Black Dandyism and the Styling of Black Diasporic Identity* (Durham: Duke University Press, 2009), 177; Clyde Woods, *Development Arrested: Race, Power, and the Blues in the Mississippi Delta* (London: Verso, 1998), 16–17.

100. Davarian L. Baldwin, *Chicago's New Negroes: Modernity, the Great Migration, and Black Urban Life* (Chicago: University of Chicago Press, 2009), 17.

101. Evelyn Brooks Higgenbotham, *Righteous Discontent: The Women's Movement in the Black Baptist Church 1880-1920* (Cambridge: Harvard University Press, 1993), 185–90. See also Baldwin, *Chicago's New Negroes*, 56; Miriam Thaggert, *Images of Black Modernism: Verbal and Visual Strategies of the Harlem Renaissance* (Amherst and Boston: University of Massachusetts Press, 2010), 3; Shane White and Graham White, *Stylin': African American Expressive Culture from Its Beginnings to the Zoot Suit* (Ithaca: Cornell University Press, 1998), 154.

102. While the turn of the century New Negro movement was mostly debated among writers and intellectuals who discussed different strategies for racial integration and civil rights, in the 1920s the movement became both more inclusive and more progressive. Its focus also shifted away from civil rights specifically to Black modernity more broadly. See Baldwin, *Chicago's New Negros*, 18–20. See also Laila Haidarali, *Brown Beauty: Color, Sex, and Race from the Harlem Renaissance to World War II* (New York: New York University Press, 2018), 7–15.

103. Ibid., 30.

104. Peiss, *Hope in a Jar*, 7.

105. White and White, *Stylin'*, 188. For further discussion about integrationist perspectives of African Americans' participation in the marketplace, see Walker, *Style and Status*, 6–7.

106. Einav Rabinovitch-Fox, "Fabricating Black Modernity: Fashion and African American Womanhood During the First Great Migration," *International Journal of Fashion Studies* 6, no. 2 (2019): 242.

107. Ibid., 243.

108. Alphonso McClendon, *Fashion and Jazz: Dress, Identity and Subcultural Improvisation* (London: Bloomsbury, 2015), 24, 93.

109. Shaw, *The Embodiment of Disobedience*, 23.

110. Rabinovitch-Fox, "Fabricating Black Modernity," 253. For further discussion about flamboyance as a political strategy, see White and White, *Stylin'*, 125–9.

111. McClendon, *Fashion and Jazz*, 24.

112. Rabinovitch-Fox, "Fabricating Black Modernity," 253; Walker, *Selling Beauty*, 70–1.

113. Zandria F. Robinson, "Gotta Sing on the Beats They Bring Us: Towards a Twenty-First Century Blues Women's Epistemology," *Issues in Race & Society* 2, no. 1 (2014): 52.

114. Shaw, *The Embodiment of Disobedience*, 78–81; Stearns, *Fat History*, 89–92.

115. Lieb, *Mother of the Blues*, 10.

116. White and White, *Stylin'*, 195, 200.

117. Rabinovitch-Fox, "Fabricating Black Modernity," 241.

118. Leib, *Mother of the Blues*, 8; Shaw, *The Embodiment of Disobedience*, 108.

119. Shaw, *The Embodiment of Disobedience*, 107.

120. Ibid., 101.

121. Bogle, *Brown Sugar*, 18.

122. Maxine Leeds Craig, *Ain't I a Beauty Queen? Black Women, Beauty, and the Politics of Race* (Oxford: Oxford University Press, 2002), 14.

123. Entwistle, *The Fashioned Body*, 11.

124. Ibid., 6–7.

Conclusion

1. "Would Foster Classification of Dress Sizes," *Women's Wear* (January 7, 1929): 11.

2. Ibid.

3. "'Stout' Said to Have Outlived Its Usefulness," *Women's Wear* (January 10, 1929): 9.

4. "Diet Decimates Stouts, Dress Producer Says," *Women's Wear* (May 5, 1930): 5.

5. Ibid.

6. See "Chubby Customers Encouraged to Shop at Lane Bryant for Specially Styled Underwear," *Women's Wear* (June 4, 1947): 17; "Chubby Fashions on Slender Lines at Lane Bryant," *Women's Wear* (August 27, 1953): 3; "Chubbies Have Their Own Fashion World," *Women's Wear* (July 10, 1957): 77; "Lane Bryant Sets Fall Style Shows," *Women's Wear* (August 6, 1958): 9.

7. Caroline Rennolds Milbank, *New York Fashion: The Evolution of American Style* (New York: Harry N. Abrams, Inc., 1989), 98–100.

8. For a discussion of the drugs that emerged in the 1930s to combat "obesity," see Schwartz, *Never Satisfied*, 191–235. Also notable during this period was the fact that "obesity" for the first time had come to be linked with other causes of mortality and other health conditions, namely heart conditions. See Seagrave, *Obesity in America*, 132–8.

9. Vigarello, *Metamorphoses of Fat*, 175.

10. For further discussion about the plus-size boom in the 1980s and 1990s, see Lauren Downing Peters, "'Fashion Plus': Pose and the Plus-Size Body in *Vogue*, 1986–1988," *Fashion Theory* 23, no. 2 (2019): 167–94.For primary reportage on this moment, see "Large-size Boom Generates Ego Consultants," *Women's Wear Daily* (January 7, 1986): 23; "Large-size Departments Told to Increase Their Range," *Women's Wear Daily* (November 16, 1984):15; "Large-Size Dresses Heat Up," *Women's Wear Daily* (March 13, 1984): 29; "Large Sizes Growth Prompts NRMA Seminar," *Women's Wear Daily* (October 9, 1984): 30; "Stores Find Large-size Dress Pickings Slim," *Women's Wear* (March 16, 1982): 10.

11. Journalist Gianluca Russo has examined the role that activists and influencers have played in advocating for the fat woman and her clothing needs, thereby buoying the contemporary boom in size-inclusive fashion. See Gianluca Russo, *The Power of Plus: Inside Fashion's Size-Inclusivity Revolution* (Chicago: Chicago Review Press, 2022). For further discussion about the role that social media platforms, specifically, have played in this process, see Lauren Peters, "Discourses of Discontent: Fashion, Activism and the Commodification of Fat Women's Anger," *Fat Studies: The Journal of Body Weight and Society*, online first (April 19, 2021).

12. Kellie Ell, "The Growing Plus-size Market Faces Itty-bitty Assortments and Lack of Options," *Women's Wear Daily* (August 6, 2021), https://wwd.com/fashion-news/fashion-features/the-growing-plus-size-market-faces-itty-bitty-assortments-and-lack-of-options-1234881354/.

13. Deborah Christel and Susan C. Dunn, "Average American Women's Clothing Size: Comparing National Health and Nutritional Examination Surveys (1988–2010) to ASTM International Misses & Women's Plus Size Clothing," *International Journal of Fashion Design, Technology and Education* 10, no. 1 (2017): 129–36.

14. See Alison Adam, "Big Girls' Blouses: Learning to Live with Polyester" in *Through the Wardrobe: Women's Relationships with Their Clothes*, ed. Ali Guy, Eileen Green and Maura Banim, 39–53 (Oxford: Berg, 2001); Katelynn Bishop, Kjerstin Gruys and Maddie Evans, "Sized Out: Women, Clothing Size, and Inequality," *Gender & Society* 32, no. 2 (2018): 180–203; Rachel Colls, "Looking Alright, Feeling Alright: Emotions, Sizing and the Geographies of Women's Experiences of Clothing Consumption," *Social & Cultural Geography* 5, no. 1 (2004): 583–96; "Outsize/Outside: Bodily Bignesses and the Emotional Experience of British Women Shopping for Clothes," *Gender, Place and Culture* 13, no. 5 (2006): 529–45; Ingun Grimstad Klepp and Mari Rysst, "Deviant Bodies and Suitable Clothes," *Fashion Theory* 21, no. 1 (2017): 79–99; Lauren Downing Peters, "You Are What You Wear: How Plus-Size Fashion Figures in Fat Identity Formation," *Fashion Theory* 18, No. 1 (2014): 45–71.

15. Calla Evans, "You Aren't What You Wear: An Exploration into Infinifat Identity Construction and Performance Through Fashion," *Fashion Studies* 3, no. 1 (2020): 3.

16. Volonte, *Fat Fashion*, 1.

17. US Patent no. 20130145516A1.

18. Douglas, *Purity and Danger*, 142.

19. Klein, "Fat Beauty," 27.

20. Lury discusses the origins Body Positivity Movement within the context of the rise of what has variously been described as "commodity feminism" and "feminist consumerism" in the early twenty-first century. For an overview of these debates, see Lury, *Consumer Culture*, 130–1.

21. Fahs points out that self-care is frequently, but problematically, posited as inherently pleasurable within neoliberal discourse. See Breanne Fahs, "Mapping 'Gross' Bodies: The Regulatory Politics of Disgust" in *Aesthetic Labor: Rethinking Beauty Politics in Neoliberalism*, ed. Ana Elias, Rosalind Gill and Christina Scharff (London: Palgrave, 2017), 94.

22. For an overview of the way that fashion has been employed as a tool of resistance and subversion within fat activist communities, see Lauren Gurrieri and Hélène Cherrier, "Queering Beauty: Fatshionistas in the Fatosphere," *Qualitative Market Research* 16, no. 3 (2013): 276–95.

23. Gianluca Russo, "Why Do So Many Plus-Size Fashion Launches Fall Short?" *Refinery 29*, July 20, 2022, https://www.refinery29.com/en-us/2022/07/11045932/plus-size-brands-inclusive-sizing-failing.

24. Ben Barry and Deborah Christel, "Radical Fashion Educators Unite: An Introduction" in *Fashion Education: The Systemic Revolution*, ed. Ben Barry and Deborah Christel (Bristol and Chicago: Intellect, 2023), viii.

25. "About Us," Chromat, accessed May 9, 2022, https://chromat.co/pages/about-us.

26. "Our Letter," Universal Standard, accessed May 9, 2022, https://www.universalstandard.com/pages/about-us.

27. The term "infinifat" was coined by fat activist and host of the *Fat Lip* podcast, Ash, and is used within activist circles to describe individuals who, due to their body size, are unable to shop at mainstream plus-size stores. See Evans, "You Aren't What You Wear," 3.

BIBLIOGRAPHY

Adam, Alison. "Big Girls' Blouses: Learning to Live with Polyester." In *Through the Wardrobe: Women's Relationships with Their Clothes*, edited by Ali Guy, Eileen Green and Maura Banim, 39–53. Oxford: Berg, 2001.

Albertson, Chris. *Bessie*. New Haven: Yale University Press, 2005.

Aldrich, Winifred. "History of Sizing Systems and Ready-to-Wear Garments." In *Sizing in Clothing: Developing Effective Sizing Systems for Ready-to-Wear Clothing*, edited by Susan P. Ashdown, 1–48. Cambridge: Woodhead, 2007.

Almond, Kevin. "Fashionably Voluptuous: Repackaging the Fuller-Sized Figure." *Fashion Theory: The Journal of Dress, Body & Culture* 17, no. 2 (2013): 197–122.

Armstrong, Tim. "Disciplining the Corpus: Henry James and Fletcherism." In *American Bodies: Cultural Histories of the Physique*, edited by Tim Armstrong, 101–19. New York: New York University Press, 1996.

Armstrong, Tim. *Modernism, Technology and the Body: A Cultural Study*. Cambridge: Cambridge University Press, 1998.

Arnold, Rebecca. *Fashion, Desire and Anxiety: Image and Morality in the 20th Century*. New Brunswick: Rutgers University Press, 2001.

Arnold, Rebecca. *The American Look: Fashion, Sportswear and the Image of Women in 1930s and 1940s New York*. London: I.B. Tauris, 2009.

Arthurs, Jane. "Revolting Women: The Body in Comic Performance." In *Women's Bodies: Discipline and Transgression*, edited by Jane Arthurs and Jean Grimshaw, 137–55. London: Cassell, 1999.

Baldwin, Davarian L. *Chicago's New Negroes: Modernity, the Great Migration, and Black Urban Life*. Chicago: University of Chicago Press, 2009.

Banner, Lois. *American Beauty: A Social History … Through Two Centuries of the American Idea, Ideal, and Image of the Beautiful Woman*. Los Angeles: Figueroa Press, 2005.

Barry, Ben and Deborah Christel. "Radical Fashion Educators Unite: An Introduction." In *Fashion Education: The Systemic Revolution*, viii–xiii. Bristol and Chicago: Intellect, 2023.

Bates, Marjory. "A Study of the Müller-Lyer Illusion, with Special Reference to Paradoxical Movement and the Effect of Attitude." *The American Journal of Psychology* 34, no. 1 (January 1923): 46–72.

Battistella, Edwin L. "The Yardstick of Manners." *Culture and Society* 46, no. 1 (2009): 363–7.

Bayle-Loudet, Aurore. "The Corset, Essential Protagonist of Modern Femininity." In *The Body: Fashion and Physique*, edited by Denis Bruna, 159–75. New Haven: Yale University Press, 2015.

Birren, Faber. "Color Perception in Art: Beyond the Eye to the Brain." *Leonardo* 9, no. 2 (1976): 105–10.

Bishop, Katelynn, Kjerstin Gruys and Maddie Evans. "Sized Out: Women, Clothing Size, and Inequality." *Gender & Society* 32, no. 2 (2018): 180–203.

Blackman, Cally. *100 Years of Fashion Illustration*. London: Laurence King, 2007.

Bogle, Donald. *Brown Sugar: Eighty Years of America's Black Female Superstars*. New York: Da Capo Press, 1980.

Bordo, Susan. *Unbearable Weight: Feminism, Western Culture and the Body*. Berkeley: University of California Press, 1993.

Breward, Christopher. *The Culture of Fashion*. Manchester: Manchester University Press, 1995.
Breward, Christopher. *The Hidden Consumer: Masculinities, Fashion and City Life 1860–1914*. Manchester: Manchester University Press, 1999.
Breward, Christopher. *Fashion*. Oxford: Oxford University Press, 2003.
Breward, Christopher and Caroline Evans. "Introduction." In *Fashion and Modernity*, edited by Christopher Breward and Caroline Evans, 1–7. Oxford: Berg, 2005.
Brottman, Mikita and David Brottman. "Return of the Freakshow: Carnival (De)Formations in Contemporary Culture." *Studies in Popular Culture* 18, no. 2 (1996): 89–107.
Brumberg, Joan Jacobs. *Fasting Girls: The History of Anorexia Nervosa*. New York: Vintage Books, 2000.
Buck, Anne. "Clothes in Fact and Fiction, 1825–1865." *Costume* 17, no. 1 (1983): 89–104.
Buckley, Cheryl and Hazel Clark. *Fashion and Everyday Life: London and New York*. London: Bloomsbury, 2017.
Buckley, Cheryl and Hillary Fawcett. *Fashioning the Feminine: Representation and Women's Fashion from the Fin de Siècle to the Present*. London: I.B. Tauris, 2002.
Burstein, Jessica. *Cold Modernism: Literature, Fashion, Art*. University Park: Pennsylvania State University Press, 2012.
Carden-Coyne, Ana and Christopher E. Forth. "Introduction: The Belly and Beyond: Body, Self, and Culture in Ancient and Modern Times." In *Cultures of the Abdomen: Diet, Digestion, and Fat in the Modern World*, edited by Ana Corden-Coyne and Christopher E. Forth, 1–12. New York: Palgrave MacMillan, 2005.
Casey, Kathleen B. "'The Jewish Girl with a Colored Voice': Sophie Tucker and the Sounds of Race and Gender in Modern America." *The Journal of American Culture* 38, no. 1 (2015): 16–26.
Christel, Deborah and Susan C. Dunn. "Average American Women's Clothing Size: Comparing National Health and Nutritional Examination Surveys (1988–2010) to ASTM International Misses & Women's Plus Size Clothing." *International Journal of Fashion Design, Technology and Education* 10, no. 1 (2017): 129–36.
Chun-Yoon, Jongsuck and Cynthia R. Jasper. "Development of Size Labelling Systems for Women's Garments." *Journal of Consumer Studies and Home Economics* 18, no. 1 (1994): 71–83.
Collins, Patricia Hill. *Black Feminist Thought: Knowledge, Consciousness and the Politics of Empowerment*. New York: Routledge, 1991.
Colls, Rachel. "Looking Alright, Feeling Alright: Emotions, Sizing and the Geographies of Women's Experiences of Clothing Consumption." *Social & Cultural Geography* 5, no. 1 (2004): 583–96.
Colls, Rachel. "Outsize/Outside: Bodily Bignesses and the Emotional Experience of British Women Shopping for Clothes." *Gender, Place and Culture* 13, no. 5 (2006): 529–45.
Coontz, Stephanie. "The Origins of Modern Divorce." *Family Process* 46, no. 1 (2006): 7–16.
Corrigan, Peter. *The Sociology of Consumption*. London: Sage, 1997.
Craik, Jennifer. *The Face of Fashion: Cultural Studies in Fashion*. London: Routledge, 1994.
Crary, Jonathan. *Techniques of the Observer: On Vision and Modernity in the Nineteenth Century*. Cambridge: MIT Press, 1992.
Czerniawski, Amanda. "From Average to Ideal: The Evolution of the Height and Weight Table in the United States, 1836–1943." *Social Science History* 31, no. 2 (2007): 273–96.
Czerniawski, Amanda. *Fashioning Fat: Inside Plus-Size Modeling*. New York: New York University Press, 2012.
Davis, Angela Y. *Blues Legacies and Black Feminism: Gertrude "Ma" Rainey, Bessie Smith, and Billie Holiday*. New York: Vintage Books, 1998.
de Perthius, Karen. "The Synthetic Ideal: The Fashion Model and Photographic Manipulation." Fashion Theory 9, no. 4 (2005): 407–24.

Bibliography

De Simone, Maria. "Sophie Tucker, Racial Hybridity and Interracial Relations in American Vaudeville." *Theater Research International* 44, no. 2 (2019): 153–70.

Douglas, Mary. *Purity and Danger: An Analysis of Concept of Pollution and Taboo*. London: Routledge, 2002.

Entwistle, Joanne. *The Fashioned Body: Fashion, Dress and Modern Social Theory*. Cambridge: Polity Press, 2000.

Evans, Calla. "You Aren't What You Wear: An Exploration into Infinifat Identity Construction and Performance through Fashion." *Fashion Studies* 3, no. 1 (2020): 1–31.

Evans, Caroline. *Fashion at the Edge: Spectacle, Modernity, Deathliness*. New Haven: Yale University Press, 2003.

Evans, Caroline. *The Mechanical Smile: Modernism and the First Fashion Shows in France and America, 1900–1929*. New Haven: Yale University Press, 2013.

Evans, Caroline. "Masks, Mirrors and Mannequins: Elsa Schiaparelli and the Decentered Subject." *Fashion Theory* 3, no. 1 (1999): 3–32.

Evans, Caroline and Minna Thornton. *Women and Fashion: A New Look*. London: Quartet Books, 1989.

Ewen, Stuart. *Captains of Consciousness: Advertising and the Social Roots of the Consumer Culture*. New York: Basic Books, 2001.

Ewen, Stuart and Elizabeth Ewen. *Channels of Desire: Mass Images and the Shaping of American Consciousness*. Minneapolis and London: University of Minnesota Press, 1992.

Fahs, Breanne. "Mapping 'Gross' Bodies: The Regulatory Politics of Disgust." In *Aesthetic Labor: Rethinking Body Politics in Neoliberalism*, edited by Ana Elias, Rosalind Gill and Christina Scharff, 83–100. London: Palgrave, 2017.

Farrell, Amy Erdman. *Fat Shame: Stigma and the Fat Body in American Culture*. New York: New York University Press, 2011.

Featherstone, Mike. "The Body in Consumer Culture." *Theory, Culture & Society* 1, no. 1 (1982): 18–33.

Forth, Christopher E. *Fat: A Cultural History of the Stuff of Life*. London: Reaktion, 2019.

Foucault, Michel. *Discipline and Punish: The Birth of the Prison*. New York: Pantheon, 1977.

Foucault, Michel. *Power/Knowledge: Selected Interviews and Other Writings 1972–1977*. New York: Pantheon, 1980.

Foucault, Michel. "Nietzsche, Genealogy, History." In *The Foucault Reader*, edited by Paul Rainbow, 76–100. New York: Pantheon, 1984.

Foucault, Michel. *The Archaeology of Knowledge*. Translated by Alan Sheridan-Smith. Vintage: London, 2010 (1972).

Gamber, Wendy. "'Reduced to Science': Gender, Technology and Power in the American Dressmaking Trade, 1860–1910." *Technology and Culture* 36, no. 3 (1995): 455–582.

Garland, David. "What Is a 'History of the Present'? On Foucault's Genealogies and Their Critical Preconditions." *Punishment & Society* 16, no. 4: 365–84.

Gilman, Sander L. "Black Bodies, White Bodies: Toward an Iconography of Female Sexuality in Late Nineteenth Century Art, Medicine and Literature." *Critical Inquiry* 12, no. 1 (1985): 204–42.

Glenn, Susan A. *Female Spectacle: The Theatrical Roots of Modern Feminism*. Cambridge: Harvard University Press, 2000.

Goffman, Erving. *Stigma: Notes on the Management of a Spoiled Identity*. New York: Simon & Schuster, 1963.

Green, Nancy L. *Ready to Wear, Ready to Work: A Century of Industry and Immigrants in Paris and New York*. Durham: Duke University Press, 1997.

Gregory, Richard L. *Eye and Brain: The Psychology of Seeing*. 5th ed. Princeton: Princeton University Press, 1997.

Griffith, R. Marie. *Born Again Bodies: Flesh and Spirit in American Christianity*. Berkeley: University of California Press, 2004.

Grossman, James R. *Land of Hope: Chicago, Black Southerners, and the Great Migration*. Chicago: University of Chicago Press, 1989.

Gubar, Susan. *Racechanges: White Skin, Black Face in American Culture*. Oxford: Oxford University Press, 2000.

Gurrieri, Lauren and Hélène Cherrier. "Queering Beauty: Fatshionistas in the Fatosphere." *Qualitative Market Research* 16, no. 3 (2013): 276–95.

Haidarali, Laila. *Brown Beauty: Color, Sex, and Race from the Harlem Renaissance to World War II*. New York: New York University Press, 2018.

Harrison, Daphne Duval. *Black Pearls: Blues Queens of the 1920s*. New Brunswick: Rutgers University Press, 1988.

Harrison-Kahan, Lori. *The White Negress: Literature, Minstrelsy, and the Black-Jewish Imaginary*. New Brunswick: Rutgers University Press, 2011.

Higgenbotham, Evelyn Brooks. *Righteous Discontent: The Women's Movement in the Black Baptist Church 1880–1920*. Cambridge: Harvard University Press, 1993.

Hollander, Anne. *Seeing Through Clothes*. New York: The Viking Press, 1978.

hooks, bell. *Black Looks: Race and Representation*. Boston: South End Press, 1992.

Huff, Joyce L. "A Horror of Corpulence: Interrogating Bantingism and Mid-Nineteenth Century Fat Phobia." In *Bodies out of Bounds: Fatness and Transgression*, edited by Jana Evans Braziel and Kathleen Lebesco, 19–38. Berkeley: University of California Press, 2001.

Jeacle, Ingrid. "Accounting and the Construction of the Standard Body." *Accounting Organizations and Society* 28, no. 1 (2003): 357–77.

Jenß, Heike. "Introduction: Locating Fashion/Studies: Research Methods, Sites and Practices." In *Fashion Studies: Research Methods, Sites and Practices*, edited by Heike Jenß, 1–18. London: Bloomsbury, 2016.

Joy, Annamma and Alladi Venkatesh. "Postmodernism, Feminism and the Body: The Visible and the Invisible in Consumer Research." *International Journal of Research in Marketing* 11, no. 4 (1994): 333–57.

Kawamura, Yuniya. *Fashion-ology: An Introduction to Fashion Studies*. Oxford: Berg, 2005.

Keist, Carmen. "'The New Costumes of Odd Sizes': Plus Sized Women's Fashions, 1910–1924." PhD diss., Iowa State University, 2012.

Keist, Carmen. "How Stout Women Were Left Out of High Fashion: An Early Twentieth Century Perspective." *Fashion Style and Popular Culture* 5, no. 1 (2018): 25–40.

Keist, Carmen N. "Stout Women Can Now Be Stylish." *Dress* 43, no. 2 (2017): 99–117.

Keist, Carmen N. and Sara B. Marcketti. "'The New Costumes of Odd Sizes': Plus-Sized Women's Fashions, 1920–1929." *Clothing and Textiles Research Journal* 31, no. 4 (2013): 259–74.

Kiaer, Christina. "The Russian Constructivist Flapper Dress." *Critical Inquiry* 28, no. 1 (2001): 185–243.

Kibler, Alison M. *Rank Ladies: Gender and Cultural Hierarchy in American Vaudeville*. Chapel Hill: University of North Carolina Press, 1999.

Kidwell, Claudia B. *Cutting a Fashionable Fit: Dressmakers' Drafting Systems in the United States*. Washington, DC: Smithsonian Institution Press, 1979.

Kidwell, Claudia B. and Margaret C. Christman. *Suiting Everyone: The Democratization of Clothing in America*. Washington, DC: The Smithsonian Institution Press, 1974.

Klein, Richard. "Fat Beauty." In *Bodies out of Bounds: Fatness and Transgression*, edited by Jana Evans Braziel and Kathleen LeBesco, 19–38. Berkeley: University of California Press, 2001.

Klepp, Ingun Grimstad and Mari Rysst. "Deviant Bodies and Suitable Clothes." *Fashion Theory* 21, no. 1 (2017): 79–99.

Kulick, Don and Anne Meneley, "Introduction." In *Fat: The Anthropology of an Obsession*, edited by Don Kulick and Anne Meneley, 1–8. New York: Penguin, 2005.

Lamanova, Nadezhda. "Concerning Contemporary Dress" ("O svremenem kostiume"). In *Against Fashion: Clothing as Art, 1850–1930*, edited by Radu Stern, 174–7. Cambridge, MA: The MIT Press, 2005.

Leach, William. "Transformations in a Culture of Consumption: Women and Department Stores, 1890–1925." *The Journal of American History* 71, no. 2 (1984): 319–42.

Leach, William. *Land of Desire: Merchants, Power, and the Rise of a New American* Culture. New York: Vintage Books, 1993.

Lears, T.J. Jackson. "From Salvation to Self-Realization: Advertising and the Therapeutic Roots of the Consumer Culture, 1880–1930." In *The Culture of Consumption: Critical Essays in American History, 1880–1980*, edited by Richard Wrightman Fox and T.J. Jackson Lears, 1–38. New York: Pantheon, 1983.

Lears, T.J. Jackson. *Fables of Abundance: A Cultural History of Advertising in America*. New York: Basic Books, 1994.

LeBesco, Kathleen. *Revolting Bodies: The Struggle to Redefine Fat Identity*. Amherst: University of Massachusetts Press, 2004.

Leeds Craig, Maxine. *Ain't I a Beauty Queen? Black Women, Beauty, and the Politics of Race*. Oxford: Oxford University Press, 2002.

Lees-Maffei, Grace. "Introduction—Writing Design: Words, Myths, Practices." *Working Papers on Design* 4, no. 1 (2010): 1–5.

Lehmann, Ulrich. *Tigersprung: Fashion in Modernity*. Cambridge: MIT Press, 2000.

Levy-Navarro, Elena, ed. *Historicizing Fat in Anglo-American Culture*. Columbus: The Ohio State University Press, 2010.

Libes, Kenna Elizabeth Mulroney. "Fat by the Wayside: Size Exclusion in Exhibitions and Collections of Dress." MA thesis, S.U.N.Y. Fashion Institute of Technology, 2022.

Lieb, Sandra. *Mother of the Blues: A Study of Ma Rainey*. Boston: The University of Massachusetts Press, 1981.

Lipovetsky, Gilles. *The Empire of Fashion: Dressing Modern Democracy*. Princeton: Princeton University Press, 1994.

Lott, Eric. *Love and Theft: Blackface Minstrelsy and the American Working Class*. New York: Oxford University Press, 2013.

Lury, Celia. *Consumer Culture*. New Brunswick: Rutgers University Press, 2011.

Mahoney, Tom. *50 Years of Lane Bryant*. New York: Lane Bryant, 1950.

Malley, Lynn and Carmen Keist. "The Origins of the New Half Sizes in the 1920s." *Dress*, online first (August 30, 2022). Accessed September 5, 2022.

Marchand, Roland. *Advertising the American Dream: Making Way for Modernity, 1920–1940*. Berkeley: University of California Press, 1986.

Margolin, Victor. "Introduction." In *Design Discourse: History, Theory, Criticism*, edited by Victor Margolin, 3–30. Chicago: University of Chicago Press, 1989.

Martin, Richard. *Cubism and Fashion*. New York: Metropolitan Museum of Art, 1999.

McClendon, Alphonso. *Fashion and Jazz: Dress, Identity and Subcultural Improvisation*. London: Bloomsbury, 2015.

McLeod, Mary. "Undressing Architecture: Fashion, Gender and Modernity." In *Architecture: In Fashion*, edited by Deborah Fausch, 38–123. Princeton: Princeton Architectural Press, 1996.

McNeil, Peter "Fashion Designers." In *Berg Encyclopedia of World Dress and Fashion: West Europe*, edited by Lise Skov, 129–36. Oxford: Berg, 2010.

Mears, Patricia. *American Beauty: Aesthetics and Innovation in Fashion*. New Haven: Yale University Press, 2009.

Melchior-Bonnet, Sabine. *The Mirror: A History*. Translated by Katharine H. Jewett. New York: Routledge, 2001.

Mida, Ingrid and Alexandra Kim. *The Dress Detective: A Practical Guide to Object-Based Research in Fashion*. London: Bloomsbury, 2015.

Milbank, Caroline Rennolds. *New York Fashion: The Evolution of American Style*. New York: Harry N. Abrams, Inc., 1989.

Miller, Monica L. *Slaves to Fashion: Black Dandyism and the Styling of Black Diasporic Identity*. Durham: Duke University Press, 2009.

Mobley, Jennifer Scott. *Female Bodies on the American Stage: Enter Fat Actress*. New York: Palgrave MacMillan, 2014.

Murray, Samantha. *The "Fat" Female Body*. New York: Palgrave MacMillan, 2008.

Negrin, Llewellyn. "Ornament and the Feminine." *Feminist Theory* 7, no. 2 (2006): 219–35.

Nicklas, Charlotte and Annabella Pollen. "Introduction: Dress History Now: Terms, Themes and Tools." In *Dress History: New Directions in Theory and Practice*, edited by Charlotte Nicklas and Annabella Pollen, 1–14. London: Bloomsbury, 2015.

Nicklas, Charlotte. "One Essential Thing to Learn Is Colour: Harmony, Science and Colour Theory in Mid-Nineteenth Century Fashion Advice." *Journal of Design History* 27, no. 3 (2014): 218–36.

O'Brien, Ruth. *An Annotated List of Literature References on Garment Sizes and Body Measurements*. Washington, DC: United States Department of Agriculture, 1930.

Overbeke, Grace. "Subversively Sexy: The Jewish 'Red Hot Mamas' Sophie Tucker, Belle Barth and Pearl Williams." *Studies in American Humor* 3, no. 25 (2012): 33–58.

Palmer, Alexandra. "Untouchable: Creating Desire and Knowledge in Museum and Textile Exhibitions." *Fashion Theory* 12, no. 1 (2008): 31–63.

Parkins, Ilya. *Poiret, Dior and Schiaparelli: Fashion, Femininity and Modernity*. London: Berg, 2012.

Patterson, Martha H. *Beyond the Gibson Girl: Reimagining the American New Woman, 1895–1915*. Urbana and Chicago: University of Illinois Press, 2005.

Pecorari, Marco. *Fashion Remains: Rethinking Ephemera in the Archive*. London: Bloomsbury, 2021.

Peiss, Kathy L. "American Women and the Making of Modern Consumer Culture." *The Journal for MultiMedia History* 1, no. 1 (1998): n.p.

Peiss, Kathy L. *Hope in a Jar: The Making of America's Beauty Culture*. Pittsburgh: University of Pennsylvania Press, 1998.

Peters, Lauren Downing. "You Are What You Wear: How Plus-Size Fashion Figures in Fat Identity Formation." *Fashion Theory* 18, no. 1 (2014): 45–71.

Peters, Lauren Downing. "'Fashion Plus': Pose and the Plus-Size Body in Vogue, 1986–1988." *Fashion Theory* 21, no. 2 (2017): 175–99.

Peters, Lauren Downing. "Flattering the Figure, Fitting in: The Design Discourses of Stoutwear, 1915–1930." *Fashion Theory* 23, no. 2 (2019): 167–94.

Peters, Lauren Downing. "Discourses of Discontent: Fashion, Activism and the Commodification of Fat Women's Anger." *Fat Studies: The Journal of Body Weight and Society*, online first (April 19, 2021). Accessed September 27, 2022.

Porter, Roy. "History of the Body." In *New Perspectives on Historical Writing*, edited by Peter Burke, 206–32. Cambridge: Polity, 1991.

Przybyszewski, Linda. *The Lost Art of Dress: The Women Who Once Made America Stylish*. New York: Basic Books, 2014.

Puhl, Rebecca, Tatiana Andreyeva, Kelly D. Brownell. "Perceptions of Weight Discrimination: Prevalence and Comparison to Race and Gender Discrimination in America." *International Journal of Obesity* 32, no. 1 (2008): 992–1000.

Quinn, Bradley. *The Fashion of Architecture*. Oxford: Berg, 2003.

Rabinovitch-Fox, Einav. "Fabricating Black Modernity: Fashion and African American Womanhood during the First Great Migration." *International Journal of Fashion Studies* 6, no. 2 (2019): 239–60.

Rasmussen, Nicholas. "America's First Amphetamine Epidemic 1929–1971: A Quantitative and Qualitative Retrospective with Implications for the Present." *American Journal of Public Health* 98, no. 6 (June 2008): 974–85.

Roberts, Mary Louise. *Civilization Without Sexes: Reconstructing Gender in Postwar France: 1917–1927*. Chicago and London: University of Chicago Press, 1994.

Robinson, Zandria F. "Gotta Sing on the Beats They Bring Us: Towards a Twenty-first Century Blues Women's Epistemology." *Issues in Race & Society* 2, no. 1 (2014): 47–72.

Rocamora, Agnès. *Fashioning the City: Paris, Fashion and the Media*. London: I.B. Tauris, 2009.

Russo, Gianluca. *The Power of Plus: Inside Fashion's Size-Inclusivity Revolution*. Chicago: Chicago Review Press, 2022.

Schilder, Paul. *The Image and Appearance of the Human Body: Studies in Constructive Energies of the Psyche*. New York: International Universities Press, 1970.

Schofield, Nancy A. "Pattern Grading." In *Sizing in Clothing: Developing Effective Sizing Systems for Ready-to-Wear Clothing*, edited by Susan P. Ashdown, 152–201. Cambridge: Woodhead Publishing, 2007.

Schwartz, Hillel. *Never Satisfied: A Cultural History of Diets, Fantasies and Fat*. New York: The Free Press, 1986.

Schwartz, Hillel. "Torque: The New Kinesthetic of the Twentieth Century." In *Incorporations (Zone 6)*, edited by Jonathan Crary and Sanford Kwinter, 70–126. New York: Zone Books, 1992.

Schweitzer, Marlis. *When Broadway Was the Runway: Theater, Fashion and American Culture*. Philadelphia: University of Pennsylvania Press, 2009.

Seagrave, Kerry. *Obesity in America, 1850–1939: A History of Social Attitudes and Treatment*. Jefferson, North Carolina and London: McFarland & Company, Inc., 2008.

Seltzer, Mark. *Bodies and Machines*. New York and London: Routledge, 1992.

Shaw, Andrea Elizabeth. *The Embodiment of Disobedience*. Lanham: Lexington Books, 2006.

Shaw, Madelyn. "American Fashion: The Tirocchi Sisters in Context." In *From Paris to Providence: Fashion Art and the Tirocchi Dressmakers' Shop, 1915–1947*. Providence: The Rhode Island School of Design, 1999.

Shilling, Chris. *The Body and Social Theory*. London: Sage, 1993.

Stearns, Peter. *Fat History: Bodies and Beauty in the Modern West*. New York: New York University Press, 1997.

Steedman, Carolyn. *Dust: The Archive and Cultural History*. New Brunswick: Rutgers University Press, 2001.

Steele, Valerie. "A Museum of Fashion Is More than a Clothes-Bag." *Fashion Theory* 2, no. 4 (1998): 327–35.

Steele, Valerie. *Paris Fashion: A Cultural History*. New York: Oxford University Press, 1988.

Steele, Valerie. "The F Word." *Lingua Franca* (April 1991): 17–20.

Steele, Valerie. *The Corset: A Cultural History*. New Haven: Yale University Press, 2003.

Steele, Valerie. "Artificial Beauty, or the Morality of Dress and Adornment." In *The Fashion History Reader*, edited by Giorgio Riello and Peter McNeil, 275–97. London: Routledge, 2010.

Stern, Radu. *Against Fashion: Clothing as Art, 1850–1930*. Cambridge: The MIT Press, 2005.

Strings, Sabrina. *Fearing the Black Body: The Racial Origins of Fat Phobia*. New York: New York University Press, 2019.

Styles, John. "Dress History: Reflections on a Contested Terrain." *Fashion Theory* 2, no. 4 (1998): 383–90.

Taylor, Lou. "Doing the Laundry? A Reassessment of Object-Based Dress History." *Fashion Theory* 2, no. 4 (1998): 337–58.

Thaggert, Miriam. *Images of Black Modernism: Verbal and Visual Strategies of the Harlem Renaissance*. Amherst and Boston: University of Massachusetts Press, 2010.

Thesander, Marianne. *The Feminine Ideal*. New York: Reaktion Books, 1997.

Toll, Robert C. *Blacking Up: The Minstrel Show in Nineteenth-Century America*. New York: Oxford University Press, 1974.

Troy, Nancy. *Couture Culture: A Study in Modern Fashion*. Boston: MIT Press, 2003.

Turner, Bryan. "The Discourse of Diet." *Theory, Culture & Society* 1, no. 1 (1982): 23–32.

Turner, Bryan. *The Body and Society: Explorations in Social Theory*. Oxford: Basil Blackwell, 1985.

Twigg, Julia. *Fashion and Age: Dress, the Body and Later Life*. London: Bloomsbury 2013.

van Campen, Crétien. "Early Abstract Art and Experimental Gestalt Psychology." *Leonoardo* 30, no. 2 (1997): 133–6.

Vester, Katharina. "Regime Change: Gender, Class and the Invention of Dieting in Post-Bellum America." *Journal of Social History* 44, no. 1 (2010): 39–70.

Vigarello, Georges. *The Metamorphoses of Fat: A History of Obesity*. Translated by C. Jon Delogu. New York: Columbia University Press, 2013.

Volonté, Paolo. *Fat Fashion: The Thin Ideal and the Segregation of Plus-Size Bodies*. London: Bloomsbury, 2022.

Volonté, Paolo. "The Thin Ideal and the Practice of Fashion." Journal of Consumer Culture 19, no. 2 (2019): 252–270.

Walker, Susannah. *Style and Status: Selling Beauty to African American Women*. Lexington: University of Kentucky Press, 2007.

Wann, Marilyn. "Foreword: Fat Studies: An Invitation to Revolution." In *The Fat Studies Reader*, edited by Esther Rothblum and Sondra Solovay, ix–xxv. New York: New York University Press, 2009.

White, Shane and Graham White. *Stylin': African American Expressive Culture from Its Beginnings to the Zoot Suit*. Ithaca: Cornell University Press, 1998.

Wigley, Mark. *White Walls, Designer Dresses: The Fashioning of Modern Architecture*. Cambridge: MIT Press, 2001.

Wilson, Elizabeth. "Fashion and the Postmodern Body." In *Chic Thrills: A Fashion Reader*, edited by Juliet Ash and Elizabeth Wilson, 3–16. London: Pandora, 1992.

Wilson, Elizabeth. *Adorned in Dreams: Fashion and Modernity*. New Brunswick: Rutgers University Press, 2003.

Woods, Clyde. *Development Arrested: Race, Power, and the Blues in the Mississippi Delta*. London: Verso, 1998.

Woodward, Sophie. *Why Women Wear What They Wear*. London: Berg, 2007.

Woodward, Sophie. "'Humble' Blue Jeans: Material Culture Approaches to Understanding the Ordinary, Global and the Personal." In *Fashion Studies: Research Methods, Sites and Practices*, edited by Heike Jenß, 42–58. London: Bloomsbury, 2016.

Woolner, Cookie. "American Excess: Cultural Representations of Lillian Russell in Turn-of-the-Century America." In *Historicizing Fat*, edited by Elena Levy-Navarro, 129–45. Columbus: The Ohio State University Press, 2010.

Workman, Jane E. "Body Measurement Specifications for Fit Models as Factor in Clothing Size Variation." *Clothing and Textile Research Journal* 10, no. 1 (1991): 31–6.

INDEX

Index

Index

Index